Praise for George Friedman and

FLASHPOINTS

"There is a temptation, when you are around George Friedman, to treat him like a Magic 8 Ball."

—*The New York Times Magazine*

"In *Flashpoints*, Friedman combines analysis with prophecy.... Some personal biography woven into poignant narratives helps reveal how geography and history have always shaped Europe's future."

—*Winnipeg Free Press*

"[Friedman is] one of the country's leading strategic affairs experts."

—Lou Dobbs

"Considering how right [Friedman's] been over the years, he's worth listening to."

—*San Antonio Express-News*

"Insightful.... Friedman vividly describes a region where memories are long, perceived vulnerabilities are everywhere, and major threats have emerged rapidly and unexpectedly many times before."

—*Publishers Weekly*

George Friedman

FLASHPOINTS

George Friedman is founder and chairman of Geopolitical Futures, which specializes in geopolitical forecasting. Before this Friedman was chairman of the global intelligence company Stratfor, which he founded in 1996. Friedman is the author of six books, including the *New York Times* bestsellers *The Next Decade* and *The Next 100 Years*. He lives in Austin, Texas.

www.geopoliticalfutures.com

FLASHPOINTS

The Emerging Crisis in Europe

George Friedman

ANCHOR BOOKS
A Division of Penguin Random House
New York

FIRST ANCHOR BOOKS EDITION, FEBRUARY 2016

Copyright © 2015, 2016 by George Friedman

All rights reserved. Published in the United States by Anchor Books, a division of Penguin Random House LLC, New York, and distributed in Canada by Random House of Canada, a division of Penguin Random House Canada Ltd., Toronto. Originally published in hardcover by Doubleday, a division of Penguin Random House LLC, New York, in 2015.

Anchor Books and colophon are registered trademarks of Penguin Random House LLC.

The Library of Congress has cataloged the Doubleday edition as follows:
Friedman, George.
Flashpoints : the emerging crisis in Europe / George Friedman.—First edition.
pages cm
1. Europe—Politics and government—21st century—Forecasting.
2. Europe—Social conditions—21st century—Forecasting.
3. Geopolitics—Europe—Forecasting.
4. Politics and culture—Europe—Forecasting.
5. Culture conflict—Europe—Forecasting.   6. Social prediction—Europe.
7. Europe—History.   I. Title.   II. Title: Flashpoints.
D2024.F75 2015   940.56'12—dc23   2014031709
•
Anchor Books Trade Paperback ISBN: 978-0-307-95113-7
eBook ISBN: 978-0-385-53634-9

Book design by Michael Collica
All maps and charts created by Stratfor

www.anchorbooks.com
•
Printed in the United States of America
10   9   8   7

This book is dedicated to my sister, Agi.

Anthem for Doomed Youth

What passing-bells for these who die as cattle?
Only the monstrous anger of the guns.
Only the stuttering rifles' rapid rattle
Can patter out their hasty orisons.
No mockeries now for them; no prayers nor bells;
Nor any voice of mourning save the choirs,
The shrill, demented choirs of wailing shells;
And bugles calling for them from sad shires.
What candles may be held to speed them all?
Not in the hands of boys, but in their eyes
Shall shine the holy glimmers of good-byes.
The pallor girls' brows shall be their pall;
Their flowers the tenderness of patient minds,
And each slow dusk a drawing-down of blinds.

—Wilfred Owen, killed at the Sambre, November 4, 1918

Contents

List of Illustrations

Preface

Between 1914 and 1945 roughly 100 million Europeans died from political causes: war, genocide, purges, planned starvation, and all the rest. That would be an extraordinary number of deaths anywhere and any time. It was particularly striking in Europe, which had, over the course of the previous four hundred years, collectively conquered most of the world and reshaped the way humanity thought of itself.

The conquest of the world was accompanied by the transformation of everyday life. Music was once something that you could hear only if you were there in person. Literacy was useless for most of human history as books were rare and distant. The darkness was now subject to human will. Men lived twice as long as they had previously and women no longer died in childbirth as a matter of course. It is difficult to comprehend the degree to which, by 1914, Europe had transformed the very fabric of life, not only in Europe but in the rest of the world.

Imagine, in 1913, attending a concert in any European capital. Mozart and Beethoven would be on the program. It may be a cold winter night, but the hall is brilliantly lit and warm with women elegantly but lightly dressed. In that grand room, winter has been banished. One of the men has just sent a telegram to Tokyo, ordering silks to be shipped and arrive in Europe within a month. Another couple has traveled a hundred miles in three hours by train to attend the concert. In 1492, when Europe's adventure began, none of this was possible.

There is no sound like Mozart and Beethoven played by a great European symphony orchestra. Mozart allows you to hear sounds not connected to this world. Beethoven connects each sound to a moment of life. Someone listening to Beethoven's Ninth Symphony must think of revolution, republicanism, reason, and, truth be told, of man as God. The art of Europe, immanent and transcendent, the philosophy and the politics, all have taken humanity to a place it has not been before. To many, it seemed as if they were at the gates of heaven. I think, had I been alive then, I would have shared that feeling.

No one expected this moment to be the preface to hell. In the next thirty-one years, Europe tore itself apart. The things that had made it great—technology, philosophy, politics—turned on the Europeans, or more precisely, the Europeans turned them on each other and themselves. By the end of the thirty-one years, Europe had become a graveyard of ruined cities, shattered lives. Its hold on the world was cracked. The "Ode to Joy" from Beethoven's Ninth Symphony was no longer a celebration of European life, but an ironic mockery of its pretensions.

Europe is not unique in this. Other civilizations have undergone turmoil, war, and savagery. But the unexpectedness, the intensity, the rapidity, and the consequences for the entire world were distinctive. And most distinctive was that this particular civilization should be capable of self-immolation. There may have been hints of this in the cruelty of colonialism, the deep inequality of European society, and its fragmentation into many pieces. But still, the connection between European high culture and death camps is surprising at the very least.

The Europeans conquered the world while conducting an internal civil war throughout the centuries. The European empire was built on a base of shifting sand. The real mystery is why European unity was so elusive. Europe's geography makes unity difficult. Europe does not consist of a single, undifferentiated landmass. It has islands, peninsulas, and peninsulas on peninsulas—and mountains blocking the peninsulas. It has seas and straits, enormous mountains, deep valleys, and endless plains. Europe's rivers don't flow together into a single, uniting system as do America's. They flow separately, dividing rather than uniting.

No continent is as small and fragmented as Europe. Only Australia is smaller, yet Europe today consists of fifty independent nations (including Turkey and the Caucasus, for reasons explained later). Crowded with nations, it is also crowded with people. Europe's population density is

72.5 people per square kilometer. The European Union's density is 112 people per square kilometer. Asia has 86 people per square kilometer. Europe is crowded and fragmented.

Europe's geography means it can't be united through conquest. It means that small nations survive for a very long time. The map of Europe in 1000 is similar to the map of 2000. Nations exist next to other nations for a long time, with long memories that make trust and forgiveness impossible. As a result, Europe has been a place where wars repeated themselves endlessly. The wars of the twentieth century were different only in that this time technology and ideology led to a continental catastrophe.

Europe is divided into borderlands, where nations, religions, and cultures meet and mix. There is frequently a political border within, but the borderland itself is wider and in many ways more significant. Consider the border between Mexico and the United States; it is a clear line. But Mexican influence, language, and people spread far north of the border, and likewise, American culture and business spread far south. In Mexico those who live in the states bordering the United States are seen as having absorbed American culture, making them alien to the rest of Mexico. Culture north of the borderland has transformed itself from Anglo to a strange mixture with a language of its own, Spanglish. The people living in these borderlands are unique, sometimes sharing more with each other than with those in their own countries.

I live south of Austin, Texas, where place-names are Anglo or German—the Germans settled the area west of Austin. When I drive south on I-35, towns tend to have German names like New Braunfels. As I get closer to San Antonio, they become Spanish, and sometimes I feel as though I am in Mexico. In a way I am, but the border is more than a hundred miles farther south, and that still has meaning.

Europe is filled with such borderlands, but the most important one divides the European peninsula from the European mainland, the West from Russia. It is a vast area that encompasses entire countries like Ukraine, Belarus, and Lithuania. Over the past century, we've seen the political border sweep far to the west, with Russia absorbing the borderland, or now far to the east, creating independent countries. No matter where the border may lie at any moment, this is a region whose people have more in common with each other than with Russia or the West. Indeed, the word *Ukraine* means "on the edge," or borderland.

This is not the only borderland, although it defines European history. There is a borderland between the French and German worlds, stretching from the North Sea to the Alps. The Balkans are the borderland between Central Europe and Turkey. The Pyrenees are the borderland between the Iberians and the rest of Europe. There are even smaller ones surrounding Hungary, where Hungarians live under the rule of Romanian and Slovakian states. There is even a water border, so to speak—the English Channel, separating Britain from the Continent. In such a small area, crowded and filled with ancient grievances, there will always be borderlands, and no place demonstrates this more clearly than Europe.

Borderlands are where cultures mingle and where smuggling can be a respectable business, but it can also be the place where wars are fought. These are flashpoints. The Rhineland is now quiet, but that was not always the case. Since 1871, three wars have broken out in the area between the Rhine and the French-speaking regions. They were flashpoints then because there were deep and serious issues dividing France and Germany. And when the flashpoint sparked, the region caught fire. Today, the borderland west of Russia has become a flashpoint. It is igniting and fires have started, but, as yet, the tinder has not caught everywhere and there is no general conflagration.

In World War I and World War II all the borderlands in Europe became flashpoints that sparked and set off fires that grew and spread. The world has rarely, if ever, seen the kind of general European firestorm that was set off in 1914, calmed briefly, and then raged again in 1939. People overflowed with terrible memories and fears, and when those sentiments ignited, the borderland was consumed and all the fires converged into a single holocaust.

Europe rebuilt itself with difficulty and with help was given back its sovereignty by the actions of others. Out of this shambles came a single phrase: "Never Again." This phrase represents the Jewish commitment to ensuring that their slaughter would never be permitted to happen again. The Europeans as a whole don't use this phrase, but its sentiment shapes everything they do. Those who lived through the thirty-one years then had to live through the Cold War, where the decision of war and peace, the decision that would determine if they lived or died, would be made in Moscow and Washington. That there was no war in Europe is worth considering later, but as the threat receded the European commitment was that the thirty-one years never be repeated. Europeans ceded their empire, their power, even in some ways their significance, to the principle that they should never again experience the horror of those years nor live on its precipice as they did in the Cold War.

The institution created to ban their nightmares was the European Union. Its intent was to bond European nations so closely together in such a prosperous enterprise that no nation would have any reason to break the peace or fear another. Ironically, Europe had struggled for centuries to free nations from oppression by other nations and make national sovereignty and national self-determination possible. They would not abandon this moral imperative, even though they had seen where its reductio ad absurdum might take them. Their goal was for the sovereignty of all to be retained, but constrained in such a way that no one could take it away. The anthem of the European Union is Beethoven's "Ode to Joy," cleansed of its irony.

The most important question in the world is whether conflict and war have actually been banished or whether this is merely an interlude, a seductive illusion. Europe is the single most prosperous region in the world. Its GDP collectively is greater than that of the United States. It touches Asia, the Middle East, and Africa. Another series of wars would change not only Europe, but the world. The answer to the question of whether Europe has overcome not only the thirty-one years, but the long millennia of conflict that preceded it, is at the center of any consideration of the future.

That's the reason I've written this book. In many ways this is the subject that has shaped my life and thoughts. I was born in Hungary in 1949 to parents born in 1912 and 1914. My family was shaped in the horrors and terrors of Europe, not only in the thirty-one years, but in their aftermath. We left Europe because my parents were convinced that there was a deep corruption in the European soul that could be hidden for a while but would always show itself eventually. As an American, I lived in a world where all things flow from decisions. As a European I lived in a world where decisions mean nothing when the avalanche of history overwhelms you. As an American I learned to confront the world. As a European I learned to evade it. My search for the answer to Europe's riddle flowed directly from the conversations of my parents at the dinner table, and the sounds of their nightmares at night. My identity crisis—a term that already tells you how American I am now—was caused by the fact that a European's approach to life was utterly different from an American's. I was both, so who was I? I have boiled this down to a single question: Has Europe really changed or is Europe fated to constantly be mocked by the "Ode to Joy"?

As a young man I chose to study political philosophy because I wanted to confront this question at the highest level possible. In my mind, the most fundamental questions of the human condition are ultimately political. Politics is about community—the obligations, rights, enemies, and friends that a community gives you. Philosophy is a dissection of the most natural things. It forces you to confront the familiar and discover it is a stranger. For me, that was the path to understanding.

Life is never that simple. In graduate school I focused on German philosophy. As a Jew I wanted to understand where men who could kill children as deliberate national policy came from. But it was the Cold War era, and I knew the European question was really now the Soviet question, and the Soviets had affected my life almost as much as the Germans. Karl Marx seemed the perfect point of entry. And since what was called the New Left (communists who hated Stalin) was at its height, I chose to study it.

In doing so I returned to Europe on numerous occasions and formed close friendships among the European New Left. I wanted to understand its philosophers—Althusser, Gramsci, Marcuse—but I couldn't sit in the library. There was too much going on outside. For most, the New Left was a way to get dates, a hip social movement. To a smaller group it was a profoundly serious attempt to understand the world and to find the lever for changing it. For a small handful, it became an excuse and obligation to undertake violence.

It is not always remembered that Europe in the 1970s and 1980s had become increasingly violent, and that terrorism predated al Qaeda. In most European countries, terrorist cells emerged, assassinating or kidnapping people and blowing up buildings. The terroristic Left existed in the United States as well, but only in a minor way. These limited groups fascinated me the most—the reemergence of political violence in Europe within the context of a movement that occasionally spoke of class struggle but didn't mean it.

One habit that emerged was "kneecapping" enemies. This meant firing a bullet into their knees. I could never figure out if crippling someone rather than killing him was an act of kindness or cruelty. For me these people were the ones to watch because in my mind they were the heirs of the thirty-one years. They were the ones who took their moral obligations seriously and rejected the values of the community, which freed them to do terrible things. In encountering some, I noted that they did not really expect to change anything. Their action was pure anger at the world they were born to, and contempt for those leading ordinary lives. They saw evil in these people and they had appointed themselves the avengers.

My time among these people made me much less at home with the growing self-confidence in Europe that the past was behind them. It seemed to me that, like cancer when the surgeon misses a few cells, given the right circumstances the disease recurs. In the 1990s, two areas of Europe, the Balkans and the Caucasus, exploded in war. Europeans dismissed these as not representative. They dismissed the left-wing terrorists as not representative. Today they dismiss the new right-wing thugs as not representative. This view, representative of Europe's pride and self-confidence, may be correct, but this is not self-evident.

We are now living through Europe's test. As all human institutions do, the European Union is going through a time of intense problems, mostly economic for the moment. The European Union was founded for "peace and prosperity." If prosperity disappears, or disappears in some nations, what happens to peace? I note that unemployment in several southern European countries is now at or higher than the unemployment rate in the United States during the Great Depression. What does that mean?

That is what this book is about. It is partly about the sense of European exceptionalism, the idea that they have solved the problems of peace and prosperity that the rest of the world has not. This may be true, but it needs to be discussed. If Europe is not exceptional and is in trouble, what will follow?

The question is posed in three parts. First, why was Europe the place in which the world discovered and transformed itself? How did this happen? Second, given the magnificence of European civilization, what flaw was there in Europe that led it to the thirty-one years? Where did that come from? Finally, once we have thought about these things we can consider not only Europe's future but its potential flashpoints.

If Europe has transcended its history of bloodshed, that is important news. If it has not, that is even more important news. Let's begin by considering what it meant to be European in the last five hundred years.

FLASHPOINTS

Part One

EUROPEAN EXCEPTIONALISM

A European Life

On the night of August 13, 1949, my family climbed into a rubber raft along the Hungarian shore of the Danube. The ultimate destination of the journey was Vienna. We were escaping the communists. There were four of us: my father, Emil, thirty-seven, my mother, Friderika, known as Dusi, thirty-five, my sister Agnes, eleven, and me, age six months. There was also a smuggler, whose name and provenance have been lost to us, deliberately, I think, as our parents regarded the truth of such things as potentially deadly and protected us from it at all costs.

We had come from Budapest by train to the Hungarian village of Almasfuzito, on the Danube northwest of the capital. Budapest, where my sister and I were born. My parents had migrated there with their families, met, fallen in love, and then were sucked into the abyss of Europe in the first half of the twentieth century. My mother was born in 1914 in a town near Bratislava, then called Pozsony and part of Hungary, which was then part of the Austro-Hungarian Empire. My father was born in the town of Nyirbator in eastern Hungary in 1912.

They were born just before World War I. In 1918, the war ended and the structure of Europe cracked, wrecked by that war. Four imperial houses—the Ottomans, Hapsburgs, Hohenzollerns, and Romanovs—fell, and everything that had been solid between the Baltic Sea and Black Sea was in flux. Wars, revolutions, and diplomacy redrew the map of the region, inventing some countries and suppressing others. Munkács, the town my father's father came from, was now in Ukraine, part of the Soviet Union. Pozsony was now called Bratislava, a city now part of a newly invented country fusing the Czechs and Slovaks.

My parents were Jews and for them the movement of borders was like the coming of weather. Pleasant or unpleasant, it was to be expected. There was something interesting about Hungarian Jews: they spoke Hungarian. The rest of the Jews in the east of Europe spoke Yiddish, fusing German with several other languages. Yiddish used the Hebrew alphabet, to further confuse matters. Yiddish-speaking Jews did not tend to see themselves as part of the countries in which they lived, and their hosts generally agreed, usually emphatically. Geography was a convenience, not something that defined them. Using Yiddish as their primary tongue represented their tenuous connection to their society, something that was both resented and encouraged by those with whom they lived.

But generally speaking, Hungarian Jews used Hungarian as their only language. It was my sister's and my first language. Some, such as my father, knew Yiddish as a second language, but my mother didn't know Yiddish at all. Their mother tongue was Hungarian, and when the borders shifted, my mother's family, all twelve of them supported by her father, who was a tailor, moved south to Budapest. In the same period the rest of my father's family moved west, out of what had become Ukraine, and into what was left of Hungary after the war. The point is that while the normal anti-Semitism of Europe flourished in Hungary as well, there was nonetheless a more intimate connection between Hungary and its Jews, far from simple or easy, but still there.

Hungary in the interwar period was not an unpleasant place—once the chaos of a communist regime followed by an anticommunist regime was completed to the usual European accompaniment of slaughter. Independent for the first time in centuries, it was governed by an admiral of a navy that no longer existed, who was regent to a nonexistent king. Miklós Horthy should have had as his family motto "Go with the Flow." The flow in Hungary in the 1920s and part of the 1930s was liberal, but not immoderately. This meant that my father, a country boy from the east, could move to Budapest, learn the printing trade, and open a print shop by the time he was twenty years old. For this time and place that was extraordinary, but it was an extraordinary time. Deep into the 1930s it was possible to believe that World War I had so chastened Europe that its darker instincts had been purged.

But demons are not so easy to purge. World War I had settled nothing. The war was fought over the status of Germany, which ever since its unification in 1871 had thrown the balance and stability of Europe into chaos. A powerful and wealthy nation had been created, but it was also a desperately insecure nation. Caught between France and Russia, with Britain subtly manipulating all players, Germany knew it could never survive a simultaneous attack from both sides. Germany also knew that both France and Russia were sufficiently afraid of it that a simultaneous attack could not be discounted. Thus, Germany's strategy had to be to defeat first one and then mass its forces to defeat the other. In 1914 Germany had tried to implement this strategy but instead had lost.

My grandfather fought in World War I, a soldier in the Austro-Hungarian army. He fought on the Russian front, leaving my father at the age of two. He returned from the war, but like so many others, he returned broken in spirit and body. Those whom the war didn't kill, it twisted into men utterly unlike those who had left home. He died shortly after coming home, possibly of tuberculosis.

Rather than settling Germany's status, World War I simply coupled geopolitical fear with ideological rage. Germany's defeat was explained as being a result of treachery. And if there was treachery, then someone had been treacherous. It was a complex plot, but Germany settled on the Jews as the malevolent conspirators, a decision that had particular implications for my family.

Geopolitically, Hitler's desire to secure German interests meant that the "flow" Horthy now had to "go with" came from Berlin. Ideologically, my parents now found themselves the major threat to the German nation. For a Jew living in Hungary it had not been a bad deal to this point. But it was now becoming a terrible one. This left my parents with a choice that had been facing Europeans for over a century—staying or going to America. My mother's sister lived in New York. I never knew how they did it, but somehow my parents managed to obtain visas to the United States in 1938. A visa like this was worth more than gold. For those who could see what was coming, it was life itself.

My father was a clever man, but he did not see what was coming. He had grown up with anti-Semites, and he knew the beatings and abuse that involved. By 1938 he had a profitable printing business in Budapest. To give that up and start over in a country whose language he could not speak was not something he was eager to do. The geopolitical reality demanded that he find an exit from the European madhouse. His personal needs dictated that he stay and tough it out. By the time it became clear that this was not your daddy's anti-Semitism, it was too late.

The result for my family was catastrophic. In Hungary, Horthy protected the nation by submitting to the German will. Hungary remained internally free so long as it cooperated with German adventures. Having defeated France in a six-week campaign, Germany now turned its attention to the Soviet Union, confidently expecting a rapid victory. Horthy, going with the flow, committed Hungary's army to the war, expecting as a reward to have returned to it the regions my family had to flee after World War I. But for the reward to be permanent, there had to be blood. Horthy understood this.

My father was conscripted into the Hungarian army. At first he was simply a soldier. But if the Hungarians were to fight alongside Germans, it was clear that Jews could not simply be soldiers. My father was transferred with other Jews to labor battalions whose assignment was, for example, to clear minefields the old-fashioned way, by walking through them. All soldiers were expected to be *willing* to die. Those in the labor battalions were *expected* to die. Horthy was no more of an anti-Semite than good manners required, and this was not something he may have wanted himself, but his duty was to preserve an independent Hungary, and if putting Jews into labor battalions was what was needed, he was going to do what was needed.

For my father and many of the men in my family, that meant a march from Hungary's eastern border through the Carpathians, toward Kursk and Kiev, all the way to the River Don, to a place called Voronezh. Most of the men in my family were dead by then, but so were many regular army troops. The Soviet Union only seemed weak. Its strength was discovered in the fall of 1942, when the Soviets, having massed enormous forces east of the Don, counterattacked against the German Sixth Army, which had taken most of the city of Stalingrad. Germany's goal was to choke off the approaches to the Caucasus, because on the other side of the Caucasus was the city of Baku, where the Swedish Nobel brothers had discovered and exploited a massive pool of oil in the late nineteenth century. Baku was still the source of most of the Soviets' oil, and Hitler wanted desperately to take it from them. The Germans knew that if they took Stalingrad and the land between the Don and Volga Rivers, Baku was theirs and the war was over.

However, the Soviets did not counterattack in Stalingrad. Instead they attacked to the north and to the south, enveloping the German Sixth Army and starving it into surrender and annihilation. My father's problem was that the Soviets' northern thrust was aimed directly at him—they knew that Germany's allies were the weak link. By the winter of 1942 the Germans depended on Italian, Romanian, Hungarian, and other allies who did not want to die for Hitler's historical vision of a Greater Germany. Therefore, when the Soviets launched their attack with massive barrages, the Hungarians broke ranks willingly. My father told me of the feared "Stalin Organ," a multiple-launch rocket system that could launch a dozen rockets from a battery, all landing within seconds of each other. Those rockets haunted his dreams for the rest of his life.

Then began the long retreat of the Hungarians from Voronezh to Budapest, a distance of over a thousand miles through the Russian winter of 1942–43. The death toll was appalling, but the Jewish death toll was almost total. My father walked back through the snows without winter clothing, without food beyond what he could scavenge, and with the knowledge that encountering German SS troops to the rear meant certain death. He explained his survival in three ways. First, he imagined his daughter, my sister, a few meters ahead of him. He was always going to pick her up. Second, city boys were soft. He was a farm boy, hardened from birth. Finally, it was luck. Enormous luck.

Hitler needed Baku. If he was to defeat the Soviets, Baku was a geopolitical necessity. It was no accident that the Germans had to take Stalingrad and no accident that the Soviets couldn't let them. It was not accidental that Germany's allies were on the flanks and not in the center, nor was it accidental that the Soviet offensive focused on them. It was not accidental that my father was at ground zero, because wherever the Hungarians were was to be ground zero, and wherever the Hungarians were, the Jews would be the most exposed. What *was* accidental was that my father survived. Impersonal forces define the larger pieces of history. It is the small things, the precious things, that are defined by will, character, and mere chance.

When my father finally reached his home in Budapest in 1943, Hungary still retained its sovereignty from Germany. Sovereignty matters. It meant that while Hungarian foreign policy was shaped by the power of Germany, there was some space, small and decreasing, for Hungary to govern itself. For the Jews it meant that while conditions were extraordinarily difficult, more difficult than for other Hungarians, who also were facing deep problems, they were not confronted by the full fury of Germany's anti-Semitism. My mother and sister were alive, and even the print shop still functioned in a way. They had a place to live and food to eat. Horthy was able to preserve that. Perhaps he could have done more, but perhaps trying would have brought the wrath of the Nazis to bear much earlier than occurred. In Europe at this time, retaining a space for Jews to survive, however precariously, was no small achievement for Horthy, or a trivial matter for my family. It was very different living in a sovereign Hungary than in occupied Poland. The sovereign nation-state could and did make the difference between life and death. I judge a man like Horthy not by the good he might have done, but by the evil that he did not commit and others did. It could have been much worse in Hungary, and much earlier. Others have judged him more harshly, my father and mother much less so. The argument still rages, but what is clear is that at the time, what he did was a matter of life and death. He, like the rest, was caught in the grip of European history gone mad, with few choices, all bad.

This was apparent when, in 1944, following his policy of going with the flow, Horthy opened secret negotiations with the Soviets over switching sides in a war that Germany was going to lose. German intelligence detected this, and Hitler summoned him to a meeting, where he threatened to occupy Hungary and demanded the deportation of Hungary's Jews, nearly a million. Horthy conceded the deportation of 100,000. In Europe at that time, this was what humanitarianism had degenerated into. A man who collaborated in killing only 100,000 but kept perhaps 800,000 others alive a bit longer was doing the best that could have been expected of him. In due course the Germans took Hungary over, and even that little was impossible. The flow of history that Horthy went with had overwhelmed Hungary. The truth was that Horthy was finished, that the fate of Hungary would now be determined by Hitler and the Hungarian fascists, and my family, along with Horthy, had run out of time.

Adolf Eichmann was sent to Hungary to oversee the "final solution" in the largest still-existing community of Jews in Europe. In the midst of a desperate war that Germany was losing, scarce manpower and transport facilities were diverted to move hundreds of thousands of Hungarian Jews north to Auschwitz and other camps, to be exterminated.

At a certain point there are actions by states that defy rational analysis. I have tried to understand Hitler's view of the Jews and imagine what he was thinking. The decision to kill Jews had a logic, however bizarre, as we shall see later. But the decision to kill the Hungarian Jews in the face of the urgent need to focus all resources, at a time when the Allies were clearly planning to come ashore in France and the Red Army was surging westward, is a decision that is extremely difficult to follow. The logic does not work.

But that is not ultimately my problem. I have two sons, and when they were small I would watch them sleep as fathers do, thinking about their future. My thoughts were at times also darker. I was imagining a time not too long before when, had they lived where I was born, it would have been the state policy of a great and civilized power to find them and kill them. What logic I can find on the broadest level dissolves in the details of two sleeping boys. Just as luck governed my father's survival and couldn't be explained by any action on his part, so a pure malevolent wickedness, not shaped by any logic whatever, would have caused men to hunt down and kill toddlers not as something incidental to war, but as a primary goal.

Geopolitics argues that people do what they must, always in the brutal grip of reality, and that the direction in which nations go can to some extent be predicted by the reality in which they find themselves. Hitler's recourse to anti-Semitism, at the broadest level, can at least be rationalized given Germany's reality. But as you come down to the microscopic level of life, to two little boys asleep, the logic falls apart. There is a discontinuity between history and life. Or perhaps, history, taken to its logical conclusion, creates horrors that are at the edge of human understanding.

My family did better than most. My father was a clever man, but in hell cleverness is not enough. He decided, or was told, that the Germans would begin rounding up Jews in Budapest, so he sent his mother and sister back to the village in the east where he was born, to keep them safe. Instead of Budapest, the Germans began rounding up the Jews in the east, and his mother and sister were among the first to go to Auschwitz. His mother was selected for gassing immediately, but his sister survived. In Budapest, the roundups came later and more randomly. In June 1944, my mother was taken, along with three of her sisters, to Austria to build roads and factories. Two of the sisters died. Two survived, including my mother, who returned to Budapest after the war weighing eighty pounds and barely recovered from typhus.

My father saved my sister and a cousin by means that I never fully understood. The Soviets were closing in on Budapest, and the German machine was frantically working to transport and kill the remaining Jews. My sister and cousin, five and six years old, were taken and lined up in the street, waiting to board trucks. My sister remembers only that a man, tall, blond, and wearing a leather coat, came looking for them and took them out of the line. This was the type of man whom even a five-year-old would know to be alien and out of place. He told the children that my father had sent him to take them somewhere safe. He delivered them to a building that was under the protection of the Swiss Red Cross. My father brought them food daily, moving through a city under siege, where he was now reassigned to the labor battalion that had taken him deep into Russia.

How he did this, no one knows. Neither my sister nor other family members know who the man in the leather coat was. Clearly my father had some influence. How he had any influence at all was never explained to me or to my sister. In that time and place, all stories of survival were tales of extraordinary good fortune or extreme cunning. Those with ordinary amounts of either did not live. This was not true just for Jews. Almost everyone who survived had an extraordinary tale to tell. But my father never spoke of it, never explained it, and went to his death with the tale. He was racked all his life by guilt over his mistake in sending his mother and sister back to the east of Hungary and his failure to protect my mother. He never forgave himself those things, and he never regarded his ability to save my sister as sufficient. I would like to think that this was the reason for his silence, but in that time and place, cunning led to darker places as well.

In due course my father was himself taken to a concentration camp, Mauthausen. But in the end my sister survived the war, and my mother and father both came home. An intact family was a miracle. Hungary was occupied by the Soviets. From the Soviet point of view, the Hungarians had the same status as the Germans. They were both enemy nations that had invaded and savaged the Soviets. The Soviet invasion of Hungary carried with it a measure of vengeance, if not on the order of what was meted out to Germany, then certainly brutal. My sister hid in a basement for six weeks during the battle of Budapest, while Soviet forces shelled the city continuously with artillery, and American planes bombed it.

The Germans held out as long as they could. Budapest and the Danube blocked a flat plain that led to Vienna, part of the Reich. The Germans' resistance was fanatical even after Budapest was completely surrounded, and the Allies' assault was relentless. In the middle was a five-year-old girl and her six-year-old cousin in circumstances that would have broken grown men. For her, as she once put it, it was all quite ordinary. The fact that a shell or a bomb might kill you at any moment was simply the way the world was.

When the devil lets go of your throat, you go back to living. In my father's case, this meant reopening his printing shop and earning enough money to eat. My mother recovered and gained back some weight, as my father was able to get food for the family, undoubtedly on the black market. My parents kept kosher, and I was told that my father once came home with pork and this was discussed as to its propriety. For me, years later hearing this story, it represented the return of some kind of normality. Could anyone have imagined a discussion of the appropriateness of eating pork a year before?

Life under the Soviets was hard. The Russians had suffered enormously in the war and had neither the resources nor inclination to be kind. They had occupied Hungary in the course of war and were there for their own benefit, not for the Hungarians'. But the geopolitical reality of occupation did not turn into a formal political reality until 1948. The Soviets were oddly scrupulous in wanting to hold elections and elect a genuine communist government fair and square. They held an election in 1948, but the communists lost. If they couldn't get it fair and square, they would get it anyway, so they held a second election, which, of course, the Communist Party won. This led to the creation of the People's Republic of Hungary, a completely sovereign state that happened to be communist and pro-Soviet.

In most practical senses, this entire election process was a farce. The Soviet Red Army had the guns and Hungary was going to do what it was told. This was the geopolitical reality. Once again, geopolitics posed a personal problem for my family. My father had been a Social Democrat before the war and was still on their lists. Lists were something your name should never appear on. The Communists hated the Social Democrats more than they hated the conservatives, because Social Democrats could potentially challenge the Communists for domination of the working class. Prior to the 1948 elections, the Communists and Social Democrats had merged, a gentle way of saying the Social Democrats ceased to exist. That meant my father (and likely my mother) had to die or be imprisoned. Hungary had voted the wrong way once, so Stalin was taking no chances.

My father had become a Social Democrat in the 1930s, when he was in his early twenties. At this time everyone was political and Jews went to the left, because the left hated them less than the right, at least in my father's view. Whatever he was in the 1930s was far removed from what he had become in the 1940s. He had seen politics and its consequences with an intimacy that made him view politics as something to be avoided at all costs. Geopolitics was something that crushed you. Politics was something that tied your hands as you tried to survive. By now my father had no politics.

Ultimately, that didn't matter. The Hungarian security police, the AVO, controlled by the NKVD, the Soviet secret police, was hunting for traitors, and they had a list—an old one but a list nonetheless. My uncle, my father's half brother, was a communist and had access to information. The two men had hated each other for years, over politics and anything else you might imagine, but my uncle let him know that there was a list, and he was on it. Even the word *list* filled your soul with dread in those days.

My parents' situation was fairly desperate. I had been born in early 1949, just before my uncle's news reached them. Giving birth for my mother had been a dangerous thing, given her physical fragility a few years before. My sister was eleven years old and had gone through her own hell. Now they faced another geopolitical disaster. They could stay in Hungary and face a catastrophic situation with the AVO or try to escape and perhaps die with their children. My parents never once explained to me their reasoning. I think they were conditioned by the Nazis to expect the crime of one to result in the annihilation of all—not necessarily a naive view of communism. They decided to leave, a desperate choice, but the only one they could see at the time.

Getting out of Hungary was not easy. Ever since the declaration of the People's Republic, the Soviets were committed to keeping people from leaving the country. The Hungarian-Austrian border was sealed shut. Minefields had been planted, guards patrolled with dogs, and guard towers were manned with searchlights and machine guns. To the north was Czechoslovakia. Like Hungary, it was Soviet controlled, and therefore the border was not quite as tightly controlled as the Austrian-Hungarian border. Czechoslovakia, too, had a border with Austria. Reaching Austria was my parents' only hope, but getting there directly from Hungary was impossible. They had to go through Czechoslovakia.

There were geopolitical reasons for the relative permeability of the Czech-Austrian border, stemming from the creation of Israel in 1948. Israel was created from territory belonging to the British Empire, and anything that weakened the British pleased Stalin. He assumed the British would continue to be Israel's adversary and thought that he might be able to create an alliance with Israel. The Soviets had always wanted access to the Mediterranean and had been sponsoring uprisings in Greece and Turkey in the hopes of breaking through. However, the Truman Doctrine, which threw American power behind anticommunists in Greece and Turkey, made success unlikely. Israel's emergence as an ally was a long shot for Stalin, but low risk. In 1949, Israel needed two things: weapons and Jews. Stalin had both. The question was, how to get them to Israel? Stalin decided to allow Czechoslovakia to sell weapons to Israel from 1947 to the end of 1949. From the Israeli point of view, anything that gave them weapons and Jews addressed their geopolitical problem, and the broader picture would work itself out.

There was a pipeline for getting weapons and Jews from Czechoslovakia to Italian ports via Austria. The Czech-Israeli arms trade is well known. As I was told years later by my parents during casual conversations at dinner, Jews were being moved through the same pipeline. They were determined to get to Bratislava in Czechoslovakia, a few miles from where my mother was born, and far more important, a few miles from Vienna. In Bratislava, my father was told by apparently reliable sources, Jews from all over the Soviet empire gathered and were then sent on to Austria and Israel. The problem was getting to Bratislava.

Soviet strategy in the Mediterranean coupled with the state of politics in Prague had given my family its opening. The challenge consisted of three parts: First, leaving Budapest without being noticed by the AVO and getting to a point where we could cross the Danube into Czechoslovakia. Second, getting to Bratislava and hooking up with the Israelis. Third, getting to Austria and getting away from the Israelis.

Leaving Budapest unnoticed was not easy, and my parents didn't make it easier. Warm coats were expensive, and they didn't want to leave theirs behind, as winter was going to come in a few short months. Unfortunately, this was August and it was a bit odd to see a family walking down a street wearing winter coats. Add to this that they had to carry enough food for four people for several days—when you're a refugee, you can't help but look like one. And most important was finding someone who would guide them across the Danube to Bratislava.

Fortunately, in this region smuggling was an industry dating back to the Romans. You will always find something is worth more on one side of the border than the other, or there are people trying to escape from something or someone. Smugglers made their living ferrying people across the Danube. By definition, these were hard men. They dealt with desperate people in dangerous places for money and had little room for sentiment. Each journey could end in their death. Such men are ruthless, and as people along all borders know, putting yourself in their hands is dangerous. But smuggling people is a referral business, and you don't get good references by robbing and killing your charges. You may get away with it once or twice, but then business dries up.

When wishing to smuggle something, including yourself, across the border, the key thing you need is a reference, someone who knows someone, who has heard of someone who might be able to do the job. My father was a man who always knew someone who knew someone. Amid the chaos in his path he found a reference who pointed him toward a man who, for a certain amount of money, could get us where we needed to go. The money was expected in cash, of course, and up front. I do not know where my father got the money and he never discussed it, but it had to be a large amount for four people.

We were told to meet the smugglers on the night of August 13, 1949, on the bank of the Danube near the town of Almasfuzito, where the railroad from Budapest ran closest to the river. The river itself was wide and slow, and in the middle an island emerged in the summer, providing a good place to hide if the searchlights were getting too close or if dawn came too early. That was how we came to be in rubber rafts on the Danube.

The risk of being caught was enormous. I was the main threat to the operation, as a crying baby in the silence of the night would mean certain death. Dr. Ungar, who loomed large in family legend, was our doctor in Budapest and was trusted with the plan. He provided my parents with sleeping powders to make me sleep and thus keep me silent. It has always awed me that my sister, all of eleven, was awake and aware throughout this escape, but then I have to remember that she had been fighting for her life since she was five. Fortunately, this part of the trip came off without a problem. We rendezvoused with the smugglers at the prearranged time and location. At nightfall we got into the boats and paddled across the river to the Czech side. From there we went to the formerly Hungarian town of Komarom, then called Komarno, a few miles to the west.

Our next task was to get to Bratislava, the capital of the Slovakian region of Czechoslovakia. Czechoslovakia itself was the creation of the post–World War I Treaty of Trianon. The treaty dismantled the Austro-Hungarian Empire, creating nation-states but leaving behind such oddities as Yugoslavia, a federation of mutually hostile nations, and Czechoslovakia, the amalgamation of the Czech Republic and Slovakia, two entities that shared a mild dislike of each other. Compounding this strange creation was redrawing Hungary's borders. Transylvania, the southeastern section, went to Romania, while the northern section was given to the Slovak region of Czechoslovakia. This is important to the tale, since the train from Komarno to Bratislava ran through Hungarian-speaking territory, which my parents knew would allow them to be less noticeable.

After boarding the early-morning train, my family settled down for the trip to Bratislava. My mother took out a salami and began to feed the family, distributing slices to my sister while feeding me. A fellow passenger leaned over and whispered to her, "Put that away. It's a Hungarian salami." Had we been traveling through a Slovak-speaking region, we would likely have been arrested immediately. Hungarian salamis were not available in Slovakia. But this was the Hungarian region and the passenger understood we were escaping and sympathized. Luckily we were warned and saved. And from this story I learned about the geopolitics of taking out one's salami.

Our smugglers were specialists; some worked the river, others worked the trains. We were supposed to meet the next set of smugglers on the train, and they were to take us into Bratislava. The family split up, the children with my mother and my father alone, as he was the prime target. He was to identify and communicate with the smuggler. Unfortunately, a clear signaling mechanism had not been set, or my father forgot it. Sitting alone on the train, he sighted a likely smuggler. With a series of facial expressions, shrugs, and slight hand gestures that passed for conversation among the hunted of the region, my father asked a question that the alleged smuggler answered, although God knows what he thought the question was. My father jerked his head to signal that he was getting off the train. The smuggler nodded slightly and got up to leave. My father followed. Meanwhile my mother, who had spotted the real smuggler at the other end of the carriage, realized what was happening too late. She turned around to see my father get off the train and discover that his smuggler was just an ordinary passenger. The train pulled out and my father was left on the northern side of the Danube, in Slovakia, alone. This was not good. Covert operations go smoothly only in the movies.

It was never clear to me how my father found us, but we all made it to Bratislava, there to join other Jewish refugees in the basement of a Jewish school. We stayed there for weeks while our Israeli handlers collected more Jewish refugees to relocate. The Czech secret police obviously knew we were there, since the building was in the middle of the city, and people kept going in and not coming out. Obviously Stalin's analysis of the geopolitical soundness of his deal with David Ben-Gurion remained intact, so we were safe.

Unfortunately, however, we had a problem: my parents didn't want to go to Israel. My father was a committed Zionist deeply in favor of a Jewish state. He just didn't want to have anything to do with it personally. Israel had only recently won the War of Independence and its survival was far from certain. My father really was tired of places whose survival was far from certain. He wanted to go to America. His reasoning was geopolitical. The United States had two neighbors, Canada and Mexico, both of whom were weak. He wanted to live in a strong country with weak neighbors, and if possible, no Nazis, communists, or anyone else who believed in anything deeply enough to want to kill him and his family over it.

Israel's national interest and my father's self-interest were now in conflict. Israel had a demographic problem: it didn't have enough people. Israel's safety depended on more Jews going there, while my father's safety depended on not going there. He was very grateful for the refuge, and definitely wanted help crossing the Austrian border, but being sent to the Negev with two hand grenades, as he put it, was not in his self-interest.

My father's situation was further compounded by the fact that the Israelis did not have a robust sense of humor. They were there to collect Jews, we were Jews, and in their view we were going to live the dream. As my father explained it, he needed the Israelis to get us across the Austrian border. His solution was to lie, pretending to be wildly enthusiastic about going to a place where people would again try to kill him, until we had safely crossed the border. In his mind there was no reason to upset the Israelis too early.

My father then executed a maneuver that only a man who had lived his kind of life could conceive, let alone execute. We were conveyed to the Austrian border in buses or trucks; I was never sure which. When we got there, the border guards on the Czech side, who were clearly used to these movements, searched our vehicle with more than usual care. They arrested my father and the rest of our family. How the guards explained it to the Israelis is unclear, but this was a major route moving a lot of people, and the Israelis probably didn't mind losing one small family, whether for political or legal reasons. The Israeli convoy rolled across the border into Austria and on to Adriatic ports and the next step in their journey.

Once the convoy was gone, we were released and allowed to cross the border ourselves. In retrospect it seems clear that my father had made arrangements with appropriate people who made sure when the convoy rolled through that we would be arrested. How my father managed to pull off this tour de force while confined to a basement in Bratislava he never shared with me, and my sister was only vaguely aware of what he had done. When I was old enough to ask, my mother insisted it was just an accident and I should stop asking stupid questions, which was followed by a slap on the back of the head. That it happened is certain, as we wound up in the Bronx rather than the Negev, but *how* is something forever lost.

This last border crossing brought us to Vienna and directly into the geopolitics of the Cold War. Europe at this point in 1949 was occupied territory. Its real shape was defined by the line drawn between the Allies and the Soviets, regardless of the degree of internal sovereignty given to any particular nation. Those countries occupied by the Soviets had communist regimes; those occupied by the Americans and British were constitutional republics of various sorts. More important, by 1949, the Berlin blockade had taken place, Churchill had made his Iron Curtain speech, and NATO had been formed. Europe was an armed camp and there was a real expectation that there would be another war.

Vienna was a microcosm of Europe. Vienna, like Berlin, was divided into four zones—Soviet, American, British, and French. Practically speaking there were two zones: Allies and Soviets. If you went down the wrong block, you could wind up in the Soviet zone and never be seen again. This happened to people my family knew. Many relief organizations were operating in Vienna, and it was a center for refugees of all sorts. The major organization for Jews was the American Jewish Joint Distribution Committee ("the Joint"), an umbrella group of other charities. The Joint assigned my family to the former Rothschild Hospital, issued papers by the United Nations Relief and Rehabilitation Administration (UNRRA), and told to wait until some country would take us.

Fortunately there were many countries looking for refugees, particularly the British settler states like Canada, Australia, and New Zealand. All wanted to increase their population, but only with white European settlers. Jews counted as part of this group, so we had the option of going to Australia or Canada. My mother just wanted to get out of the refugee camps and would happily have gone to either country, but my father didn't want to go to either Australia or Canada. He knew that Australia had come too close to being invaded by Japan during World War II, and was saved by the United States. In his mind Canada was weak and dependent on the United States not invading it. Albert Camus had said that he wanted to be "neither a victim nor victimizer." My father would have regarded Camus's view as delusional. In his experience there was nothing other than victim or victimizer, and it was definitely better to be the victimizer rather than the victim. He wanted to go to the United States. Other choices like Cuba or Brazil were dismissed out of hand, as was settling in Austria, which had too many former Nazis around for comfort.

So many refugees wanted to immigrate to the United States that then, as now, getting accepted was not easy. The United States had quotas based on country of birth. Having spent the last decade on the run, my father never considered illegal immigration. He had to go to the United States legally. But that required waiting. Time, as well as space, was my father's enemy—he was too close to the Soviets and in time he knew this would be disastrous. He smelled war coming and he wanted to have his family out of Europe. He did not want to wait.

Europe was filled with intrigue. The Soviets were working hard to expand the communist parties in countries like France and Italy and to penetrate the recently revived German military and intelligence services. Stalin also focused on infiltrating the newly formed CIA and rounding out his already deep penetration of Britain's intelligence services. The Soviet intelligence services were superb, and for Stalin, information was power. If he could subvert and paralyze the Allies, a war might not be necessary or might be easily won. At the very least, his intelligence services would give him warning of American and British intentions.

The Americans had become obsessed with the Soviets, particularly after 1948, with the Berlin Blockade and the Greek and Turkish conflicts. Any illusions about how the postwar world would work had evaporated.

World War II's devastation, following on World War I and the Napoleonic invasions, convinced the Soviets that a buffer zone to absorb the shock of attacks from the West was essential. For the Soviets, that buffer zone was the line from the Baltic Sea to the Adriatic Sea, and it ran through the center of Europe in Germany.

From the American point of view, the presence of Soviet troops in the center of Germany raised the specter of a Soviet conquest of Western Europe. The Soviets had a large military that had ground the Wehrmacht to dust, massive communist parties in France and Italy, and the best intelligence service in the world. If the Soviets dominated the European peninsula, the result would be a combination of Russian resources and European technology and industrial sophistication that would challenge American security, especially when those resources were used to build a navy and air force. Preventing that from happening became the foundation of American strategy.

America faced two very real problems: its forces were dwarfed by the Soviets' forces, and it had an almost complete lack of intelligence on the Soviet Union and what was happening on the other side of the fence. The United States compensated for the first with atomic bombs, and the second it compensated for by making deals with people like my father.

The United States had to build an intelligence capability from scratch. During World War II its focus had been mostly on France and Germany, but now the problem was farther east. It was critical to recruit people who knew something about the East and the Soviet Union and had connections there. Merely being able to speak the language would have been useful as well, as this skill was sorely lacking on the American side. As distasteful as it was, men like Gerhardt Gehlen, who ran the German military intelligence program on the Soviet Union, were indispensable. Others who were even more despicable, such as men from the SS, which ran its own intelligence operations, were also critical to the United States at this time.

But the war had been over for four years, and former German intelligence officers didn't know what was happening in the buffer states that the Soviets had established. In addition, the Americans had a fantasy that they could overthrow some of these regimes and roll back the Soviets. The plan was to recruit refugees to return to the countries they had left and foment risings, or at least serve U.S. counterintelligence services blocking Soviet operations in the West.

The plan, known as Operation Rollback, had two weaknesses. First, destabilizing a regime and starting a riot don't undermine the Soviet army that is occupying the country. Second, the Soviets were sending their own operatives across as refugees, dangling them in the hope they would be recruited. You could identify them by the fact that they left without their families, who were at home serving as hostages. It took a while for the West to catch on, and in the meantime the operation was penetrated, and all the American-controlled agents who went east were captured and tortured, and they talked.

Thus, from an intelligence perspective this operation was a bad idea, but not, it would appear, from my father's point of view. While the Soviets obtained cooperation by keeping families as hostages, the Americans offered citizenship papers and green cards. Things become very murky here, but from what I can reconstruct my father made some sort of deal that would allow my mother, sister, and me to leave Vienna and go to the United States. We first went to Salzburg and from Salzburg we flew (extraordinary for us) to Bremerhaven, where we boarded a navy ship and were given the captain's cabin for the voyage to the United States.

My father stayed behind. The official version was that my mother, although Hungarian, had been born in Czechoslovakia and could enter the United States with the children under the Czech quota, but my father could not, as he was under the Hungarian quota. The problem with this explanation is that the United States did not separate families, particularly those who held UNRRA cards. The unofficial version consisted of a slap on the back of the head and the assertion that I wouldn't understand. Much later in life, when I got to know my father better, he said things about Austria and those "idiotic American jackasses," or words to that effect. This much is known from papers my family kept and from which I was able to reconstruct our history in later years: on the same day my mother registered for her papers in New York City, my father reported in as a refugee in a place called Hallein. This was close to where Hitler had had his home on the Obersalzberg and Goering's looted art was stored in salt mines. It was also close to the headquarters of the 430th Army

Counterintelligence Corps Detachment. This was a key unit in the Cold War at the time, running operations against the Soviets.

My best guess, and that's all it is, is that my father had cut a deal to get his family out of harm's way in return for running errands for U.S. counterintelligence among Hungarian refugees. It is the only thing that explains what he did, and the murkiness of his existence at this time tends to confirm it. If this was true, he was one of thousands, and his dislike of college boys playing spy, which he voiced to me on several occasions, indicated some knowledge of the breed. Clearly he didn't do anything important since he stayed alive, and the Soviets had completely penetrated these low-level operations. My father's situation must have distressed him greatly. Delighted that his family was safe, he was still too close to a major geopolitical fault line with Soviet tanks on one side, American bombers on the other.

In 1952 my father was able to come and join us in the United States. About that time U.S. operations in Eastern Europe were falling apart. An attempt to infiltrate Albania, raise a guerrilla force, and take the country failed at the moment of infiltration. Soviet intelligence was waiting on the beach. Did my father do stuff like this? We have a picture of him on a ship, wearing an armband and surrounded by a group of men best described as thugs. He had no explanation for the ship. His explanation for the armband was that he led the group because he could speak English. The flaw in this explanation is that he couldn't speak decent English even twenty years later, when he was setting type at the *New York Times*.

Immediately on his arrival in America, my father found a job as a printer. We lived first in the Bronx. It was not as bad as it later became, but it was a tough neighborhood. We then bought a little house in Queens, which had a tiny garden that my parents loved. Later we moved to another small house on Long Island's South Shore. My sister married an engineer and had three children. I went to school and eventually grew up.

In the 1960s Pete Seeger wrote a song ridiculing small suburban tract homes as all looking the same and all made out of "ticky tacky." My father heard me playing it and asked me what it meant. I explained that Seeger's dislike of cheap, mass-produced homes reflected his dislike of cheap, mass-produced people. How you lived defined who you were. We were becoming mass-produced people. We were in the backyard of our house, and I will never forget his response: "And this is what Americans worry about?"

The answer was yes. When you are safe and powerful, then you worry about losing your identity. My father never lost his identity. His fear was losing his life. My father loved America because except in his dreams, he was safe. He emerged from Europe with the elemental knowledge that life is precious and that the greatest enemy are the men who would deprive you of it. For him the world was simple. Europe was a place filled with wolves and people they preyed on. America was filled with people who were not afraid. For him that was more than enough to expect from life.

My father never forgave the Russians for perpetuating the terror the Nazis had begun. He never forgave the French for being weak and corrupt and losing a war in six weeks. He never forgave the Poles for counting on the French instead of themselves. And above all, he never forgave the Germans. My father never forgave Europe for being monstrous, and he never forgave Europeans for how easily they forgave themselves. For him, Europe was a place of monsters, collaborators, and victims. He never returned to Hungary, or to Europe. He had no interest in going there. When I was in college I asked him why he refused to recognize that Europe had changed. His answer was simple: Europe will never change. It will just act as if nothing happened.

When I look at the European Union now, I think of my father's words. It is an institution that acts as if nothing happened. I don't mean by this that it doesn't know what happened or isn't revolted by it. I mean that the European Union—as an institution and idea—is utterly certain that all that is behind it, that it has willed its demons to depart and they have listened. I doubt that history is so easy to transcend. This book is about the darker corners of Europe, where my father was certain the real Europe still lived. The story is more complicated than modern Europe would have it, and even more complicated than my father made it out to be. But the task of this book is to try to make sense out of my family's lives as Europeans. We must start in a very small town in Portugal.

2

Europe's Assault on the World

There is a place where Europe ends. It is called Cabo de São Vicente, and it is the westernmost point of the European peninsula, a cliff jutting into the Atlantic Ocean. The Greeks, according to Herodotus, called the waters beyond Gibraltar "Atlantic," after the god Atlas. This was his realm—vast, powerful, and profoundly mysterious. When you stand at Cabo de São Vicente, you understand why this seems like a good name. There is a presence there that hints at a world both monstrous and enchanted.

The Romans called it the Promontorium Sacrum, or Sacred Promontory, and they prohibited people from being there at night. They thought that this was the end of the world and that demons from the Atlantic came ashore at night to seize people's souls. It is not difficult in the darkness to imagine demons from the nothingness of the Atlantic seizing you. During the day it is still a desolate place, with a Portuguese naval communications center and some stalls selling nothing much to the handful of tourists who still visit the end of the world. This banality belies the importance of the place.

There is a second cape less than a mile to the east, just south of a small town called Sagres. A man known to history as Henry the Navigator built a palace there in the fifteenth century. Only a chapel, likely built later, and a large circle on the ground survive. The purpose of the circle is unknown, but it makes clear that there was once something important here. This was the point from which Henry oversaw the beginning of Europe's great adventure—the exploration and domination of the world.

Cabo de São Vicente was the end of the Old World. Sagres was the beginning of the new one.

Sagres was the place where the Europeans finally banished the old demons of Rome and where Europe's new demons would first emerge, demons that haunt Europe to this day. Empires always spawn demons, and this was the beginning of the magnificent and terrifying European empire. It rose to unthinkable heights and committed unquestionable crimes. We are still living in the shadow of Europe's rise and fall. And it all began at Sagres and the Atlantic.

Prince Henry of Portugal, better known as Henry the Navigator (the son of King John I of Portugal), built a school for the navigators who probed the Atlantic for decades. It is said by some that among his students were men such as Vasco da Gama, who found the path to India, Ferdinand Magellan, who sailed around the world, and even Christopher Columbus, who was once shipwrecked and rescued, and spent some time at Henry's school. It is difficult to tell what sort of school this was, who actually attended and what was myth, what attendance meant, and how much time Henry himself spent here. Very little survives but a certain hard collective memory—that at this place the conquest of the world by Europe began, as Portugal spent its national treasure probing the Atlantic, searching for wealth in the unknown.

Portuguese exploration was a vast national enterprise. A great deal of money was staked on an unknown prize. The Portuguese were motivated by internal politics, international rivalry, religion, ideology, and the sheer glory of it. Whatever else Henry attempted, he kept meticulous records of every failed and successful voyage. Each ship went a little farther, was built a little better. There was no great leap, but decades of increasing knowledge. It was an exercise in engineering, seamanship, finance, and bureaucracy. It was also an exercise in glory.

Thinking of Sagres reminds me of NASA in its heroic days. NASA, too, was stunningly expensive, motivated by politics, geopolitics, and ideology. And like Sagres, there was the sheer majesty of it. Mercury, Gemini, and Apollo, space programs named after Greek gods, were run by men who hid the romance beneath the prosaic fabric of engineering, piloting, and bureaucracy—the romance of choosing to battle demons in an unknown realm with skill and grace. Survival demanded that they discipline themselves to move carefully, each step a little farther, each ship a little better. Sagres and NASA were made up of men who lived poetically rather than men who wrote poems. The Europeans began not with myths but with the will to shatter them. This was the beginning of empire. The resurrection of myth in the twentieth century was the end of empire.

It is unlikely that anyone other than a prince would have the standing and resources to undertake this kind of venture. Henry had access to the very rich Order of Christ, the Portuguese successor to the Knights Templar. Building ships was expensive and losing them more so. It took a man with Henry's nature to command such wealth and not squander it with impatience and impetuousness. But Henry, a careful, meticulous, religious, and thoughtful man, was also patient. When he founded his project, the world had a completely different sense of itself from that which emerged in the following centuries. Between the late fifteenth century and the late nineteenth century, there was hardly a part of the world that had not been occupied, or heavily influenced, by a European power at some point.

Perhaps more important than the mere conquest, the Europeans transformed the world from one that did not know itself into one that did. The idea of a common humanity could not exist in a world where no one was fully aware that there were other civilizations. The Incas had never heard of the Cossacks, the Tamils did not know the Scots, the Japa-

nese were not familiar with the Iroquois. In a world filled with seques-
tered civilizations no one was in a position to be aware of them all. These
barriers were smashed with the European assault. Even the smallest cultures were brought under European control or influence, made part of
this humanity, and denied the right to think of themselves as unique and
alone. The discovery of a single humanity was to become a revolutionary
force under the Europeans. It was also to become a bloody one.

   Such an enterprise as conquering the world and inventing humanity
carried with it a price. No one is certain how many died through the
direct impact of European imperialism, from military action, starvation,
disease, and other causes. Some experts estimate 100 million dead over
the course of four centuries of empire building, but no one really knows.
The dead were drawn from a world population much smaller than exists
today, making the price even more staggering. But so was the wealth
extracted, accumulated, and put to work in Europe. When I walk the
streets of London or Paris, the almost magical uses of the wealth Europe
extracted from its empire can be seen in each building—or in a single
street lamp. The price the world paid was enormous, but so were the
possibilities created.

   There is a quote attributed to Honoré de Balzac: behind every great
fortune there is a great crime. The same can be said of empires. The crime
of the European empire was not simply the number dead. It was the loss
of control over the futures of everyone they encountered. Whatever they
touched, and Europe touched everything, some measure of choice and
possibility was lost by those they visited. This was true of civilizations
and individuals. The charges that can be laid against European imperialism are vast. The possibilities that European imperialism opened up to
humanity are also vast. Just as a person's life should be judged, in the end,
on the whole, that is how, in the end, we will judge Europe. Judging great
things is not easy, not when done properly.

   Why did a school in Sagres, at the farthest end of Europe, start this revolution? Other civilizations could have done it. At the same time Henry
was founding his school, the Chinese had constructed a fleet potentially
capable of sailing the blue waters and compelling all they met to submit to their will. The Romans or Norsemen might have been able to do
this. The technology was not unique to the Europeans or to the Portuguese. Yet the others didn't do it, and the Portuguese and other Euro-

peans did. So we need to understand what caused first the Portuguese and then the rest of Atlantic Europe—Spain, France, the Netherlands, England—to undertake an adventure of such enormous proportions.

Europe, Islam, and the Origins of Exploration

A great deal of the story has to do with Islam. Europe was Christian, the place where Christ was worshipped. Another religion grew up alongside Christianity: Islam. Christianity dominated Europe. Islam dominated a far larger region ranging from Morocco to Mindanao, from Central Asia to Zanzibar. The two religions were intimately bound not only by the shared Old Testament but also by trade, politics, war, and even alliances. At a time when tensions between the Muslim and Christian worlds are intense, it is important to see how, alongside the tension, the two religions collaborated with and shaped each other.

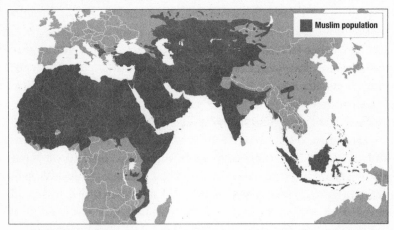

The Spread of Islam

Islam had created one of the most widespread civilizations in human history. It was not a single, integrated empire. Still, if any entity ought to have conquered the world, it was Islam. Many Muslim societies had developed merchant fleets and warships, but they didn't need to develop deep water navies. It was possible to travel from one end of maritime Islam to the other using coastal vessels, ships that traveled within sight of the coast or not far from it. They didn't have to support the cost of developing and building oceangoing vessels. They could make port regularly, mostly in Muslim countries, for trade and provisioning. The Muslims did not feel economic pressure to take the risks that Portugal now needed to take as they controlled a vast space by using smaller ships more efficiently and developing effective land routes.

Portugal's own problem originated partly in the challenge posed by Islam's strategic position. Christianity and Islam confronted each other almost from the beginning of Islam's rise. Christianity dominated the northern shore of the Mediterranean; Islam dominated the southern one. In 711 Muslim armies went north into Spain, ultimately occupying it and crossing the Pyrenees into France. In 732 Charles Martel, in a defining battle, defeated the Muslim armies, forcing them back behind the mountains and confining them to the Iberian Peninsula. Had Martel lost that battle, Europe would have been a very different place.

It is interesting the extent to which the two coexisted, even in war. *The Song of Roland*, a French poem from the middle of the twelfth century that is the oldest existing piece of French literature, tells about the war between Christian and Muslim in Spain. It is set in the city of Saragossa. Charlemagne, grandson of Charles Martel, is fighting the general Marsilla, a Muslim. Marsilla offers to convert to Christianity if Charlemagne leaves Spain. Charlemagne, tired of war, agrees. Roland, a great Christian warrior, rejects the peace. In the tortuous and complex tale, he sets out to sabotage the agreement, leading to a massive battle, a Christian victory, and Roland's death. What is most fascinating about the poem is the similarity between the Christian and Muslim warriors. They live in similar feudal social orders, have similar values of loyalty and chivalry, and could engage in political expediency while seeking to serve God.

They are, in many ways, mirror images of each other. Islam and Christianity were mortal enemies intertwined in conspiracies, alliances, and betrayals. Each conquered the other, seduced the other, and transformed the other. Neither Europe nor the Muslim lands can be understood without recalling both their endless wars and endless collaboration. European history cannot be understood without understanding Muslim history, and at this moment, events at either end of Europe were driving decisions in Sagres.

In 1453, the Muslim Ottomans captured Constantinople. In 1492, thirty-nine years later, the Spaniards captured Granada, the last Muslim city in Spain. Constantinople's fall represented a mortal threat to Christian Europe. But the capture of Granada gave the Iberians the confidence and resources to try to do something about it in a very unexpected way.

Europe craved spices, the ultimate luxury in late medieval times, which came primarily from India. Spices were used to flavor and preserve food, as well as for medicine and aphrodisiacs. Pepper was the most significant imported spice, as it was both a food preservative and was believed to prevent disease, in a time when the Black Plague stalked Europe. Pepper was believed to prevent the Plague, and whether it did or not, its price was staggering, comparable to that of gold.

Asia and Europe were linked by land and by sea. Ships brought spices by sea from India, and the Silk Road brought silks overland from China. The Silk Road was and still is a vibrant route, now filled more with pipelines and oil than silk. In the old city in Baku, Azerbaijan, there are restored caravanserai, hostels where travelers on the road could rest and eat. These are substantial buildings that could not have existed without customers, which meant the route was heavily traveled, and that a great deal of money could be made.

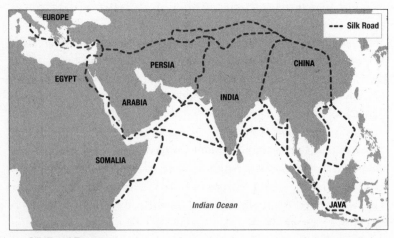

Silk Road Routes

Both the sea and land routes terminated at Constantinople, where another sea route made its way to Italian ports for further distribution of goods to the rest of Europe. At each stage in the road, merchants added to the price. What was inexpensive at the source became enormously expensive at its destination. With money came political power, and the main trading posts, like Mogadishu in Somalia, became powerful. A caliph who wanted to control the spice trade to Europe founded Cairo in the tenth century. It became the single point where spices passing through the Red Sea were collected for shipping into the Mediterranean. Europeans paid for the spices with silver and wool, both available in Europe and prized in India and China. The spices not only shaped trade, they created cities that lasted for millennia.

The caliph was, of course, Muslim, and Constantinople was Christian, so the wealth generated by their trade was distributed between Muslims and Christians. But a new force arose in the region four hundred years after the founding of Cairo and the beginning of Muslim-Christian collaboration. When the Ottomans conquered Constantinople they not only subjugated the Christians but became the dominant naval power in the eastern Mediterranean. The Ottomans had already interfered with the spice trade before their victory. Once they controlled Constantinople they squeezed the Europeans by first blocking and then imposing extremely high tariffs on goods transiting the Silk Road.

There were religious reasons certainly, but their motivation wasn't entirely religious. To control the Mediterranean, they needed allies. Although they had been previously allied with a number of Mediterranean powers, by the mid-fifteenth century the Ottomans found their most significant ally to be Christian Venice. Together the Ottomans and Venetians drove the price of spices higher and higher. With the Silk Road unusable, Europe's land trading system with Asia was broken. With the Mediterranean closed to it, so were its sea lanes. If the Europeans could find a way to bypass the Ottomans, they could not only regain access to India but also capture the profits now going to the Ottomans and Venetians.

The growing power of the Muslims and the rising price of spices were two of the forces driving Henry. He mounted a series of expeditions, led by captains and navigators whose training and experience he

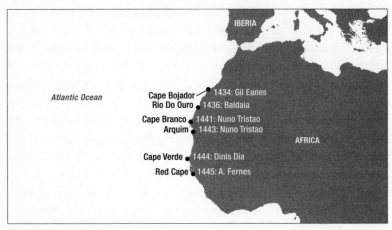

Portuguese Exploration of West Africa

had financed. Many of these men and ships were lost as they probed southward.

Legend said it was impossible to navigate past the point of Cape Bojador because the temperature of the water rose so high that it boiled. The failure of expeditions to return prior to 1434 seemed to substantiate this claim. In fact the region was dangerous because Muslims held the coast, and there were few opportunities for getting needed provisions. But the water didn't boil. Each year the Portuguese pressed farther south until by 1445 they had rounded the hump of West Africa, in the process increasing their skills and their power in the Atlantic.

At this point the Portuguese weren't yet looking for the path to India. They were looking for gold to finance the purchase of spices. Mali was believed to be a tremendously wealthy country, filled with gold, and the Portuguese were trying to find a route—a river, perhaps—that would allow them into the interior of Africa to reach these riches. The Portuguese thought this was true, but they didn't know for sure. When we speak of the world not knowing itself, the fact that the sophisticated Portuguese had no clear idea what lay inside Africa, only 150 miles to their south, is extraordinary. This is the ignorance the Portuguese were overcoming as they moved into the world beyond the West African coast, step by careful step.

Henry and Portugal had another motive besides spices—defeating the Muslims. The Muslims held West Africa, and while they were not deepwater sailors, they could and did capture Christian boats that sailed too close to shore. In order to probe south the Portuguese therefore had to navigate farther from the coast, out of the reach of the Muslims. In the course of moving away from the coast they discovered and seized the Azores in the Atlantic, a prize in itself. But Henry sought the more important prize. Going out to sea and then south would allow the Portuguese to outflank the Muslims to the south. Henry was a crusader. He had commanded the forces that conquered Ceuta in Morocco, and he lived during the time when Iberia was throwing off Muslim rule. For Henry, the pursuit of wealth and the defeat of the Muslims went hand in hand.

Legend told of a vastly powerful and wealthy Christian monarch somewhere in Africa named Prester John who was besieged by infidels and needed aid from Christian armies. In another version he had conquered the infidels and could aid in Europe's struggles. His legend lasted centuries, which is odd when you think about it. Nevertheless, going around the hump of West Africa and trying to find the path to Mali held out the possibility of making contact with Prester John and launching a Christian crusade from Africa's interior into North Africa.

We should also consider the geopolitical situation in Iberia aside from the Muslims. Cut off from the rest of Europe by the Pyrenees, the Iberian Peninsula was an isolated mass jutting into the Atlantic. Once Spain had united and expelled the final Muslims from Granada, it was a more powerful country on land than Portugal, but less powerful at sea. Due to their rivalry and the importance of the sea routes, the larger Spain needed to become a naval power. The smaller Portugal, unable to compete with Spain on land, was driven to become even more powerful at sea.

Portugal was not motivated by any one of these reasons alone but by a combination—containing Spain, reaching India, finding gold in Mali, making contact with Prester John, spreading the word of Christ, and seizing islands in the Atlantic. This complexity of motives remained one of the hallmarks of European imperialism. There were many goals; some were illusory, some were contradictory, but logical or not, combined they propelled the Portuguese forward.

The Spaniards came late to the game. They had struggled against the Muslims in Spain for centuries and were finishing the process of expelling the last Muslims from Granada and uniting their country. Portugal had become the predominant maritime power while Spain was preoccupied. But a united and peaceful Spain was much larger and more powerful than Portugal. Portugal had taken advantage of a window of opportunity. Spain wanted to close it. Their competition drove the process of exploration even harder.

The Portuguese controlled the southern route around Africa, and Spain wasn't yet in a position to challenge them there. But Christopher Columbus provided Spain with another option, arguing that China and India could be reached by going due west. The problem was that no one in Europe was sure how long it would take to reach India and China via the western route or if it was even possible. Columbus proposed this route to the Portuguese, but they rejected it. The southern route was more promising and, in addition, they controlled it. They didn't need to roll the dice. The Spaniards, also wanting to reach India and not wanting to challenge the Portuguese on the southern route, accepted Columbus's proposal. They were prepared to roll to play in the game and backed Columbus.

The southern route paid off for the Portuguese. Vasco da Gama reached Calicut on the Malabar coast of India in May 1498. He announced his presence with authority. His shelling of the city with guns terrified Calicut, which quickly agreed to trade with Portugal. Da Gama's voyage to India had included finding and sinking a "Mecca Ship," a ship carrying pilgrims to Mecca, killing all aboard. Hostility to Islam and desire for wealth remained intermingled. In India he found Hindus who were as hostile to Muslims as he was. Da Gama certainly achieved Henry's goals of creating a new route to India and bypassing the Ottomans. He also set the stage for centuries of European domination of India.

This would seem to have been the pinnacle of Iberian success. It wasn't. Columbus's voyage would prove more important, difficult as that might have been to imagine at the time.

In spite of its disappointment with his first voyage, the Spanish court funded others. They were to discover something even more valuable than a path to spices—the other half of the world—and in time they found that it was filled with gold and silver. Spain did not trade in spices. It could steal the wealth of the misnamed Indians.

The Portuguese had found the way to something whose existence was already known. Columbus had stumbled onto something totally new—an unknown part of humanity. Discovering that there were massive unknowns in the world revolutionized European thinking. The Portuguese, having reached India, appeared to have won the game. The Spaniards, having encountered something for which they had no frame of reference, had actually won the greater prize.

When Odysseus started the journey that Homer chronicled, he entered a world that was not only unknown to him but filled with wondrous beings. There were Cyclopes, Lotus Eaters, and an endless array of beings nearer to the gods than he was. He was in an enchanted world, as the German philosophers Max Horkheimer and Theodor Adorno put it. Odysseus discovered the unknown world, came to understand it, and ultimately dominated it. He tore away the veil that covered it, and with it its enchantment. He came to know it, and as it became familiar it lost its magic. This was Odysseus's tragedy, that the act of learning about the world destroyed its enchantment and made it prosaic. It became less than it might have been. This would be one of Europe's tragedies as well, as the discovery of an enchanted world devolved into mere business devoid of magic.

Columbus's discovery of an entirely unknown and exotic part of humanity resurrected the Homeric sense of an enchanted world. His discovery excited the lust for wealth, but more deeply, the lust for the unknown, the enchanted, that was out there, beyond the oceans. The world that he discovered enthralled Europe. It excited fantasies in the minds of ordinary men ground into the dust of everyday life. The oceans had been seen as filled with unknown and terrifying things. Columbus lifted the veil, ever so slightly, off the world on the other side of the dreaded oceans. It was a world that held secrets—and wealth—that made the oceans worth enduring. Countless Europeans after Columbus crossed these oceans, the first seeking enchantment, then tearing away the veil and creating a new, but prosaic, world. Columbus discovered the enchanted, but not the secret of knowing it without destroying it.

What, after all, is European science if not the belief that the world contains within it and beyond it cleverly hidden and enchanted things? What is science but the lust to uncover these things? This lust gripped Europe, best symbolized by the myth of Faust, who made a deal with the devil in exchange for knowledge—not power, not money. Faust became Europe, and it started with Columbus arriving in a place he did not know and seeing things he could not understand or imagine.

But first, the explorers had to give way to the next wave of Europeans, the tough guys, the conquistadors.

Hungry Men Well Armed

The Extremadura is dry and hot and one of the poorest places in Spain. This region bred many of the men who explored and conquered the New World. Their names ring through history: Pizarro, who conquered the Incas in Peru; Balboa, who went to Panama and first saw the Pacific from the New World; and de Soto, who went north and discovered the Mississippi. But perhaps the greatest and most important of them was Hernán Cortés, who conquered Mexico.

Cortés was the opposite of Henry the Navigator in most ways. Henry was well fed, Cortés was hungry. Henry was moderate in demeanor, Cortés was a bravo, just this side of an outlaw. Henry wanted to preserve his family's power, Cortés lusted for the wealth and power he didn't have. Henry came from the highest ranks of society, Cortés came from near the bottom. One was patient, the other was a ruthless man with an urgent determination to succeed. The two men, one refined and the other thuggish, were the two faces of Europe for the next five hundred years. They shared one trait: a deep Catholicism, sharpened in the wars against Islam, and a source of faith, obligation, and fear.

Henry lusted to know the world, but it was a patient lust and a methodical one—step by careful step, never giving up, but never going too far too fast. It prepared the ground for men like Columbus and allowed them to remove the veil. Cortés was both clever and a brute. He manipulated his enemies and then defeated and enslaved them without mercy. Where Henry was patient, Cortés was in a hurry. But then one was rich and the other poor. Europe approached the world with a mixture of caution and calculation, fearing what it might hold—and then loosed a raging force on its shores that took what it wanted in a rush of hunger for triumph. Neither would have been possible without the other. Together, with their cannon, they were invincible for centuries.

With men like Cortés, the metaphorical assault on the world now turned into an actual assault. This was the first time Europeans had encountered a completely unknown continent and civilization. The core of the Aztec empire around its capital of Tenochtitlán consisted of about 200,000 people with a ruling class and subordinate tribes. Aztec warriors were brave and trained and not a force to be trifled with. Their economy was substantial and the Aztec capital was more sophisticated and complex than most European cities.

Cortés landed on the island of Cozumel off the Yucatán cost, near where Cancún is today, with its hotels and cruise ships. This was Mayan territory, and if you leave Cancún and drive for about eighteen hours on the back roads, into the mountains of Chiapas, you will find that descendants of the Mayas still live there and still resist the government in Mexico City. Cortés landed with five hundred men and some slaves. Legend has it that when he landed he burned the boats that brought them. He told his men that there was no going back. They would triumph or die; it was a battle with no retreat. Whether the boats were burned or not, I don't know. But with five hundred men against an empire, he would either be annihilated or, a preposterous thought, he would triumph. There was no middle ground and Cortés must have known that.

It is said that when they saw the Spaniards and their horses the Aztecs believed the god Quetzalcoatl had returned. Imagine seeing a UFO landing. Strange creatures wearing clothing made out of unknown and wondrous metals, speaking an utterly unknown tongue, emerge from a craft no one has ever seen before. Now envision the terror of the natives reacting to their first encounter with these creatures—a terror commercialized by Hollywood many times over.

Cortés had weapons the Aztecs had never seen, and the direction from which he came had never before presented danger. While the conquistadors' guns and cannon could not have withstood a determined assault by masses of Aztecs, it was psychologically difficult to confront what appeared to be magical. The sense of enchantment ran both ways.

The sound, fire, and death unleashed by these weapons had no frame of reference for the Aztecs. The conquistadors projected a sense of inevitability to the Aztec elite because their power was incomprehensible. Only the gods possessed incomprehensible power, and the Aztecs felt as if enraged Gods had fallen upon them.

Though such an overwhelming event may have sapped the will of the Aztecs, they rallied and resisted. Once the shock had abated, they recalled who they were, great warriors who had conquered many. There were only five hundred Spaniards, and even if they were armed with guns and cannon, thousands of warriors could have overcome them. The reason for the Aztec defeat rests in this fact: Cortés was actually attacking with thousands of warriors, neither Spanish nor Aztec.

The Aztecs had risen to power a little more than a century before. Their rule was brutal and exploitative and there are indications of human sacrifice, with the victims selected from subordinate tribes. Aztec rulers were deeply feared and resented, and for many, the arrival of the Spaniards was salvation. The Aztecs' capital—Tenochtitlán—was in the central Mexican basin where Mexico City is now. Their rule didn't reach to the Yucatán, and they had not yet conquered the Mayans. But the Mayans still feared a future with the Aztecs in power, and they joined the Spaniards. Thousands from other tribes, including tribes already subject to Montezuma, the Aztec ruler, joined them as well. Montezuma didn't want to wage war because it was far from clear that all his own forces were loyal to him. He tried diplomacy, not because he remained psychologically stunned by the Spaniards' arrival, but because his power base was fragmented and in many cases hostile. A flashpoint to the south of the Aztec empire had been ignited by the arrival of Cortés, and it destroyed the Aztecs.

Cortés's skill was neither military nor psychological. It was diplomatic. He was able to exploit the weakness of Montezuma's regime because it rested on a base of sand. Pizarro, who was in the process of conquering the Incas in Peru, faced precisely the same situation. The Incan empire was also based on a coalition of tribes, many of whom saw themselves as victims of the Incas rather than as beneficiaries. Pizarro exploited the brutality of the Incan rulers to recruit a force that could defeat them.

This is vitally important for understanding why the Europeans conquered the world. They did not merely impose injustice. Injustice already existed. Local rulers operated by the same methods as the Europeans did. They subordinated neighbors and used power and fear to control them. When the Europeans came along, sided with those who were oppressed, and offered wealth to others, the local political structure collapsed. The Europeans exploited this collapse and imposed their rule. Five hundred men did not conquer the Aztecs. Five hundred men and thousands of Aztec enemies conquered the Aztecs. The Spaniards exploited Aztec or Incan weakness and imposed their own brutal regime to replace it. But there was nothing new in that for Mexico or Peru.

Another element was at work here: the sheer barbaric will and nearly insane courage of the conquistadors. Elsewhere I have argued that civilizations are divided into three phases. The first phase is barbarism, a time when people believe that the laws of their own village are the laws of nature, as George Bernard Shaw put it. The second phase is civilization, where people continue to believe in the justice of their ways but harbor openness to the idea that they might be in error. The third phase, decadence, is the moment in which people come to believe that there is no truth, or that all lies are equally true.

The conquistadors' actions didn't make them barbarians, but rather they were able to do what they did because they were barbarians. They believed in their religion with deep conviction and without doubt, not with the sophistication of a theologian but with the simplicity of those to whom God is both terrible and familiar. For Cortés, God was not a metaphor, but a being. This view is not unique to Catholicism. Muslims, Protestants, Jews, and others at various points shared this sensibility and used it to achieve things that appeared to be beyond their powers. The pure, unenlightened will of the barbarian is his power.

Roman Catholic doctrine revolved around the notion of "Two Swords." Put forward by Pope Boniface VIII, the doctrine holds that there is the sword that wields power in the material world and is held by the state. There is also the sword held by the Church that wields power in the spiritual world. This does not mean divided rule. Each sword supports the other. It means that where one goes, the other goes as well, and that political and spiritual power can't be divided. This drives the evangelical spirit of the Church. Christianity was prepared to use the sword to convert, but it also saw conversion as being led by clerical evangelists who brought Christianity to the heathen. Christianity seduced the heathen by the richness of its thought, and the discipline and conviction of its warriors. Christianity, like Islam, was not only something to submit to, but something worth emulating.

It is hard to believe that the conquistadors took risks out of pure self-interest. No matter how much they were motivated by greed, the prospects of defeating the Aztec and Inca empires must have appeared hopeless. How, after all, could any rational person have expected to win against those odds? The conquistadors were Catholics and believed they were acting as the worldly sword of the Church. It is easy to dismiss this as simply justification for the pursuit of wealth, but that would be to misunderstand and underestimate them. They were quite serious in their dual mission, and conversion by the sword did not strike them as ironic. They had seen it on both sides in the war with Islam. Moreover, the likelihood of their survival was so small it would have required a miracle. Belief in a miraculous God is the only psychological explanation for the risks they took.

Christianity was intimately bound up with the European conquest of the world. It was needed partly to drive the conquerors, partly to subdue the conquered. The Aztecs were stunned by the arrival of men in metal, riding horses and carrying tubes that belched fire. This mattered. But the other dimension of the psychological attack was that the Spaniards claimed to speak in the name of a god greater than theirs. The presence of this god, validated by the victory of the conquistadors, was the more important element in the shattering of their self-confidence. It also shepherded them into submission and obedience. But still, the rising of those whom the Aztecs oppressed was central to their fall.

It is easy to see this as a condemnation of the Spaniards or of Christianity. However, the Aztecs they destroyed had taken power only a few generations before, supplanting peoples and gods that went before them. Itzcoatl founded the Aztec empire by conquering key towns in the Mexican valley. When he died in 1440, Montezuma took power and in the final battle of his ascendancy took five hundred prisoners and sacrificed them. The Spaniards were not morally inferior to their victims, who a generation before had been the victimizers. But they were operating on a grander scale and ultimately found in the two-swords doctrine an efficient engine not only for conquest but for domination.

The Spaniards exploited the political divisions that existed among the natives of Mexico, Peru, and other places. But the Europeans had their own divisions. The Portuguese also laid claim to their share of South America, and battles broke out there between them and the Spanish. A treaty, negotiated by the pope, divided Latin America between Spanish and Portuguese zones. Brazil speaks Portuguese today. Most of the rest of South America speaks Spanish. The tension between Portugal and Spain persisted and drained each of them. The wealth exploited by the Spaniards in the New World gave them the power to seek to unite Europe. In the end it was not enough. Their failure to dominate and unite Europe freed France, Britain, and the Netherlands to pursue their own imperial strategies.

The Spaniards' mistake was that they took too much back home and left too little on which to build a society in the New World. The English, in particular, would reverse this, creating little New Englands in North America. But the English, too, lacked the strength to impose their will on Europe and unite it. Ultimately the ability of Europeans to conquer the world but their inability to conquer themselves would prove part of their fatal flaw. This is the point to which Sagres brought Europe.

The Portuguese and the Spaniards began the conquest of the world for a host of reasons. One was technological. They were able to construct ships large enough to sail on the high seas, carrying supplies that would last for months and guns with which to stun their enemies. But the real reason that they undertook the journey was that they needed to. The route to India and China had been impeded, and whoever found another path would become fabulously wealthy and powerful. They had the means and they had the need, and in the end it boiled down to this.

The story of Henry the Navigator, Vasco da Gama, Columbus, and Hernán Cortés is, of course, a tiny fraction of the story of the conquest of the world by European powers. Between 1492 and 1992, when the Soviet Union collapsed, five hundred years passed. In 1492 the first global power appeared. In 1992 the last European global power collapsed. There were three phases to this conquest. The first was the Iberian. The second was the northwestern European, which lasted until America expelled the

British and South America the Iberians. This began the final phase, the conquest of Africa and parts of Asia, particularly by Britain. My story is not about the conquest, but about how it all finally collapsed. The opening act of this story will suffice to allow us to understand who the Europeans had become, and what kind of men could do such enormous and terrible things.

But this will not simply be a story of the physical conquest of much of the world. It is about the European obsession with the world, and its hunger to own it. This does not simply mean dominion over Latin America or India, but over objects as small as bacteria, and as vast as galaxies. The European obsession with possessing everything and where it comes from and where it leads to—the reasons Faust made a deal with the devil—is my concern here. Bear Cortés in mind because there are many like him. Bear Henry in mind as well; there were fewer like him, but they were important in the meticulous rise of the East India Company the British used to exploit their colonies. But among the engineers, the scientists, the artists, and the warriors of Europe, there was a Faustian hunger for everything, a love of the enchanted, a desire to know, that turned the world into a prosaic and uninteresting place, and the European into something much weaker than he appeared.

3

The Fragmentation of the European Mind

When Henry's soul merged with Cortés's, what emerged was an intellectual who was also a swashbuckler. It was someone who lived the life of the mind but who took that life where he chose, beyond the limits of custom and revealed truth. Like the swashbuckler, he refused to accept any boundaries save those set by his conscience, his reason, and his will. In the hands of great minds, this opened the door for the discovery of the hidden, magnificent, and dangerous truths about nature and the human condition. The best of them understood the danger and took care in proclaiming the truths. Lesser minds shattered noble and necessary lies as if there would be no price to pay. The most dangerous were the ordinary, mediocre minds who used the insight of the great thinkers to claim the right to believe anything they chose, and argued that anything offensive was by nature true. Mediocrity claimed the rights of genius simply because it respected nothing. In the hands of both the great and the pedestrian, Europe fragmented into infinite pieces, a few brilliant, most dull and banal. The fragmentation of the European mind would in due course reflect the fragmentation of Europe's geography. Eventually, it would cost Europe its empire and its soul.

In 1500 Christianity dominated the European mainland and Catholicism the peninsula. Catholicism was both utterly accessible and infinitely mysterious, as is the case with all serious modes of thought. In the mass it was a set of rituals binding custom and superstition. It provided fear and comfort in proper proportion. At its intellectual depths it was subtle, complex, and contradictory. It sought both political and spiritual authority. It had to engage in political life, a life of struggle and compromise. Spiritually, it had to reconcile Christ with the political, while still understanding the meaning of his life. The former demanded that compromise and corruption be distinguished from each other. The latter demanded that the meaning of all this be understood through the prism of Christ's sacrifice. It was an edifice as complex and beautiful as a medieval cathedral, as difficult to construct and as expensive to maintain.

In the Treaty of Tordesillas of 1494, Pope Alexander VI divided the world between Spain and Portugal. We should pause and consider the incredible hubris behind this. Not only did the Vatican ignore other Catholic countries, but it ignored the claims of the native inhabitants, even those who had converted to Catholicism. The subtlety of Augustine and Aquinas appealed to the deepest sensibilities of the Church, and the simple religious, as they were called, resonated to its beautiful and seductive ritual, but at this time and place, it was the claim to universal political authority over humanity that is the most striking.

From a spiritual and pastoral point of view—as well as the political—this was the high point of the Catholic Church. It dominated the European peninsula. It was converting the heathen. It had triumphed over the Muslims in Iberia. But there were things gnawing at the Church. The Treaty of Tordesillas was necessary to prevent war between two great Catholic powers. The discovery of the vastness of the world, most of whose inhabitants had not heard the name *Jesus*, raised potential questions about the tension between humanity and the Church's claim of universality. Small political and intellectual rifts were opening but not yet fully visible. Behind it all, the merging of Henry and Cortés opened the door to the intellectual swashbuckler who would set his own terms and his own rules and disrupt the European intellectual order.

It began with three intellectual blows to European self-certainty, all three in the fifty-one years between 1492 and 1543. There were three certainties in the popular culture of the European peninsula: the world was the center of the universe; Europe was the center of the world; and the Church was the center of Europe. In the course of fifty-one years, the European intellectual framework would receive a series of blows from radical and irresistible ideas that would lead to a revolution in the European mind, and ultimately to its fragmentation. It didn't happen in a neat sequence, but it happened very quickly in the time frame of human history.

Shocks and Consequences

In 1492 Columbus's voyage drove home the fact that the world was round. The fact that the world was physically round was not unknown, of course. But Columbus showed it to be round in a deeper sense. He opened the door to a world filled with other, quite advanced civilizations, none of whom had heard of Europe, and none of whom had heard of Christianity. It was not simply that they had rejected Christianity, as the Muslims had. They had simply never heard of it. The world was round not only in the sense that its surface could have no center, but that no one civilization was its pivot. Europeans could claim that their civilization was the first among many, but they could draw no comfort from a geography that contained civilizations ignorant of and indifferent to their very existence. If Christ was the savior, then how could it be that Christianity had never been revealed to the majority of humanity? The world was far larger, less centered, and more diverse than they had previously believed. Over the centuries the idea that European civilization was inherently superior to the "noble savages," in Rousseau's terms, became more and more dubious, until all cultures seemed of equal value.

Twenty-five years later, in 1517, Martin Luther nailed his Ninety-Five Theses to the door of a church, initiating the Protestant Reformation, which challenged the idea that Rome was the center of Europe. Luther's ultimate argument was that the Bishop of Rome did not have a unique relation to God, and that each person could approach God on his or her own without the intercession of a priest. People could read the Bible as individuals, guided by conscience and the gift of God's Grace, to reach their own conclusions. Rather than being the center of Christianity—something always challenged by Christian Orthodoxy—Rome was now challenged inside the European peninsula. Just as Europe lost its psychological primacy in the world over time, Catholicism lost its primacy in the parts of the European peninsula it had dominated.

Twenty-six years after that, in 1543, Copernicus demonstrated with clarity and subtlety that the earth was not the center of the universe but revolved around the sun. This was more than a cosmological insight. There were others who had argued this. But Copernicus's demonstration was so powerful that it raised this question: If God created the world so that he might make men in his own image, why did he not place his masterpiece, the purpose of the entire universe, at its center? Centuries later, it was pointed out that the world was in fact insignificant, located on the rim of an ordinary galaxy, one of trillions. Copernicus's insight led to a sense of human insignificance that challenged the teachings of many religions, but none more so than a religion whose beliefs held that God gave his only son to man.

The Catholic Church had taught that men came to knowledge of God through the teachings of the Church, as illuminated by the hierarchy and the priesthood. Martin Luther, at the Diet of Worms, said, "My conscience is held captive by the Word of God. And to act against conscience is neither right nor safe." This pronouncement and its introduction of individual responsibility, conscience, and doubt reshaped the entire structure of Christianity and set the stage for a revolution in Europe that had endless unexpected consequences.

For Catholicism, the teachings of the Church represented the word of God and no individual could interpret the Christian faith outside the framework of the Church. Luther introduced the idea of conscience, the private convictions of individuals. This was an argument for the individual's right and authority to study the word of God, the Bible, and interpret it as his or her conscience dictated. There is no way to minimize the significance of this, although Luther sought to avoid complete subjectivism. This was still Christianity, but it elevated the individual Christian to the center of Christianity and demoted Rome, changing the spiritual landscape of Europe.

All this took place in the context of a technical revolution. The printing press was invented sometime before 1440. By 1500 there were some one thousand presses in Europe. Until the invention of the printing press, the written word was rare. Illiteracy existed not only because people couldn't learn to read, but because there was nothing for them to read. Now the Bible was available for all to read, and to read in the vulgate, the native languages of their birth. That simple act undermined the authority of the priest more than any other. People could read the Bible daily in their homes, rather than waiting for Sunday and for the priest to read and interpret the Word. They could now read it and disagree on its meaning and, from the disagreement, break not only with Rome but with each other. The Church on the European peninsula did not merely schism, it began to fragment, and this fragmentation came along increasingly national lines. Language, the ability not only to speak but to read, created broader bonds among people for whom a common language had not yet developed political meaning.

The printing press allowed Luther not only to translate the Bible into German, but to distribute it. If Christianity was the conscience confronting the word of God directly, the printing press made that confrontation possible. It also made it possible to print pamphlets, arguments, and debates and distribute them among the public, who could for the first time participate directly in the life of the mind.

One consequence was the legitimation of the ordinary languages of Europe. They were no longer simply vulgar, with the pathway to God marked by Latin signs, but were equally valid not only for writing, but for thought. An idea conceived in German was no longer inferior to one in Latin. And the common characteristic of speaking German or English or any other language bound people together in a community broader than their village. People could read or have read to them in their native tongues thoughts created by people they had never met. Language was the common denominator, and language became the foundation of the nation, and an additional factor in creating European flashpoints.

Luther spoke to Germans in German. The Germans stopped being a minor problem for dynasties to manage and became a political engine in their own right. There was a German movement that wished to recover the memory of historical Germany, and Lutheranism was the foundation of this movement, and integral to emerging German nationalism. Protestantism was the beginning of the popular nationalisms that would lead to Europe's crowded geography. Each nation was based on language and each language was equal in God's eye. The European mind was fragmenting.

The heartland of the Reformation was Germany, but it spread throughout the northern periphery of Europe, the British Isles, and

Scandinavia. But its north German roots were always there. It is interesting to note that Copernicus was German/Polish, Luther was German, and Gutenberg was German. Without pressing this point too far, I'm reminded of the way Germanic tribes resisted the Romans and retained their independence. It is interesting that the Germans began the rebellion against Rome and reasserted their independence.

The Reformation also bred another sort of fragmentation. Conscience and faith were personal things, private to the person thinking the thought. By anchoring faith in conscience and elevating the individual, the Reformation opened a door to this question: Whose interpretation of the Bible was correct? An element of doubt entered in two ways. First, how could you judge the sincerity of conscience and faith? And more important, how could you choose between interpretations? Luther galvanized the Reformation. He was not its culmination. The reformers were themselves challenged by reformers. There were differences between national forms of the Reformation, differences between major factions, and endless small factions breaking off and forming their own churches. If faith and conscience were the guides to the Bible, then no man's interpretation was authoritative. Each man had to measure each idea by his faith and conscience. Not only was each man free to do this, but conscience demanded he do so.

Where the Catholic Church bound believers into a single fabric of faith and action, Protestantism opened the door not so much to doubt as to uncertainty, and not so much to skepticism as to caution about all claims of authority. This was a major break with the past at a time when many things were in flux. It provided the theological underpinnings to another emerging intellectual movement—the scientific revolution.

Luther had argued that the time of miracles had ended with the early Church's founding. That meant divine intrusions no longer disrupted the natural order that God had created. The world was predictable and stable—the laws of nature governed. If natural laws governed the world, then the question became how we could know those natural laws. The Bible was one path, but the Bible dealt less with nature than with the supernatural, with God and his will. But if you followed the logic that flowed from Lutheranism, then there was another realm that had to be studied and could not simply be studied via the Bible: nature. And that meant science.

Science and Enlightenment

The scientific revolution included many thinkers and strands. It was not simply a Protestant movement by any means, but it was a movement that had some of its roots in Protestantism, both in terms of its view of nature, and in terms of its elevation of conscience and the individual to the center of the moral and intellectual universe. In addition the single most influential figure in the early scientific revolution was a Protestant, a political figure, and a supporter of Elizabeth I and James I. It's in this sense that the birth of science was bound up with the Reformation and politics.

Francis Bacon was born in 1561, fifteen years after Luther's death. In *The Great Instauration*, Bacon proposed a new approach to knowledge. While acknowledging the primacy of God and spirit, he proposed a way of looking at the world that was primarily material, based on what the human senses could perceive. The end of miracles meant that the material world and its laws ought now to be seen as in some ways the final word of God. The deductive reasoning that had driven scholasticism in the Middle Ages had to give way to inductive reasoning. It was now necessary to look at the world and the things hidden there, rather than at the writings of those who had reflected on the mind reflecting.

Bacon laid out a method for uncovering the secrets hidden in nature. The scientific method that he devised was based on the doctrine of observation of nature and reasoning based on that observation. Hypotheses were posed, and proven or disproven based on observation and experiment. The scientific method was driven by the principle of increasing human knowledge by doubting what might have been believed in the past and testing that belief through rational analysis. The heart of the scientific method was an insistence that any proposition about the material world must justify itself through evidence and reason. This laid the philosophical foundation of science explicitly. It also made this point: in the physical world, at least, all ideas were subject to challenge and doubt.

Oddly, while Bacon appeared never to challenge Christianity, these lines appear in his work:

Atheism leaves a man to sense, to philosophy, to natural piety, to laws, to reputation; all which may be guides to an outward moral virtue, though religion were not; but superstition dismounts all these, and erecteth an absolute monarchy in the minds of men. Therefore atheism did never perturb states; for it makes men wary of themselves, as looking no further: and we see the times inclined to atheism (as the time of Augustus Caesar) were civil times. But superstition hath been the confusion of many states, and bringeth in a new primum mobile, that ravisheth all the spheres of government.

Science is not necessarily atheistic. It does not have to deny the existence of a spiritual realm that it cannot provide guidance to. But there is a temptation in science to elevate the material over the spiritual because it can be studied with precision, while spiritual studies are less disciplined. We all believe that what we do is the most important thing, and science values nature. Luther challenged authority by way of conscience, of individual thought. Bacon moves further down this path by turning thought—reason—into a machine that can understand all of nature. The enemy of science is superstition, beliefs based on authority rather than evidence. Bacon defends atheism against superstition, leaving it to us to figure out if he is thinking of all things spiritual as superstition.

Bacon does something extraordinary. When Luther said that the age of miracles had ended, he never intended to imply that the spiritual realm wasn't real and of primary importance. Nor did he intend to free men from the constraints of biblical teaching when he declared each man and his conscience free and required to confront the Bible directly. However much it might appear that he was speaking in favor of the law of nature as the thing we ought to concern ourselves with, or that he was freeing men to be freethinkers, Luther was not doing that. He was freeing men to a pious consideration of God's will through the Bible.

Bacon made the critical break. First, he focused men on nature. Second, he created a method based on reason for understanding nature. And finally, he opened the door to thinking about the world without recourse to God. Bacon sought to disenchant nature and place it under the control and will of human reason. Whatever his outward piety or political leanings, Bacon elevated human reason to the center of the universe, and he knew he was doing it. And in so doing, he was opening the door not only to knowledge, but also to the destruction of the certainty of Europe.

Thomas Hobbes was an acquaintance of Bacon. Hobbes wrote in his book *Leviathan*, published in 1651, that "there is no conception in a man's mind which hath not at first, totally or by parts, been begotten upon the organs of sense." In other words, all ideas come from the senses—and since God can't be sensed, by implication, he can't be known. Hobbes called man's natural life "nasty, brutish and short." Hobbes posed a fundamentally new view. If nature was as dangerous as he said, then nature was the thing to be overcome. The means of overcoming nature, Bacon taught, was through technology. Hobbes's view laid the groundwork for applying science and technology to the task of overcoming all the defects of nature. And that set the stage for modern technological culture.

The scientific revolution had one irresistible virtue. It was useful. Bacon never intended science to be contemplative but to provide benefits to mankind. When we looked at Sagres, we saw where Europe's conquest of the world began. When we look at Bacon, we see where Europe's conquest of nature began. The transformation of the way humans moved, communicated, healed, and learned was rooted in Bacon's scientific method, extended to technology. It transformed humanity's relation to nature in the same way as European exploration and imperialism changed humanity's relation to itself.

The Enlightenment arose from the three shocks, and it swept the Western European peninsula from the mid-seventeenth century to the end of the eighteenth, representing a revolution in human thought. The Enlightenment sought to bring clarity to the world by revealing what had been obscured by superstition. It wanted to redefine man, society, and humanity, first intellectually and later politically. There was enormous growth in what the world understood about nature, and in the complexity and sophistication of thought. That increased understanding of nature survived.

There were so many figures and trends during the Enlightenment that it is almost impossible to say anything about it that can't be contradicted. For example, the Enlightenment was ultimately antireligious. But René Descartes, one of its key figures, remained a devout Catholic, even though this contradicted much of what he said. As Jean-Jacques Rousseau once wrote, "I have seen these contradictions and they have not rebuffed me." Rousseau's argument was that reality wasn't elegant. It was filled with contradictions, small fragments of truth that opposed each other. The Enlightenment was at war with religion. It was also at war with itself—the European mind fragmented.

At the heart of the Enlightenment was reason, the idea that human reason could understand the universe and humanity. There were things not yet known, but there was nothing that could not, in principle, be known by reason. If reason was the razor that sliced through everything, then the best people were those who reasoned best. Traditional society rested on the aristocracy, and the European aristocracy was determined by birth. The argument in favor of it was that heredity determined virtue, and therefore rule by an aristocracy selected by birth. For the Enlightenment, birth was an accident, and the greatest injustice was allowing accidents of birth to determine someone's fate. For the Enlightenment, the only aristocracy was that of talent, and talent was based on the ability to reason. It may have been the result of birth, but no one's fate ought to be determined even prior to birth. And this is where the Enlightenment planted the idea that transformed the celebration of reason into a revolution against the old regime.

Europe developed the concept of merit. If reason was the only standard by which to judge men, then those men who had reason should rule. The first stage in the development of rule by reason was the enlightened despot, a king who ruled both by birth and intellectual excellence. The second stage was the republic, in which the best men, selected by an electorate with certain qualifications, were selected as most suited to represent them in systems of government designed to restrain even their passions. This was the foundation of European liberalism. But it took Europe forward, to a more radical idea.

If Galileo had the right to think as he pleased, then everyone had the right to think as they pleased. And short of harming others, why didn't they have the right to act on those thoughts? In the end, who was to say what the line was between genius and mediocrity? One path led to democratic revolutions. The other led to meritocracy, rule by the most rational of people. Both paths were difficult. The Enlightenment celebrated reason as the only standard by which people could be judged, but it never provided an indisputable method for distinguishing the rational from the irrational. The freedom to think and speak without the ability to respect superior thought fragmented the European mind.

It opened the door to the superiority of the most persuasive, not the most rational.

The Enlightenment devolves into radical individualism, but the individual's wisdom could not be guaranteed. Even if he could live by himself, life would be nasty, poor, brutish, and short. Individualism was an abstract concept. It had to be rounded out by community. What kind of community could there be? Obviously its leaders had to be bound to their followers. It had to be republican in representation, and democratic in choice. The organization of the community doesn't answer the question of what decisions were just and proper. The dynastic kingdoms and empires were delegitimized. No state ruled by a despot could govern individuals. The right to self-government was fundamental. But equally confusing was the question of what constituted the geography to be governed. Who was a citizen? Who was not? Who could vote and who could govern? What was left to work with derived from Luther: the legitimacy of language, culture, and history. In other words, what was left was the nation. The problem was that the nation was in some ways antithetical to the Enlightenment. It was built on birth more than on individual virtue. A German was German, a Frenchman was French, all without any test of reason or talent. He just was. The nation provided a human with the things that are most human—language and a past that stretched back before his birth. Enlightenment and nationalism were not simply incompatible, they created a tension not always easy to bridge. The bridge was national self-determination—democracy—but democracy can be as ruthless and limitless as despotism. In the twentieth century we saw the nation in its rawest form, driven by national self-determination.

Whatever the tension, men needed a place to be born, nurtured, and protected. Those things became vital to all men. There is a concept that is critical in understanding this: love of one's own. The first loves of humans are the things they were born to—parents, language, religion, and village. These are things a man didn't choose, they were his by birth and he was theirs, and unlike romantic love, which is chosen, these are the first, simplest, and most powerful loves—the ones beyond even thought, let alone choice. The Enlightenment wanted to break the bonds of birth, to free men from the limits of those identities, the things they were born to. Yet in breaking those bonds they created men who were lost in their own thoughts. Freeing men from superstition meant freeing them from religion in its lowest, irrational sense. However, these men still needed to be part of a place where community, obligation, and history existed, lest their solitary thoughts wreak havoc.

Here was the problem. Science and enlightenment had reduced humans to their physical nature and appetites. If that is all they were, then what were their obligations to each other and themselves? What is moral and how do you know it? The inability to answer this question made men dangerous. They were no different from animals. Somehow, atomized men had to reenter society and they needed a reason. There was no good reason, but it was still necessary. Men had to be seduced to return to their community and history—had to be told tales that were enchanting to save them from themselves and the banality of their lives. They needed fairy tales, something to explain to their souls who they were.

German parents—and those in many other European countries— told their children tales both terrifying and electrifying. "Hansel and Gretel" is a story about two children, a boy and a girl, born to a poor woodcutter. Their mother dies and he remarries. The stepmother persuades her husband to take Hansel and Gretel into the forest and abandon them there so that the parents might have more to eat themselves. Overhearing the conversation, the brother decides to put pebbles in his pocket so that he can trace his way home after being abandoned. When the children return home, the stepmother convinces the father to again abandon them, and this time they can't go outside to gather pebbles, so the brother leaves a trail of bread crumbs. In the forest, they encounter a witch who decides to put them in an oven and eat them. The boy is to be baked in an oven as a feast for the witch. The girl, understanding what is to happen, pushes the witch into the oven, where she dies screaming. The children take the witch's jewels and return home, led by a bird. When they get there they discover that their stepmother has died, and their father welcomes them and their jewels home. They live happily ever after.

There was a political message in these tales of German victimization and cleverness. The stories begin with injustice, incredible poverty, which forces Germans to behave terribly to those they should love the most. Then the source of the injustice is confronted and destroyed. Along with the victimization is a celebration of German courage, cleverness, and ultimate triumph. The cleverness is more evident in the children, who are the future, than in the corrupt parents, who represent the past. They are also tales of European history, and of the Germans seeking to reclaim their wealth from those they believe stole it from them. Children were reading these stories—and still read them today. In their horror, there is a bridge between the family and the broader community.

The Grimm brothers' tales were more pagan than Christian and drew on a pre-Christian heritage that went back to the primeval forest. Here was the link to the Enlightenment. Both were pagan rather than Christian. The Enlightenment increasingly dispensed with religion in the name of progress, and in the end, it was, as Peter Gay put it, a form of paganism. The Grimm brothers went back before Christianity to the German forests, filled with dangers and triumphs. It was a romantic place, more myth than real, and the romance of history became the foundation of modern European nationalism.

The Enlightenment sought to rid the world of myths, but the nation could not justify itself without them. Romantic nationalism addressed the problem and to a great extent solved it, but then created a new problem. If people are obligated to the nation, what are the limits of that obligation and, more to the point, what are the limits on the right of the nation in relation to other nations? This inevitably leads to a belief by some that their own nation is more beautiful than others or that they have been victimized by lesser nations.

Romantic nationalism magnifies a sense of greatness and a sense of victimization because it is about beauty more than about reason. Chopin delivers the justification for Poland in a sonata, not in a treatise. Sonatas touch the soul, but what the soul does with the sonata is not always predictable. Art is ruthless in a different way from reason. Reason goes to its logical end, no matter how absurd. Art demands adoration, no matter how defective it might be. Reason leads you to your conclusion. Art *is* the conclusion because beauty is an end in itself.

In the end, as we shall see when we consider the rise of fascism, the nation itself became the work of art and the party leader the artist. The fascists created a fairy tale about the nation, similar to the rational

Enlightenment in that both created ideologies, but these ideologies were wildly different in their roots and their consequences. Both were dangerous, as reason driven to its extreme logic, and art freed to pursue a ruthless love of beauty can create terrible things. Consider Stalin and Hitler. But in the end, men needed community and that community was the nation, and that nation was a jealous master.

The three shocks to European culture—Copernicus, Columbus, and Luther—ultimately shattered the European order, freeing Europe and then mankind and creating a single global culture. The greatest change was placing man at the center of the universe. By elevating reason to the center of life, it elevated man, who embodied reason, and the sciences and technologies that flowed from reason. But in placing men at the center of the universe it created a fantasy. Men can be at the center, but they can't be alone. In the end the triumph of the individual contradicted his need for community. Community had to be reinvented and men persuaded to participate. European man had become so unnatural and fragmented that his moral compass was broken. When he embraced the nation intellectually, based on art and myth, he was not quite whole. The moral compass was left out. Art did not know the difference between good and evil. And so the invented nationalisms that were so beautiful and seductive replaced the lonely individual. But neither knew right from wrong. What Columbus, Luther, and Bacon shattered had to be bound together in some way. This was accomplished partly through the technology that Bacon celebrated and the integrated economic life that followed. The other part was the nation and the integrated moral life that followed. Neither fit well with the other. It was a world of tensions.

It was magnificent to behold, contradictions and all. Triumphant over the earth, and triumphant over the mind—Europe revolutionized everything and by the beginning of the twentieth century stood astride the world in seemingly absolute dominion over nations and nature. In 1913 it seemed inconceivable that this could change. But it did. It had to. The vast array of nations had come to life, each knowing the beautiful and mistaking it for moral behavior. This paved the way for horror. And it all flowed logically from the unintended consequences of three shocks, each fully praiseworthy, each celebrating reason, but together taking the European mind to a place where it shattered.

Part Two

THIRTY-ONE YEARS

4

Slaughter

Life was good in 1912, the year my father was born in the little town of Nyirbator, near the Hungarian-Ukrainian border. There was enough to eat. The violence was not excessive, and it had been a while since armies had rampaged through the town. It wasn't Paris, but the Enlightenment had touched even this place, one of the bleakest on the European peninsula. The local doctor was said to have read Spinoza. There was a train station, and the train went to Budapest. It was possible to live, it was possible to plan, it was possible to hope—within reason. If this is where you were to be born, this seemed a good time for it.

The year 1912 was a very good one for Europe, and particularly the western part of the peninsula. Europe had been mostly at peace since 1815, almost a century. Not a perfect peace by any means, but more peace than it had seen for a while. Republican ideas had spread widely, and even in a country like Germany, with a kaiser, there was a parliament with power, a free press, great universities, and prosperity. Economic growth had been astonishing. Technological progress had been even more astonishing.

Europe ruled the world.

Europe had colonies totaling 40 million square kilometers. Britain ruled 25 million of those, tiny Belgium controlled the Congo, the Netherlands governed tens of millions of people in today's Indonesia, and France had its own substantial empire in Africa and Indochina. This list does not count areas of the world that Europeans did not formally rule, but that they informally controlled or shaped, like Egypt or China.

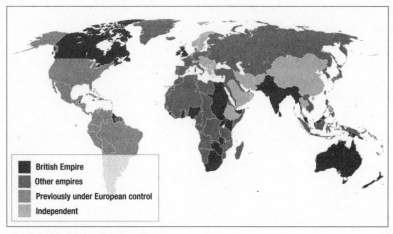

British Empire
Other empires
Previously under European control
Independent

Europe's Global Empires 1914

Nor does it include colonies that had broken free. Europe was a colossus astride the world, wealthy, creative, and powerful.

No one expected what came next. Suddenly, in August 1914, Europe turned into a slaughterhouse. By 1945, 100 million were dead, countless injured, and the entire continent shell-shocked. The scale and speed of the destruction were both unprecedented. Europe, the center of the Enlightenment, the place that saw itself as having reached the highest development of the human spirit, was the last place where anyone expected this. That this place at this time should have descended into hell was as startling as the idea that this place some four hundred years earlier should have begun transforming the world and humanity. Now, in the twentieth century, Europe squandered it all with an unprecedented savagery lasting thirty-one years.

By 1945, the European peninsula was occupied territory, its sovereignty suspended, shattered by war, collaboration, and resistance. Europeans were stunned by the monsters they had become and some by the cowardice and others by the weakness they had shown. But all were stunned by the realization that the greatness of the years immediately preceding the outbreak of World War I had been merely a veneer over a much darker Europe than they had imagined possible. And with that realization, the Europeans' dominion over the world slipped away. In the end, they willingly gave it up. The empire they had fought over for more than four hundred years, and which exacted a staggering price in effort and lives, appeared to have become pointless. After battling for dominion, Europe lost the ability to care.

As in all great tragedies, the virtues responsible for Europe's greatness were precisely those that destroyed it. The principle of nationhood and the right to national self-determination celebrated by the Enlightenment evolved into rage at the stranger. The enormous intellectual advances in science were driven by a radical skepticism that challenged all moral limits. The technologies that transformed the world created systems of killing previously unimaginable. The domination of the world led to constant conflict with it and for it. Every act of greatness had the seeds of catastrophe within it.

This wasn't visible even as the catastrophe was looming. Norman Angell, a famous author and Nobel Prize winner in the 1930s, published a brilliant book in 1909. In *The Great Illusion,* Angell argued that war in Europe had become impossible due to the intense level of interdependence between European countries in investments and trade. He postulated that a war would devastate Europe simply because of the economic disruption it would cause. Therefore, war was impossible.

The argument was clever and greatly appealed to the financial elite, not only because they believed in economic relationships but because it made the financial elite into masters whose interests determined history. It was the financial elite who determined the fate of the world and protected the world from its base, militaristic instincts by creating webs of relationships that would protect it from itself. Then, as now, it was all about making money and the belief that if you were allowed to make money, there would be no war. Angell was clever, but wrong.

Angell had missed the point. When two nations share economic interests there is always concern that one side will take advantage of its position or withdraw from the relationship to work with someone else, or fail to keep its agreements. The more interdependent countries are, the more they try to ensure that their partners remain committed to the relationship and don't, in an extreme scenario, seek to blackmail them. This distrust mounts and nations look for more effective levers to use, sometimes ending in war. Interdependence can create security—or insecurity and war.

In 1900, beneath all the interdependence, there was a fundamental reality: Germany had emerged as the leading economic power on the peninsula, rivaled only by Britain across the Channel. And Britain and Germany towered over the rest of Europe in exports—the British with their empire, the Germans without one.

Germany's power was so great, growing so rapidly and translated so easily to military power, that it frightened all other countries on the European Plain. Ironically, Germany was just as frightened by its neighbors. Surrounded by Russia to the east and France to the west, with few natural barriers, and with only forty years since unification, Germany was worried that enemies from both directions would attack it simultaneously—regardless of cross-border trade or investment.

Germany's unification and rise had destabilized the European system, and a flashpoint was born along its eastern and western borders. It changed the economic order and created strategic fears that could not be calmed by diplomacy and press releases. The fears were real and were fed by the vulnerability created by interdependence. Angell was simply incorrect that war was impossible. Friction was created by competing

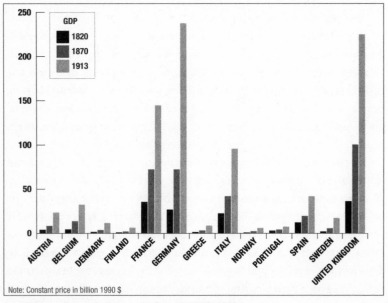

Western Europe's Economic Growth 1820–1913

demands that increasingly made war necessary. Either Germany must be weakened, or the European system must adjust to give Germany greater security. Europe had been dealing for centuries with these kinds of conflicts. There was nothing new here. What no one had reckoned with was the kind of war that would be fought.

The Normalization of Slaughter

Germany calculated that a two-front war initiated at a time and place of their enemies' choosing would be disastrous. Although they had no hint that the Franco-Russian alliance was planning such an attack, the Germans understood that intentions change and that if Germany continued to surge economically, its rivals might feel threatened and choose war. Germany couldn't risk that. The solution was to preempt it by initiating war at a time of Germany's choosing, rapidly destroy one of their enemies, then deal with the other at their leisure. Germany started the war out of fear that others would initiate it. If that sounds paradoxical, it is also commonplace, as was the German plan developed by Field Marshal von Schlieffen and named after him.

The Schlieffen Plan called for Germany to attack France first, rapidly forcing its capitulation. Germany would attack through neutral Belgium, with the weight of its thrust on the right flank, and sweep down the Channel coast to the rear of Paris, isolating the French army and capturing the city. This had to be achieved before the British could intervene. The Germans expected the Russians to attack from the east and were prepared to retreat, even if it meant the temporary loss of East Prussia. Once France was defeated, the forces in France would be rushed to the east on the Germans' superb rail network and deal with the Russians.

Germany envisioned a short war, as did everyone else who had considered how such a war would be fought. But the war did not go the way the Germans expected. Rather than a quick, clean war, it degenerated into a stalemate and slaughter unlike anything Europe had seen since the Mongol invasions. Between September 6 and September 14, 1914, there were about a half-million casualties on the Western Front alone.

Three things had changed. First, technology created the ability to conceive of and implement new weapons. Second, industrialism permitted the mass production of those weapons. Third, the psychological power of the nation-state allowed the three major European nations—France, Britain, and Germany—to maintain control over their troops and motivate them to fight in the face of a level of slaughter that made life on the battlefield nasty, brutish, and short.

Consider the machine gun, which was invented as a solution to the problem of the rifle. Except in extremely well-trained hands the rifle is incredibly inaccurate. While its accuracy couldn't be improved, you could compensate by firing a lot of bullets in rapid succession, saturating the horizon. The American Gatling gun of the Civil War was an early prototype. Hiram Maxim invented the modern machine gun. In 1882, an American told Maxim that if he wanted to make a lot of money, he should invent something "that would enable these Europeans to cut each other's throat with greater facility." A single machine gun facing a charging enemy could kill and wound dozens before they could close to its position. But to stop an enemy army, vast numbers of these new guns would be needed.

Although the idea of the machine gun had been around for a while, the ability to produce large numbers of machine guns had not. The concept was meaningless without mass production. Mass production made all modern warfare possible—mass production of canned food, of artillery pieces and shells, of trucks and shovels. It was the combination of the industrial revolution and technological advancement that revolutionized war, increasing its deadliness by orders of magnitude.

War was also revolutionized by the willingness of men to fight and go to an increasingly likely death as deemed fit by the state. All the technology in the world would not create a bloodbath among soldiers unwilling to put nation above themselves and see the state as the moral embodiment of the nation. The nation became more than a language. It became a moral bond and a universal administrative system. The moral bond was derived from many concepts that emerged from the Enlightenment, from the social contract to the romance of language. The idea of the individual became submerged in the idea of the nation, and nothing personified it more than the mass army.

In the past, armies had consisted of a mixture of reluctant subjects and mercenaries. Now they consisted of citizen soldiers acting from moral principle, the embodiment of the national spirit. Betrayal of one's duty was betrayal of one's own soul. A nation's administrative structure, the rational embodiment of the political system, was perfected in its military. The nation was the army, and the army was the nation. So men were prepared to die, and continue to die, because the nation had been elevated to a transcendent moral principle, and with it the army and duty, pride and honor. The soldier was prepared to die rather than betray all that. This was truer of mature nation-states like Germany, France, and Britain than for the polyglot empires. But even in Austria-Hungary the Austrian core felt the pull. In Russia, the pull was light and the regime fell.

Death has always been a normal part of war, but the First World War changed the scale, the speed, and the likelihood of death. Such large numbers were killed in such short periods of time with such efficiency and will that what transpired in the First World War transformed not only the magnitude of war, but the relationship between man, the state, and death. The quantity of deaths changed the quality of death. Death ceased to be tragic. When tens of thousands die in a day, it becomes banal. Now it happened each day, and it ceased to shock the numbed soul of Europe. It became a routine event, and with it the taboo against mass murder was broken by its ordinariness.

The willingness of Europeans to die and kill en masse lasted a long time and changed things forever. But exhaustion, and the arrival of a million Americans who weren't tired at all, brought the war to an end. On the Eastern Front, the war ended sooner. The soldiers of the Russian army were not yet modern and had not yet gone through the Enlightenment, so they endured and then, without shame, revolted. Going home meant much more than national honor. But in the West the war went on until 1918 and then ended. There was only one thing all sides had in common: the soldiers all felt first relieved and then betrayed.

The war achieved little that anyone had intended. Germany failed to eliminate the threat of a two-front war, and France failed to dismember Germany. What did happen was completely unexpected. Four empires— German, Austro-Hungarian, Ottoman, and Russian—collapsed. As a result, a host of nations previously submerged in empires emerged.

Europe After World War I

The end of the First World War represented the triumph of national self-determination. Nations that had been submerged into polyglot empires passed into nationhood, ready or not. And those nations had to determine their fate, not an easy task in countries that had not had national rule—even by a tyrant—for generations. Poland existed again after centuries. But Poland always had a common language and religion that bound it. And Chopin and the other romantics had revived its national pride early in the nineteenth century.

But other nations such as Estonia or Romania, knowing they were nations, had to struggle with what that meant. Even harder to decipher were some of the strange creations formed by the various treaties. Czechs and Slovaks were merged into one country. All the Slavs of the western Balkan Peninsula were joined together into Yugoslavia, a particularly troubling decision since Catholics, Orthodox, and Muslims shared a mutual loathing of each other. Europe was more packed than ever before with sovereign states that had bad memories of and grievances with each other. And in the West, nothing was settled, and whatever the fantasies of the war to end all wars, most knowledgeable observers thought, as did Marshall Foch, that the end of the war was only a twenty-year truce.

Europe was at a loss. European liberal democracies were economically shattered, and their public had little confidence in their leaders. Germany was bitter at its defeat, at the regime that led them there and the forces they thought had stabbed them in the back. Russia had undergone a massive revolution that had taken a marginal movement, Marxism, and put it in control of the European mainland. The chaos was not nearly as violent as the war, but it was more dangerous. Europe was seething, exhausted, resentful, and lost.

Only the new Soviet Union had a clear purpose: the creation of a radical equality made possible by industry's conquest of nature. By overcoming scarcity, equality could be achieved. Leaving aside the fact that the Soviet Union was as far from the conquest of nature as could be imagined, Marxist philosophy was the summation of the Enlightenment. Science and technology would radically transform the human condition, opening the path to equality, and overcome artificial distinctions among men and the accidents of birth.

The Enlightenment had invented ideology, a secular belief in justice built around a rational analysis of humanity, creating an internally consistent and coherent explanation of how the world worked, and what people should do. The secular aspect was critical. The Enlightenment was at odds with religion, and by eliminating God the framers of ideologies were free to define justice and analyze the human condition as their reason dictated.

A need for internal consistency meant that ideologies defined all aspects of thought, from the nature of marriage to what was beautiful in art to how steel ought to be smelted. If you began with a set of core principles and applied them ruthlessly to all things, then everything could be explained and all actions defined. The more ambitious the vision, the more consistent the logic and the more ruthless its application. Karl Marx himself was a man who had never committed a violent act. As an intellectual he contemplated the use of violence to compel others to follow the ruthless logic of his thinking, but in looking at his life it is not clear that he understood in his gut what he was saying. The same was not true for his heirs, who understood exactly the implications of ideology in general and this ideology in particular, and who applied it with a ruthlessness that would have been hard to imagine before 1914.

Ideologies led to something else: revolution. The Enlightenment's love of systematic thought led to a love of systematic politics, which led to the desire to impose systems on the world. From the French and American Revolutions onward, the idea of revolution as a moral imperative gripped Europe. But the revolutions, even the French, were modest. Revolutionaries killed thousands in a desire to create and perfect the new regime. These revolutions appeared apocalyptic, but only to someone who did not see what would come after.

World War I redefined what was reasonable in terms of revolutions. It eliminated boundaries to processes that were inherently boundless, and it eradicated limitations on imaginable casualties. It also undermined institutions that might have held the slaughter in check, such as churches and families, as well as sheer common sense. After what traditional institutions had permitted, they had no right to rule anything out of bounds. The war turned loose soldiers fresh from the battlefield and unleashed intellectuals to shape the world according to their imaginations, which were breathtaking in their scope and ambition.

Communism and fascism were organized on the idea of the mass. This was a vision of men not as individuals but more of humanity as a mass of men, differentiated by function, but driven by appetites, illusions, and fears. It was the purpose of the party and the state it created to take the unformed mass and turn it into the future of humanity. In both the Communist Party and the Nazi Party, an elite used the mass as an instrument of power for its own good. Footage of the mass rallies in Moscow or Nuremberg show the appetite, managed by the illusion, always with fear lurking somewhere nearby. The Nazi and Communist parties were World War I armies out of uniform but operating on the same principle. Armies of massed men, mere quanta to be used and disposed of at the will of the state. Their appetite was to survive. Fear of their own leaders and fear of the enemy caused them to do what was needed. From the mass would emerge a better man. But first there would be blood.

The Communist Party of Russia emerged based on two classes, neither envisioned by Karl Marx. There were soldiers who had mutinied and created the revolution, and intellectuals who dominated the revolutionary parties. The soldiers went back after the war to the factories and farms of the Soviet Union, but they had been shaped by their military experience. They had learned two things. The first was discipline in the face of terrible hardship, the second that death was routine and massive numbers of deaths were to be expected. These men were ready to plunge into the civil war that immediately followed the revolution; they were prepared to take their roles in an essentially militarized society and to face death at the hands of their own state. They had done that before.

The leadership of the Party was in the hands of intellectuals like Lenin, who wrote a book called *Philosophy and Empiro-Criticism*, impossible to read and certainly qualifying him as an intellectual. The Enlightenment had elevated intellectuals to the center of the moral universe, replacing the priests who had been there before. Reason was at the center of the Enlightenment, so those who made the exercise of reason their calling were the quintessential figures of the Enlightenment. And the intellectual at the center of the firmament had the temptations of the priest. If his work was at the center of things, wouldn't it be better if he ruled? Plato had talked about philosopher-kings but had never really meant it. The Enlightenment believed that the most radical of ideas was possible, and therefore the intellectual might rule, with rationally deduced ideology replacing revealed scripture.

Lenin embodies the intellectual who moved into the vacuum left by the war and sought the power to change the world. Lenin was the opposite of the disconnected and gentle intellectual. He was no absent-minded professor but viewed the world through the prism of ruthless logic. Intellectuals in service to reason are capable of enormous savagery. Lenin once said that the purpose of terror was to terrify. The Party was built to terrify, and it did. Trotsky, his colleague in revolution, wrote a book on Baudelaire that was quite good. He also organized the Red Army and oversaw the civil war.

These were a new type of man—the intellectual in action. For them the world was a canvas on which to create a new and better humanity. What had previously existed on the canvas was to be erased, both in thought and in action. For men like Lenin and Trotsky, ruthlessness flowed from logic, and sentiment could not be allowed to limit it. Love of humanity required cruelty to individuals. As Lenin put it, you can't make an omelet without breaking eggs.

The Enlightenment's logic was powerful, but it was really World War I, which had desensitized Europeans to death and suffering for a greater cause, that shaped what followed. It is estimated that 9 million people died in the Russian civil war. Prior to 1914 that number would have been unimaginable. However, after the slaughter on the European peninsula between 1914 and 1918, this was no longer an inconceivable number. The slaughter was logical, and Lenin was not restrained by moral considerations. What happened in World War I made unlimited slaughter something real and beyond theory. There were no limits. What had to be done was done, logically and ruthlessly.

The intellectuals who created and ruled the Party after the revolution debated and disagreed as intellectuals are wont to do, and none could hold on to power. The single, powerful figure among them who was not an intellectual, the Georgian Joseph Dzhugashvili, who changed his name to Stalin, systematically eliminated the intellectuals once Lenin died. He had them killed. And the Russian soldier, forged in battle since 1914, responded far more enthusiastically to Stalin than he had to the czar. He was persuaded that this time he was killing and dying for a magnificent future that was his own.

Stalin continued and intensified the tradition of extravagant slaughter. In addition to the intellectuals, Stalin killed peasants for their grain, moved potentially hostile nationalities about at will, and terrorized both the working class and military. He might have been a communist in the sense that he knew that without the survival of the Soviet state, communism would die. But his preservation of the state required a reign of terror difficult to fathom. In 1937 alone, 681,692 people, mostly Party members, were executed. Some, like Robert Conquest, an Anglo-American historian of the Soviet Union, have said that the number was closer to 2 million. These were simply those arrested and summarily executed for real or imagined crimes. During the 1930s about 20 million others died of planned starvation in Ukraine and elsewhere.

At least there was some sort of rationality, however tortured, behind these deaths. The Soviet Union faced another war in the 1930s. If it did not industrialize, it would lose that war. Grain was critical to feed the industrial workers and to sell in order to buy technology from the West. As there was not enough grain for both these critical purposes and to feed the peasants, Stalin expropriated the grain and left the peasants to die. The intellectuals were not united or ruthless enough for the task. Bukharin, one of the original Bolsheviks and not faint of heart, was appalled at what was being done to the peasants. Therefore, Stalin's thinking went, he and the others had to be killed in order to move forward.

The left-wing intellectuals in the rest of Europe forgave Stalin his murders in part because they denied they were happening, in part because they couldn't believe that it was possible, and in part because they sympathized with his logic. Whether they would have felt that way had they witnessed the deaths or been asked to carry out the killings is another matter. Logic is often best managed at a distance from its consequences. But as vast as the slaughter was, there was a reason.

What is extraordinary about this time and place is that the Soviet Union was not the only slaughterhouse in Europe. Were that the case, then it would have all been very simple—the Russians were a backward people and their brutality was understandable. Most surprising, the Germans, who had perhaps reached the highest intellectual, social, and economic level of development on the European peninsula, also entered the nightmare. They forged their madness alongside that of the Soviets but did not start mass killing until later.

In Russia the revolution was taken from the hands of the soldiers. In Germany, the revolution was created by soldiers—not the old military nobility, but the men who served in the trenches, who began with little and were left with nothing. There has been much debate over what made Hitler so powerful in the German mind. At root, it was that he was a corporal who served in the trenches and endured the war with honor, winning the Iron Cross. He went into the war with nothing, and he came out of the war nearly blinded by poison gas. Like many soldiers in many different times, he felt that all his sacrifice was for nothing, that the rewards had been stolen from him. He could not accept that after all he and the others gave, they could lose the war. The idea of sacrifice and failure was unacceptable, particularly when coupled with the foolish peace made at Versailles that shattered Germany economically and left it in the hands of a government of liberals that had no idea what to do. It also left Adolf

Hitler and his comrades alive, shell-shocked, bitter, and, in many ways, missing the army.

Heinrich Heine, a German born a Jew, anticipated at the turn of the nineteenth century what would happen in Germany:

> The German revolution will not prove any milder or gentler because it was preceded by the Critique of Kant, by the Transcendental Idealism of Fichte. These doctrines served to develop revolutionary forces that only await their time to break forth. Christianity subdued the brutal warrior passion of the Germans, but it could not quench it. When the cross, that restraining talisman, falls to pieces, then will break forth again the frantic berserker rage. The old stone gods will then arise from the forgotten ruins and wipe from their eyes the dust of centuries. Thor with his giant hammer will arise again, and he will shatter the Gothic cathedrals.
>
> Smile not at the dreamer who warns you against Kantians, Fichteans and the other philosophers. Smile not at the fantasy of one who foresees in the region of reality the same outburst of revolution that has taken place in the region of intellect. The thought precedes the deed as the lightning the thunder. German thunder is of true German character. It is not very nimble, but rumbles along somewhat slowly. But come it will, and when you hear a crashing such as never before has been heard in the world's history, then know that at last the German thunderbolt has fallen.

The German thunderbolt was perhaps the last straw in Europe. As Heine points out, it came from a country filled with philosophers and cathedrals. And it produced a crashing sound unlike anything ever heard.

Men who experience war are traumatized by what they went through, and yet also frequently miss it. Particularly in their memories, the war and the military were a place of friendship, belonging, discipline, and order. For those on the losing side, demobilized into a world that regards them as having lost the war, a world in which they don't belong and filled with disorder, the memory of what might never have really been leaves them longing for their lost comradeship.

All able men in Hitler's generation served in the military. Most felt rage and contempt toward Versailles and the Weimar government. Versailles imposed a cost that Germany couldn't live with. The economy of Germany made beggars of men who had looked forward to comfort and honor after their service and, equally as bad, made beggars of their parents. When the poor lose everything, their life changes little. When the middle class loses everything, their lives are transformed. Germany had lost the war, and it was the ordinary man, certainly not the aristocrats and black-market hustlers, who paid the price. Weimar's liberalism was a form of mere impotence.

Adolf Hitler was a German, Austrian born, who fought, risked his life, was wounded, and returned to a Germany without honor for the soldier and a giant vacuum at its political core. German aristocrats and industrialists still existed, but like elites throughout Europe, they had lost their credibility in the war. Liberalism had lost its credibility in the 1920s when it failed to either reject the Versailles treaty or compel the elites to make certain that the rest of the country had a minimal ability to live. Hitler also lived in a time of cultural disintegration, when a kind of intellectualized hedonism ruled and the principles of the army were discarded.

Hitler was an intellectual not in an academic sense but in the sense that he lived within his mind, a self-taught man with idiosyncratic observations of the world. Dismissed as a crank by credentialed intellectuals, he developed a view of history and the world that possessed tremendous power. A man like Martin Heidegger, a towering intellectual figure of the twentieth century, bent his knee to Hitler. Many have dismissed this as pure opportunism by Heidegger. Perhaps so, but he didn't have to do that to survive. I suspect he did it because he was to some degree persuaded, if not by the academic sophistication of the analysis, then by what he thought of as powerful, if undeveloped, insights.

A massive void had been created in the German nation, with the delegitimization of institutions. The Left held them in contempt because the institutions had plunged Germany into the war. The center was mostly exhausted, struggling to stay alive, and cynical. The Right thought that if it could resurrect the monarchy and aristocracy, it could roll back the clock. Hitler redefined the problem. He posed the question in a different way, speaking not of institutions but of the nation itself. Romantic nationalism rested on a commonality of culture, language, and religion, something it had in common with all other countries; thus, it was not superior to any. Therefore romantic nationalism could no longer move a cynical and exhausted country, angry about what had happened.

Hitler believed that to resurrect Germany he had to resurrect pride. He redefined the foundation of the nation, from culture to blood, from real history to total myth. Hitler argued that nations were defined by blood, a vague concept related to heredity. Blood and the race it gave rise to were the core of the nation. He further argued that all blood was not equal, and that the Nordic people, and Germans in particular, had by nature unique talents that entitled them to rule the world. Hitler also invented a history for Germany, not the one that involved the Holy Roman Empire or Lutheranism, but the history of the Teutonic knights, of the German forest, of heroes who might well have existed but were resurrected in order to frame the concept of blood and race. History became a work of art, artificially crafted, untrue in many ways, yet having a truth that resonated with the German spirit. The Grimm brothers saw myth as an element of the nation. Hitler saw myth, along with blood, as its essence.

Blood, race, and myth filled the space left by collapsed institutions. They swept aside the exhausted center and the impotent Weimar Republic. They confronted and overwhelmed the communists in street fights that were very much in keeping with how to motivate a soldier. Having torn down his self-image in training, you reconstruct it bit by bit with tales of the glorious past of your unit, and pride in your unit and your country's excellence. It is important to remember that Hitler was a soldier speaking to his generation of soldiers, calling them to arms to right the wrongs of the past, and assuring them that they could master any other race. The German soldier had gone through basic training. The German nation had seen itself as one with the army. Hitler's themes resonated just as his methods and indoctrination did.

So too did his call to ruthlessness. A soldier must be able to kill without remorse. That was learned in the trenches. Now Hitler made it a principle of history. Christianity was said, both by Nietzsche and Hitler, to sap the will by filling a man with mercy. Hitler's intention was to wipe away the weakness of Germany. It had to be replaced not by Christian charity, but by Aryan ruthlessness and pitilessness. Waging war wasn't simply an option of national policy. It was the test of the fitness of a soldier and his nation. Hitler joined the Enlightenment in his hostility to Christianity and his resort to paganism, but with a very different focus, inequality among races.

In World War I the German army had distributed copies of Nietzsche's works to soldiers. The doctrines of the Overman could be found there, along with attacks on Christianity. Nietzsche had an additional doctrine, the idea of horizons. Nietzsche argued that men needed horizons, an optical illusion that reduces the world to a manageable size. The Enlightenment had created humanity, and humanity is far too vast a place for a man to find himself. He needs a smaller place. It is certain that Hitler had read Nietzsche, and while I don't think Nietzsche would have admired Hitler, Hitler admired Nietzsche. In *Mein Kampf* he created a horizon, and as with all effective horizons he forgot that it was an illusion. It was nihilism in its purest sense: Hitler believed nothing, so he was free to believe in anything. He believed in what Germany needed to believe the most, the overwhelming greatness of Germany. How could Germany, the land of Schiller and Beethoven, believe such things? It was because Schiller and Beethoven, and the Enlightenment as a whole, could not lead Germany out of the abyss that geopolitics, war, and failure had brought it into.

Weimar was the Enlightenment personified. Hitler hated Weimar, believing it a sign of defeat and weakness in the face of defeat. Fascism was a revolt against the Enlightenment. The Enlightenment refused to judge people by birth and rejected inequality. It elevated the individual. Hitler embraced blood, inequality, and the mass. In a sense he rejected science and technology even as he used them, replacing them with a vague and uncertain mysticism. Hitler knew that the Enlightenment, and modern science, had both given him the tools to conquer the world and corrupted the German soul by stealing its depths and replacing them with materialism, which was incompatible with a national myth of blood and race.

For Hitler, the Enlightenment, just like Christianity, had sapped the will of the German people. Liberals and socialists had stabbed the German army in the back. If race was at the center of human life, then there had to be a racial explanation. Hitler found it in the Jews. The Jews were a race, but a unique one, in that they did not have a homeland but blended into other nations while retaining their racial identity. His explanation was that the Jews were everywhere and they brought sorrow wherever they went, because their strategy was to exploit the nations in which they lived, enriching themselves by bringing catastrophe on their hosts. Hitler saw the Jews as the great beneficiaries of the Enlightenment. The Jews had been outcasts until the Enlightenment discovered that all men were equal and men like John Locke wrote essays on toleration. The Jews had then flourished during the Enlightenment, Spinoza creating some of its greatest work, the Rothschilds creating the greatest bank, and Marx creating the most extreme reductio ad absurdum of a materialist revolution. When Hitler charged the Jews with being responsible for both capitalism and communism, he saw both as flowing from the same source, the Enlightenment.

The charge against the Jews was that they created the modern world for their own benefit. This was false. They had benefited from a modern world that was created by Bacon, Copernicus, and Luther. A space was created for the Jews, and they gained from it in many ways. But in the work of art that Hitler was creating, the Jew didn't simply benefit as others did. In Hitler's mind the Jew was the architect of this world. It was in this world that Germany had suffered the stab in the back, from Jews controlling banks, communism, and liberalism as well. Why had there been a war in 1914? Because the Jews conspired to make one. Why did Germany lose the war? Because the Jews undermined Germany. Why did they do that? So they could enrich themselves.

There were many questions that had to be answered, the most important of which for Hitler was what was in Jewish blood that made the Jews this way. But this was not a scientific treatise. This was a seductive work of art that was judged not by its logic or justification but by the way it resonated. And it resonated so well that it did not require proof or logical consistency. It simply had to be a stunningly seductive and effective work of art.

Bear in mind that this argument persuaded Germany, a nation of extremely well-educated and sophisticated people. It may appear to be nonsense now, but it was superbly suited to that time and place. Hitler energized a people to reconstruct itself. It also opened the door for limitless horror. The work of art, like radical ideology, brooks no limits. Hitler had created the basis for the idea that Germans were inherently superior even if they were victims and that Jews were subhuman even if they had triumphed. He was engaged in a great rectification, restructuring Europe based on his vision. The Wehrmacht rolling across Europe was not merely an army. It was the embodiment of a work of art.

It seems insane, but World War II can simultaneously be seen as a geopolitical event and a work of art. The *Einsatzgruppen*, the special troops who followed the Wehrmacht into the Soviet Union to round up and kill "subhumans," were redrawing Europe based upon the sketches of Hitler, the man who wanted to be an architect. The Wehrmacht was engaged in war so as to enable the artist to create the work of art.

The question of Europe is how the civilized Germans could descend into such monstrosity. The answer is that the logic of European greatness, empire, and enlightenment had made the monstrosity a logical outcome. The European empire was built on the base of a civil war inside Europe that culminated in World War I. The Enlightenment had created sciences and technologies that made that war an unprecedented horror. It also had a radical limitlessness that ultimately undermined its own commitment to reason but opened the door to the idea that reason itself was an illusion.

German monstrousness took a peculiarly German form, but I would argue that while the specific outcome of European history depended on which country emerged from World War I both decimated and powerless, it was inevitable that some country would emerge in that state. And it was inevitable that it would then be left to resurrect itself by creating a work of art for its horizon. I am also arguing that works of art are ruthless and untamed beasts when they are pseudo-histories of countries, painted in order to allow their resurrection. I am therefore arguing that as much as my family suffered from the Holocaust, while another nation in Germany's position might not have painted the same picture that resulted in Auschwitz, another picture with a similar end would have been painted, perhaps with the victims changed, perhaps not.

The Soviets were bringing history to its conclusion and mankind to its redemption. No price was too high for that. The Germans were perfecting the nation by purging not only those who were outlanders, but even more, those who had no nation, who were homeless, and who undermined the nations they infested. No price could be too high for that either. Compare the cost of transcendence to World War I, which yielded nothing but misery. At least this was for something, or at least so the Nazis and Marxists thought.

Ideology is ruthless and prides itself on its willingness to go wherever its logic demands. This is true of all ideologies and religions as well. One would imagine that any religion that saw itself as having a transcendent mission would go to any lengths. Consider the Hebrews crossing the Jordan, Christian crusades, Muslim jihad. Their logic was limitless. But religions could and did limit themselves. Ideologies could be governed by common sense—consider the United States. But there was a class of ideology that had no limits, and it emerged in Germany and the Soviet Union.

The Twilight of the Gods

World War II was simply the continuation, expansion, and intensification of World War I, with a very similar pattern. An insecure Germany, caught between France and the Soviet Union, began by attacking France, this time through the Ardennes Forest. Unlike in World War I, France collapsed in six weeks. Britain refused to make peace with Germany, and the Germans, unable to cross the English Channel, decided instead to eliminate the Soviet Union. They almost succeeded, but in the end the vastness of the European mainland swallowed up Hitler's armies, and Soviet manpower ground them to dust. Germany declared war on the United States, which entered the war and after more than two years invaded the European peninsula across the English Channel (a less significant invasion of North Africa and Italy had, of course, taken place prior to that). The Germans were overrun and occupied by the Americans and the Soviets. The causes of both wars were the same, the outcome was similar, but the scale of slaughter was much greater this time. For Germany it was an even more catastrophic end; so too for Europe.

The First World War was essentially European. The Second World War was truly global, with the Pacific as well as the Atlantic basin involved. But most important, the war was more intense. No one can be certain of exactly how many died in Europe in World War II, but a reasonable number is 51 million, soldiers and civilians, from genocide, bombing, and the normal cost of war. In 1939, Europeans numbered about 550 million, including neutral countries. A staggering 10 percent of all Europeans perished during the six years from 1939 to 1945.

This doesn't quite capture the horror. Poland lost over 16 percent of its population, Germany about 10 percent, the Soviet Union about 14 percent. The greatest losses were on the border between the European peninsula and the mainland, where the bulk of the fighting took place. Countries like the Baltic states, Romania, Hungary, and Czechoslovakia took the greatest blows. But even countries to their west like France lost half a million, and Italy and Britain lost almost a half million.

War had reached its most extreme point; it had become industrial. Factories that produced the weapons were more dangerous than any individual weapon. Workers were therefore more deadly than trained troops. As industrialism became more important, it created the means for destroying itself. When the manned bomber was introduced, it ended the distinction that Europe had made between civilian and soldier. First, the civilian was engaged in war by working in factories. Second, bombers were extraordinarily inaccurate. In one early bombing raid by the British on Germany, the Germans couldn't figure out what the British were trying to bomb, as they attacked empty fields. If bombs are inaccurate and factories must be destroyed, then large numbers of bombs must be dropped by large numbers of bombers. The result was inevitable; many civilians unattached to war industries were killed as well. By the end of the war, Germany's cities looked as if they had been deliberately demolished, so little was left standing.

But the most hideous casualties were inflicted by the Germans. Waging war is a natural condition of nations, to paraphrase Plato. But the manner in which a war is waged involves choices. At each point the Germans chose to be as ruthless as possible. If they were by blood the master race, then what they did to inferior races was not a moral issue. Poland's treatment after their defeat was brutal, and the manner in which the

Germans waged war on the Soviet Union was stunning not only in its ruthlessness, but in its lack of necessity. Ukrainians resented Russian rule and Soviet ideology. They had suffered incredibly under Stalin when he raised funds from the export of their grain. The Ukrainians could have become German allies. But Hitler did not want the support of the inferior Slav, so convinced was he that the defeat of the Soviet Union was readily at hand. So instead he brutalized them. He was gentler with the French and the Nordic occupation, but that too fit with his ideology.

It is hardest to write on the Holocaust. It had no military purpose. While everything else Hitler did could, with some strain, be fitted with some military logic, the industrialized killing of 6 million Jews and millions of others could not be. A place like Auschwitz did nothing to help with the war effort and used up massive resources, if not for food for the inmates, then for manpower, trains, and the rest.

But if we go back to Hitler's thinking, there's a strange logic. If the Jews were intertwined with the nations of Europe, and by blood and nature lived by exploiting and ruining the nations that took them in, then ridding Europe of them was essential. Hitler had argued that the Jews had caused the First World War, but he also believed they had started the Second World War. He believed that they wanted to finish what they hadn't completed in World War I. They had done this by forcing Britain and France to go to war over Poland, then blocking Britain from making peace with Germany.

Hitler sketched a work of art whose power was not in its truth as much as its power to move men, and was trapped in it. He genuinely believed that what he said was true. He warned that if the Jews started another war in Europe, they would suffer catastrophic consequences. Hitler believed that they had started a war and that to put an end to their wickedness, he had to eliminate their threat.

If you combine the technology of the Enlightenment with pagan mythology, certain outcomes that seem insane become reasonable. It took the myth for Germans to want to kill. It took industry to make it possible to kill millions. And if the myth was believed, then all Jews suffered from the same racial defect, and therefore the smallest child was as dangerous to Germany and Europe as a man in his prime. So Hitler sent large numbers of men to look for Jewish children, take them to places where they could be killed en masse, and kill them.

The wars had reached a terrible climax. In Hiroshima and Nagasaki together, over 100,000 people died in an instant. In Tokyo that number died in three days of conventional bombing. The atomic bomb had taken war making to its limits. If industry was the foundation of war, and industries were in cities where there were workers, then destroying cities made sense, and the invention of an atomic bomb that could efficiently destroy cities was logical and necessary. But Hiroshima, which some have compared to the Holocaust, was different in a fundamental way. Whether we agree or disagree with the military logic, it was believed that the war would not end without the invasion of Japan, and that incalculable numbers on both sides would die. I think this is true, but there are reasonable people who do not. The point is that Hiroshima had a plausible military purpose.

What made the Holocaust unique was that it had no plausible military purpose except a justification so preposterous it is hard to imagine that anyone believed it. Hitler's myth of blood and race was dismissed by some Germans, but most accepted its logic. When young Germans look back on what their grandparents believed, they are genuinely aghast. But they did believe it. Other societies had believed some ethnic, religious, or political groups to be dangerous. The Spanish Inquisition killed hundreds or even thousands, but it lacked the technology to kill millions. In the end it was not myth but technology that made the Holocaust possible, the technology of killing.

What would have been horrifying in 1913 was no longer so. Combining the 55 million dead from World War II and over 16 million from World War I, in the thirty-one-year period from 1914 to 1945 approximately 71 million Europeans died in general warfare. When you add roughly 20 million killed or starved under Stalin, the number rises to 91 million. Add in the Russian and Spanish civil wars, and sundry other conflicts hardly worth mentioning, such as Turkey's war with Greece and Armenia, and the number of 100 million is conservative. A million more or less was simply not noteworthy.

These numbers also signaled the twilight of Europe, which never recovered from the slaughter. At the end of the war American and Soviet troops massed throughout most of the European peninsula, with Americans also in Britain and the British in Europe. The peninsula was occupied, shattered and exhausted, no longer the arbiter of its own fate. Who controlled Europe's fate depended on where the armies on each side had stopped. Europe's empire was still there but would not remain for long.

In thirty-one years Europe had gone from the invincible center of the global system to a place where poverty was as common as self-confidence was scarce. In 1945, as Europe awakened from its orgy of violence, stunned by what it had done, the world's map was changing as dramatically as Columbus had changed it, and Europe was no longer at its center.

5

Exhaustion

On May 5, 1945, Adolf Hitler committed suicide. It ended the war in Europe and brought to a close the thirty-one years. It also brought to a close 450 years of history. The European peninsula was occupied by the United States and the Soviet Union, its sovereignty compromised. Over the next decades its empire would disintegrate and its global power disappear. Only the Soviet Union's global power would survive, but eventually it too would dissolve. The flashpoints of Europe, the fires that had been raging, suddenly went out, with one potential borderland and one flashpoint remaining, in the center of Germany.

In 1913 the unimaginable had happened. Europe, always fragmented, had torn itself apart in thirty-one years of war, near war, and illusory peace, planned starvation and civil wars, until it was unable to feed its people, heat their homes, or in many cases put a roof over their heads. The leader of the global economic system was now poorer than most of the world. Ironically, the center of power had become powerless.

Rudyard Kipling, the poet of the British Empire, sensed this was coming and warned of it in his poem "Recessional."

Far-called, our navies melt away;
On dune and headland sinks the fire:
Lo, all our pomp of yesterday
Is one with Nineveh and Tyre!
Judge of the Nations, spare us yet,
Lest we forget—lest we forget!

If, drunk with sight of power, we loose
Wild tongues that have not Thee in awe,
Such boastings as the Gentiles use,
Or lesser breeds without the Law—
Lord God of Hosts, be with us yet,
Lest we forget—lest we forget!

Europe had certainly let loose with wild tongues. And even those who were victorious in Europe and hadn't loosed wild tongues (unless some of Churchill's early speeches are deemed wild) had really lost the war. Europe's arc from 1913 to 1945 was perhaps the most precipitous decline of a power of its magnitude that we can imagine.

One of the extraordinary things about World War II in Europe is how suddenly it all ended when Hitler died. Germans fought fanatically while he was alive. With his death resistance ceased in hours and days at most. Hitler had written a mythic history in which his life force had reached deep into the past to create a German renaissance. In the tale he told, his will was Germany and Germany was his will. With his death, there was nothing left but a region that spoke German. The cord that tied Germany to its heroic past was cut and the German will evaporated as if it were magic. This was the moment that the German nation as art and fantasy died.

The romance of the British Empire died as well. The idea of the British Empire as a vast global movement, civilizing the lesser breeds, died with it, if not as suddenly as Germany's, then just as surely. Part of it was economic. The war had shattered the Empire's economy. But part of it was the realization that they were on the winning side but had lost the war. Events since 1914 had exhausted the British not only economically, but also morally. There was little confidence left by 1945 about the British carrying the "white man's burden." There was little belief in the wisdom of the government. However inspiring Churchill had been, he was voted out of office as soon as the war ended.

Twice the United States had intervened in Europe, and twice Britain had been diminished by it. The first time the Americans had not been in Britain. During World War II American troops were there for three years. The problem with the Americans, it was said, was that they were "overpaid, oversexed, and over here." It was a joke that wasn't a joke. The Americans not only had the power the British had lost. They also had the swagger, the worst part of which was that they didn't know they were swaggering. The Americans had come to save an isolated Britain, and they expected the British to be grateful. The terrible thing was that they were grateful.

The French had bled for four years in World War I. But in the end, even if the Americans were more decisive than the French could admit, the French were clearly among the winners. In 1940 they were defeated in six weeks. Whatever truths and myths existed about the resistance and collaboration, the fact was that their army was defeated in six weeks, and the Americans, British, Poles, and others had liberated them. There was a French contingent, and there was a resistance, but it was the vast matériel of the Americans and the swelling American force that dwarfed the British and certainly the French, that had given them back their sovereignty. The French drew their lineage from Charles Martel, who defeated the Muslim army at Tours, and from Napoleon, who, while defeated, was defeated gloriously. There was little glory for France in World War I, and none in World War II. They knew it, and deeply resented it. Charles de Gaulle appeared arrogant and ungrateful when he refused to read a speech written for him to broadcast to France on D-day. But de Gaulle was playing a desperate game, trying to resurrect French sovereignty from defeat, occupation, and even liberation. Gratitude can be a bitter pill.

Most of the rest of Europe was in shock, whether it was Spain under Franco recovering from its civil war, Italy recovering from the petit grandiosity of Mussolini, or Poland suffering through tragedy after tragedy, losing its sovereignty and borders to the Soviet Union. Those who had greatness lost it. Those who hoped for greatness failed to gain it. Those who simply hoped for a little peace and safety were denied it. In thirty-one years, the reasonable and unreasonable dreams were shattered.

The end of a war would normally mark a moment of hope, at least for someone. It must have for some in Europe. But for most the end of the war brought with it the realization of what had been lost. For many Europeans life hovered between life-threatening poverty and mere penury. Forgetting empire, sovereignty, nationalism, the sheer human toll could not be measured. Entire families had been annihilated, had ceased to exist, their names expunged from human history. Of course I am thinking of Jews, but how many Germans were incinerated in the bombings, how many Russian families were killed by SS looking for partisans? How many children were orphaned without a single blood relative left?

Europe was in a state of shock that haunted a generation until its death. I knew a Jew who had hidden as a young man in a forest in Poland, protected by a Polish Christian family. He had come from the city of Lodz, where his entire family perished. After the war, he came to America. His exhaustion was perpetual until moments when the horror and the guilt poured out and he would say, "There is no hope." His madness and grief clung to him like the necktie he always wore.

I also know a woman who as a small child lived in Hamburg. The British strategy was to firebomb cities at night. Hamburg, the great seaport, was one of those cities. Her father had gone to war and was in the SS and never came home. Like my sister, she sat in the basement as the enemy tried to kill her. When I got to know her, she was strangely self-contained, needing and wanting little. She had one great love in her life to whom she gave herself utterly and clung until he died. For her, exhaustion limited what she had to give and then she gave to excess. Her perpetual loneliness haunted her.

I speak here of a Jew and a daughter of the SS, both equally guiltless in my eyes, both the shredded humans that were the real result of the thirty-one years. I hold the Germans guilty of what they had done. I cannot hold her guilty of anything. This is the paradox of nationalism. A five-year-old girl is always guiltless. Her nation is not. The nation is its history, not simply those alive now. My two acquaintances both suffered equally in my eyes. They were equal in another sense. In all the years I knew them, and I knew them well, I never saw either weep.

We Americans like to use medical terms to describe the human condition. Being staggered by horror is now called posttraumatic stress disorder. It is what these two suffered from, in its incurable form. Multiply this a million times, with a million memories erasing a million possibilities, and the real consequences of the European rampage against itself can be measured. Take a man who died in madness and a woman who trusted almost no one, and the price of the thirty-one years can be measured. Empires matter. But this is the truth. The smugness of 1913 led directly to the despair of 1945.

The war was over and life went on. The kind of life that was to be lived differed according to where you lived, who you were, and who had conquered you. A handful of countries escaped the fury of the thirty-one years. Sweden, Portugal, and perhaps Ireland are in this handful. Some suffered less. Some were a slaughterhouse. But all of Europe was poor, and the fate of everyone was to be shaped by those who now occupied it, essentially the Americans and the Soviets. Both countries had experienced the thirty-one years very differently. The Americans entered the wars late, and there was no damage to their homeland. The Soviets experienced the First World War, the civil war, the purges and famines, and the Second World War. The Americans emerged more powerful than before, while the Soviets were among the worst victims. It mattered a great deal who occupied your country.

The United States held the wealthiest part of the European peninsula,

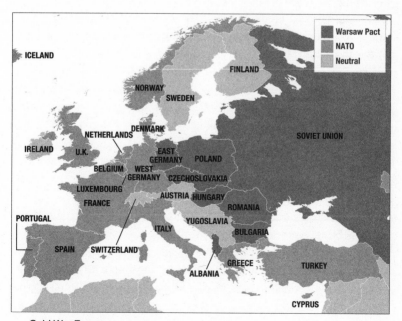

Cold War Europe

but in many ways, that responsibility was a hardship. At first Americans wanted to do the same thing they did after World War I: go home. The Soviets held the poorer part of Europe, but there was no doubt in their minds what they had achieved. First, they had won the war at a terrible price. Second, they had pushed farther west than ever before.

The Soviets were frequently brutal occupiers. In the misery of 1945, the Soviet state began dismantling industries in their zone and shipping them to Russia. Soviet soldiers stole watches and shipped them home. They were obsessed with watches, a symbol of wealth and enlightenment for peasants who had not been fully familiar with the idea of time. Soviet soldiers were overwhelmed by the wealth of their captives. Many had never seen indoor plumbing and regarded the homes of ordinary citizens as opulent. They envied what they saw, and this gave the occupied a psychological sense of superiority. Even though they were conquered, they were envied. The envy was real. And so was the misery that left its mark for many years.

It was different with the Americans. They shipped German scientists and weapons home, but otherwise had no need for European factories. American soldiers undoubtedly stole things as soldiers do, but it was souvenirs rather than sustenance they sought. It is reasonable to say that American occupiers gave more than they stole. They had more to give and the Europeans had little that Americans wanted.

The Soviet soldier was in awe of European wealth at a time where there was little. The American soldier was in awe of European culture, at a time when it was less certain of itself than ever. After World War I a generation of American intellectuals were drawn to Paris. It was memorialized in Hemingway's *A Moveable Feast*. Soldiers who had read that and heard their fathers' stories wanted to relive it. Some did, in Paris, Rome, or Florence.

At most, the Americans wanted to see the sights before they left. More than anything, American troops felt pity for Europe. It was expressed in casual gifts of chewing gum, chocolates, and food to children and the acquaintances they had made. This was not simply for women. The American soldiers had a great deal, and they were not as bitter at the Europeans as the Europeans were with each other. A can of Spam that an American soldier was tired of eating could mean life to a European and they didn't begrudge it, save the expectation of effusive thanks that were deserved, although they embittered the recipient. For many Europeans the wealth of the American soldier was a sign of how little Americans had suffered.

Soviet troops were as hungry as those they conquered. Few Polish or Hungarian women married Soviet enlisted men or even officers. For the most part it was forbidden; for another part it offered no escape. In Germany, the memory of the mass rapes of revenge by the Red Army created profound barriers. Many German, Italian, British, and other European women married Americans. One estimate is that 300,000 European women became "war brides." For the women it was a means of escape. For Americans it was exotic. For many European males, it was a betrayal of European men by the women, and presumptuous of Americans. This was as true in the countries that won the war as in the countries that had been occupied and those that had been enemies.

To the Europeans, the Americans seemed shallow and superficial while at the same time being as powerful and technically sophisticated. Anyone who had seen the American military pour into Europe's skies and streets could not dismiss them. But even the American officers were seen as unsophisticated. The European sense of sophistication was still class based. The way the upper class behaved, what they had read, what they valued, were for the Europeans the definition of sophistication, as it might be anywhere.

White Americans descended from refugees from Europe, those who had no place there. They descended from the wretched refuse that Emma Lazarus wrote about. English adventurers and rebels, Scots-Irish peasants, starving Irishmen, unemployed Italians, and so on. Dwight D. Eisenhower grew up in poverty in Kansas, Omar Bradley even poorer in Missouri. Even George Patton, who was born to wealth, and who wrote poetry, was rough and uncultured by European standards. To the Europeans the Americans were cowboys. The Europeans had learned about cowboys from American movies produced frequently by transplanted Europeans who had never actually seen a cowboy or an Indian. They had, however, read the incredibly popular novels of Karl May, a German writer who once visited the United States for six weeks, although never the American West.

The Europeans had invented a myth about Americans and believed it. The cowboy was rough, quick to anger, and uneducated. Above all he had a simplistic notion of the world, thinking in terms of black and white, unable to see the subtleties and complexities, and resorting to violence as a first resort. While it is ironic that the Europeans viewed the Americans as violent and themselves as sophisticated, given their history it also made sense. Europe might be shattered, but submission comes hard. However powerful the Americans might have been, however genuinely grateful Europeans were for American generosity, being able to look down on the lack of American sophistication was a defense—and in a certain way it was valid. The Americans were not sophisticated in the European sense. Nor did they want to be.

It was easy to confuse them with unsophisticated Europeans. But they weren't Europeans any longer. They were, rather, sophisticated Americans. Europe and America had evolved profoundly different cultures and values in everything from education to table manners. American culture focused on the technical. An American boy would tinker with a car, whereas a well-born European boy might study the classics. The European would regard the American as a tradesman at best. The American would look at the Europeans as losers. The war had been won by technology and mass production, and the boy with his car was far more important to American civilization than would have been a well-educated classicist. Gratitude, envy, resentment, and contempt were all present on the European side, condescension and indifference on the American.

The Russians were powerful, dangerous, and hungry. Many European leftists romanticized Stalin and the Soviet Union, ignorant of or forgiving his mass murders. For those under Soviet occupation there were no illusions about the Soviets. They were there, in plain sight, and the difference between Germans and Russians was at best a matter of degree. For the east, life would be hard. But there was little of the psychological complexity in the relationship between the occupied and occupier. The occupied feared and looked down on the Soviets. The Soviets were generally kept separate from the occupied. The Americans and Europeans had a complex and splendidly ambivalent relationship. The Soviets and their Europeans kept it simple.

Strategy and Domination

Unlike the Germans, neither the Soviets nor the Americans tried to rule occupied countries directly, but permitted them to formally retain their sovereignty. For the Soviets, there was much pretense but little expectation that the pretense would be believed. Elections were held and when they didn't yield the expected results, as was the case in Hungary, intimidation took place, they held a new election, and they got the desired results. There was no question from the Soviet point of view but that the nations it occupied would serve the strategic interests of the Soviet Union.

The Americans had no direct interest in Europe. However, they had an enormous negative interest: they didn't want it united under a single hegemon. America had learned that the European balance of power no longer sustained itself because since 1914, a single power, Germany, had twice toppled the balance in Europe. The Soviets had now taken the place of Germany. Absent the United States, they would be able to militarily conquer the rest of the European peninsula, as no native military force could stop them. The Soviets could also undermine the rest of Europe through political influence via powerful communist parties, which had long-standing strength forged in the underground war against the Germans.

There was no way the United States could permit this to happen, and therefore the idea of repeating the complete withdrawal of World War I rapidly dissolved. The United States knew, in spite of occasional fantasies, that the Soviets could not be dislodged in the east. Therefore it needed to buttress the west. The inclinations of the countries under American domination, unlike in the east, were for the most part compatible with what the United States wanted. These countries did not want to be conquered by the Soviets or have communist governments imposed on them. The borderland had shifted far to the west.

They certainly understood that if the Soviets gained control of the peninsula, no power, including the United States, could or would want to spend the resources to invade Europe again. It was also understood that the United States would help the region recover economically, if only to strengthen its strategic position. In this sense, there was far more alignment in the sector occupied by the United States than there was in the Soviet sector. The border between American and Soviet power in Europe became the new flashpoint, and this one had a potential nuclear ignition.

The Cold War was based on mutual fear. The Americans dealt with their fear by creating a system of alliances in which allies played the primary role in blocking Soviet expansion, backed by the United States. The Soviets' strategy was to rely primarily on themselves, creating a massive ground force focused, as in 1914 and 1939, on Germany. The great dread for the United States was a Soviet attack that would overrun Germany, roll on to the Channel ports, effectively seal off the peninsula, and consolidate it into one bloc. In that nightmare scenario the Soviets would achieve what had never been achieved before: a united peninsula and mainland. The Europeans had to face the possibility of another war, this time completely out of their control.

After living through the Great Depression and fighting in World War II, Americans just wanted to get on with their lives. While the United States military had to attend to the immediate humanitarian needs of Europe, on the whole they did not see themselves as responsible for Europe's reconstruction. The United States was captive to the geopolitics of the Soviet Union. Whatever Western intellectuals thought about Joseph Stalin, his will controlled Russia and a state controlled by Stalin was not one that would be constrained. In fact, the Soviets had no choice. They had extended their control to the center of Germany. They needed the strategic depth and they needed to control and divide Germany, which itself had been constrained to twice invade Russia in thirty-one years. But the farther west the Soviet armies went, the more vulnerable they were, since they were operating on an extended line of supply that ran through the hostile territory of the other countries they occupied, particularly Poland.

Strategy was built around potential moves and supposed intentions between the United States and the Soviet Union. The Soviets' solution was to retain an extremely large force in Germany, both to suppress resistance and to protect its forward position from potential American attack. The Soviets needed a counter to American nuclear power but did not yet have their own weapons or a bomber force that could deliver a nuclear strike on the United States. If there was a war it would be fought in Europe. The Soviets' best defense was an offense that rapidly captured western

Germany, France, and the Low Countries, creating a fait accompli that American nuclear weapons couldn't reverse, or so the reasoning went.

The Soviets did not want a war. They were exhausted by the last one. But they could not be sure of American intentions, and they hoped that a massive forward deployment might deter them. It was their only option. Whatever the subjective intention of the Soviets, they had created what appeared to the Americans to be the ability to overwhelm Western Europe in a rapid blitzkrieg as the Germans had done. The United States could not be indifferent to the Soviet threat and the possibility that they could occupy the entire Eurasian landmass. That would shift the balance of power dramatically, as the long-term U.S. control of the sea might be threatened and with it U.S. national security. Between 1945 and 1947 U.S. strategy shifted from the postwar withdrawal from Eurasia to a strategy designed to contain Soviet expansion all along its periphery, but particularly to confronting it in Europe, the center of gravity.

Two crucial problems arose from this strategy for the United States. In order to protect Europe against Soviet invasion, the United States needed to defend Germany, and that required control of Dutch, Belgian, and French ports. It required air bases in Britain, far enough away to provide warning of attack but still within range of the potential battlefield. The Soviets had to be prevented from sending their naval forces into the Mediterranean, which meant the Bosporus had to be secure. Therefore Greece and Turkey had to be secure. In order for the United States to use naval power in the Mediterranean, Italy had to be in the alliance structure, as Sicily could block access to the eastern Mediterranean, just as Spanish seizure of Gibraltar could seal off the Mediterranean altogether.

The Cold War was beginning to take shape by 1946. Communist insurgencies in Greece and Turkey, with Soviet troops on their borders, had forced the United States to send supplies and covert support to the two countries. Geographically, the Soviets were blocked from sending significant naval forces into the Mediterranean. This meant that southern Europe, particularly Italy with its large Communist Party, was secure, and that the Suez Canal could not be blocked. If either Turkey or Greece turned communist, the Soviets would have access to the Mediterranean, and the United States would face a much more complex strategic challenge. Therefore, in 1947 the Truman Doctrine was announced, providing guarantees for the security of Greece and Turkey. The United

States had concluded that the Soviet Union was a threat to the European peninsula and was committed to blocking the Soviets.

What made the Cold War different from the previous thirty-one years was that there was never an actual war between the two key powers. The explosion never happened; there was a point, but it never flashed. The issues were geopolitically and ideologically of the highest order. Both sides were used to fighting wars and were well armed, and war appeared always to be on the horizon. It seemed to some as inevitable. But it never happened. Neither the Americans nor Soviets were as pressed geopolitically as the Europeans had been. Both had room to maneuver.

There was another reason, rarely mentioned. American and Soviet politicians were much more careful than the Europeans were in 1914 and 1939. They had seen the thirty-one years and understood nuclear weapons. They were meticulously careful in not going too far and in pulling back when they did. One sign that the world had changed decisively in 1945 was the prudence of the new potential combatants compared to the recklessness of the Europeans before them.

Fate of Empire

World War II was fought on the basis of total war. In total war the entire weight of society—industrial, social, military—must be thrown into the battle. When the Europeans were conquering the world, or fighting with each other, total war was unnecessary and impossible. Even with Napoleon the total society was not mobilized for war, nor was the entire society at risk. In World War II this was no longer the case. Indeed, one of the things that broke European power was that the effort of total mobilization for war had broken the Europeans economically and emotionally.

The Europeans, with their empires, were now operating on a global scale in a world filled with other powers of vaster size and organization. The Americans and Soviets were both well organized for efforts far beyond what any European state could manage by itself. World War III would also be a total war beyond the scale of World War II. It's in this context that Kipling's fear became real.

Much united the British and American strategies in World War II, but they were deeply divided on one point. The British were fighting the war to protect Great Britain, defeat the Germans, and preserve their empire. The United States wanted to protect the British and defeat the Germans, but had no interest in protecting the British Empire. This had caused increasing friction over strategy. The United States had favored an invasion of France. The British were hesitant. First, they feared a repeat of the bloodshed of World War I, which they knew would destroy what was left of their ground forces. Second, they had a heavy focus on the Mediterranean. For the British, Gibraltar and the Suez Canal were the highway to India. Preserving that highway was a priority for them. It led them into North Africa, and the invasion of Sicily and Italy. The United States wanted a direct blow against Germany. Britain preferred an indirect attack, through Italy and Yugoslavia, both to preserve their forces and guarantee control of the Mediterranean.

The United States had signaled its intentions regarding the British Empire even before entering the war. America's Lend-Lease program had two components. The first was lending the British destroyers with which to protect the North Atlantic sea lanes against German U-boats. Under the lease portion, the British leased all their naval bases in the Western Hemisphere, save the base in Halifax, Nova Scotia, to the United States. In effect, this meant turning over their empire in the Caribbean to the Americans. They retained formal control, but these islands were now under American domination. The United States was simultaneously aiding the British and using that aid to whittle away at its empire.

After 1945 unrest emerged in much of the European imperium. India had been agitating for independence for years. Indochina resisted returning to French rule after Japanese occupation. In the Netherlands East Indies, agitation broke out against the Dutch. Particularly in Asia, there was resistance to returning to European rule after the Europeans had been defeated by the Japanese in Southeast Asia. Vietnamese and Malayans objected to a return of their rule; Indians and Chinese wanted to be rid of them. The unrest was not confined to Asia but also began to rise in the Arab world and sub-Saharan Africa.

Although the Cold War froze Europe in place, conflict began to swirl in what became known as the third world. These nations were not advanced industrial powers and not part of the Soviet bloc and included the recently freed European colonies, but also colonies freed more than a century earlier in Latin America. From the 1950s to the 1980s there were constant struggles in the third world between the United States and the Soviet Union over who would become the heir to the European empire. Multiple borderlands, like the Korean Peninsula or Vietnam, or Afghanistan, became flashpoints that drew the two superpowers in.

There was something ironic in this. Both the United States and the Soviet Union were founded as anti-imperial enterprises, trying to break imperial rule. Now they found themselves drawn into an imperial role, albeit with anti-imperialist rhetoric. The United States was trying to save countries from Soviet domination and oppression. The Soviets were trying to save them from American imperialism. In the end, the logic had nothing to do with the moral mission of either nation. It had to do with the fact that the European frontier, down to Turkey and Iran, was frozen solid, and the only advantage to be gained was in the unstable third world.

By 1970 the European empire had virtually disappeared—it was mostly gone by 1960. Europe had ceased being a global force. Except for the Soviet Union there was no European power at all that could be considered a global power. At the same time Europe had recovered economically, particularly that part of Europe dominated by the Americans. Europeans learned to do well and live well without their empires. Indeed, they eventually came to the conclusion that they had pioneered a new dimension of human existence, prosperity without risk and without war.

As the Cold War ground to its conclusion in 1991, when the Soviet Union collapsed, the Europeans had recovered their pride, a pride based on the lessons they believed they had learned from the thirty-one years of destruction: that the benefits of power were not worth the price. They also believed they had learned that no matter how crowded Europe was with states, it was now possible to do the thing that had been previously impossible: integrate Europe into a single entity and abolish European wars permanently.

The European Union intended to achieve what the Romans, Charlemagne, Napoleon, and Hitler had all failed to do: create a united Europe. They planned not only to achieve this but to achieve it without blood. In one sense Europe had abandoned its dreams of radical solutions through war. In another sense it became more radical, dreaming of the same solution without war: the integration of Europe.

6

The American Origins of European Integration

The winter of 1945–46 was one of the coldest on record in Europe. Coal was scarce. So was winter clothing and food. Homeless refugees wandered Europe, desperate and dangerous. In some places, like Germany, it appeared that many would not live through the winter. In other countries, like France or Britain, things were better. All they faced was dire poverty.

To the extent that there were European institutions, they were based on the old nation-states. Governments, frequently of returning exiles, were reestablished. But there was little they could do about the human disaster all around them. In the east, Europe was under Soviet domination, united by occupation. In the west, Europe was fragmented. No one thought about unification. Their minds were on survival and re-creating national governments.

The Americans had not given much thought to occupation. There is a myth that the United States, immediately after the end of the war, was planning the Cold War with the Soviets. If that were true, demobilization would not have taken place. Franklin Roosevelt had genuinely believed in the United Nations, and however dubious it became, there were no alternative strategies. The United States responds to events, sometimes disproportionately. Only infrequently does it plan them. It takes a long time to change an American strategic dogma. Roosevelt may have been dead, but he still governed.

Since the United States had a presence in Europe, with troops stationed amid the chaos, it almost reflexively felt obligated to provide aid. And frankly, when you examine the record in Congress and elsewhere, there was a genuine feeling that something should be done. The primary channel for this aid was the United Nations Relief and Rehabilitation Administration (UNRRA), and the first aid went to countries other than Germany. The United States could be brutal in other ways too. At the end of the war it designated surrendering Germans as Disarmed Enemy Forces rather than Prisoners of War. POWs had to receive the same rations as American troops. DEFs didn't have to receive any. But as the winter of 1946 wore on, the United States realized that a human catastrophe was under way in Germany as well as the rest of Europe and provided help.

The United States was caught between conflicting desires to leave and to help. The need to remain for strategic reasons had not yet coalesced into an intent. This is a decision that retroactively is easy to dismiss or treat as part of American Cold War strategy, but in fact it was simply what the United States, at that time and place, did. Either way it helped shape European perceptions of America. The cost was bearable and public opinion was in its "something must be done for those poor people" phase. Sometimes American actions can only be understood as altruistic. But rarely for long.

I remember hearing as I was growing up the story of when we were refugees in Vienna and were given surplus American cheese, still being supplied in 1949. It wasn't very good cheese, according to my parents, and it was very yellow. My mother wouldn't feed it to me, but the rest of the family ate it. It was undoubtedly surplus Wisconsin cheddar cheese, purchased by the U.S. government to help dairy farmers, and shipped to Europe. But the United States helped when few others had the resources to help. The cheese was still discussed in my family many years later.

Over the years, American generosity turned into strategy. By 1947 it was increasingly clear to the United States that the Soviets were both imposing their ideology in Eastern Europe and trying to spread their power, particularly to Greece and Turkey. The United States began making plans for resisting what it saw as a Soviet strategy. Western Europe's economic condition was no longer a matter of charity but of national security for the United States. An economically fragile Europe would be subject to social unrest and vulnerable to the power of the communist parties. The West also wanted to demonstrate that capitalism was more productive and provided a better quality of life for their citizens than did communism. More important, the United States did not want to block the Soviets by itself. It wanted the Europeans to rearm, and they needed a stronger economy in order for that to happen. The United States started planning.

In 1947 William Clayton, Under Secretary of State for Economic Affairs, wrote a memo to Secretary of State George C. Marshall:

> Without further prompt and substantial aid from the United States, economic, social and political disintegration will over-whelm Europe. Aside from the awful implications which this would have for the future peace and security of the world, the immediate effects on our domestic economy would be disas-trous: markets for our surplus production gone, unemployment, depression, a heavily unbalanced budget, on the background of a mountainous war debt. These things must not happen.

He went on to say:

> Such a plan should be based on a European Economic Federation on the order of the Belgium-Netherlands-Luxembourg Customs Union. Europe cannot recover from this war and again become independent if her economy continues to be divided into many small watertight compartments as it is today.

Clayton was a key architect of the Marshall Plan, an attempt to revive Europe's economy with infusions of cash and encouragement of trade. The Marshall Plan formalized and vastly expanded what the United States had been doing before in response to the confrontation with the Soviet Union. It was also the true beginning of European unification.

The final legislation for the Marshall Plan contained the following passage:

> Mindful of the advantages which the U.S. has enjoyed through the existence of a large domestic market with no internal trade barriers, and believing that similar advantages can accrue to the

countries of Europe, it is declared to be the policy of the people
of the U.S. to encourage these countries [receiving Marshall aid]
through a joint organization to exert common efforts. . . . which
will speedily achieve that economic cooperation in Europe which
is essential for lasting peace and recovery.

The Marshall Plan did not envisage a United States of Europe. Nor
did it envision an elaborate administrative system. But it did envision
a European free-trade zone as well as some sort of joint organization to
coordinate economic development. Free trade and collaborative policies
required some sort of common interest if not a common identity. This
was the conceptual foundation of the European Union.

The Europeans welcomed American aid, but they were not comfortable with American plans for European economic integration. Britain in
particular was dubious. The British had created a free-trade zone in their
empire, built around a unified currency, the pound sterling. In 1947 and
1948, the British had not conceded that the British Empire was finished.
For them, it remained the foundation of their economic system, allowing the British to set currency values at advantageous rates within their
empire. For those in Britain who still believed the empire could survive,
the answer was to retain the empire and exclude the Europeans.

For centuries the British had survived behind the English Channel
by managing the balance of power on the peninsula. A united European
peninsula, especially one including France and a large part of Germany,
was a threat the British had long handled by maintaining their distance
and manipulating the two countries. The idea of integration was appalling. The thought of being caught between a revived Germany and France
in a single economic structure made them reflexively recoil.

Britain was one of the victors in World War II, which in the minds of
the British allowed them to continue as they were. They did not accept
that their empire was gone or that basic British strategy had become irrel-
evant. American discussion of European integration struck the British as
naive and dangerous. Given their deep alliance with the United States,
they expected to participate in the Marshall Plan, but on the same bilat-
eral terms in which they participated in Lend-Lease, and with the same
degree of priority. Britain could not accept being reduced to a power on
the level of France or Germany, both defeated nations.

The French were equally dubious about cooperation, particularly if it involved the Germans. After three wars, the French were not interested in Germany's recovery. Add to this the Gaullist focus on recovering French sovereignty. But the French had been defeated and badly needed the Marshall Plan even if they didn't like it. They wanted to hold on to their empire, but they knew that they couldn't revive their economy alone.

Whatever fear the French had of a revived Germany, the United States was focused on defending Europe against the Soviets, and the map decreed that West Germany be the bulwark. German manpower and a German army were needed to build the defense and that meant a strong German economy. By 1947 it appeared to many in Europe and the United States that a war was coming. Others believed the only way to avoid a war was creating a bulwark in Germany.

The French grasped the logic of this but were understandably frightened by the idea of Germany's rearmament and reconstruction, and the resurrection of the Franco-German flashpoint. Americans viewed Franco-German hostility as a problem to be solved, not one to be respected. If it couldn't be solved, Germany would remain shattered and weak, which would make European economic recovery impossible. Europe must have both German economic recovery and Germany's integration with the rest of Europe, particularly France. On the surface this seemed like Norman Angell's theory, but embedded in American thinking was the idea not just of interdependence, but of formal structures binding Germany with France.

The French didn't like it, but they understood the reality they were facing. They also realized that the entire architecture of Europe had to change if economic development was to happen and war to be avoided. However much they loathed the Germans, France and West Germany's interests aligned. And politically, if the French government didn't alleviate postwar poverty, the communists, already powerful in French politics, might take over the government and would certainly undermine France's ability to defend against the Soviets.

France had two other considerations. First, with Britain opting out of integration, France was the leading power in Europe. It was better off leading the process than reluctantly following. Second, the French understood they could not recover their sovereignty on their own. If France stood alone, the overwhelming power of the United States could force it into actions that were not in France's interest. In order to counterbalance the United States they needed to be in a coalition with other European countries. The answer, the French realized over time, was to be the leading force, shaping an increasingly integrated Europe, rather than attempting to follow or stand alone.

American strategy in the event of a Soviet invasion was to have its European allies do the bulk of the fighting. The United States would position some forces in Europe but would mostly provide reinforcements, airpower, logistics, and, in extremis, nuclear weapons. Any Soviet invasion would come west through West Germany. Therefore West Germany had to be involved in the alliance system, as its territory would be the critical battleground. Two organizations were necessary to execute this strategy. One was a military alliance that integrated Western Europe's increased military under joint command dominated by the United States. Second, it needed an integrated economic structure. And Germany would ultimately have to be part of both of these.

In July 1947 the Europeans met in Paris and created the Committee on European Economic Cooperation. The plan did not include what the Americans wanted, integration and transnational institutions to manage Europe's reconstruction. Instead it was a council without power, a forum for independent states to discuss joint projects. But it was the beginning. Later in the year, it was the French who shifted their position and embraced American ideas not only on integration with Germany but on an integrated approach under the Marshall Plan. Where the British continued to dream of empire, the Germans waited for others to decide their fate, and the rest of Europe clung to a dubious prewar model, the French were the first to shift their position.

The credit for creation of the EC has always gone to Robert Schuman, who was prime minister of France at the time and was deeply committed to European integration. But behind Schuman was de Gaulle, who knew three things: First, that Europe could not resist the Soviet Union without the United States and some sort of collective defense system. Second, that in the end Germany would have to be resurrected if NATO was to be effective, and that therefore French participation in Germany's resurrection and an intimate relationship with Germany were a necessary step. And finally, he recognized that if France led the integration of Europe and had Germany in its orbit, France could use its position to dominate

Europe and shape Europe not only into an effective force against the Soviets, but also into a counterweight to the Americans. The road to this goal would be difficult and de Gaulle would not be in power as it unfolded, but he understood its logic.

De Gaulle's influence was substantial, and Gaullism was powerful. Schuman envisaged a United States of Europe. De Gaulle had no interest in that, but he was interested in France using Europe for its own ends. Therefore it is not a surprise that the French allied themselves with the Americans on this. France defined the future model for Europe—an integrated Europe in which the leading powers used Europe for their own ends. It was a new phase in European history, combining the nationalist interests of the past within a new framework that balanced nationalism and Europeanism, addressing all the forces driving integration without abandoning the principle of national self-interest. Or at least that's what it tried to do for as long as it was possible to do it.

The French played the dominant role in organizing the Committee, but it was weak and bound together by U.S. pressure and fear of the Soviets. Some of the participants had a vision of what Europe might become, but the vision wasn't widespread and it lacked vigor. Narrow national interests, opportunism, and a sense of resignation toward American pressure dominated. The defeated mingled with crumbling empires and with countries seeking to create a coalition to enhance their own power.

Ultimately, it was the Americans who drove both military and economic integration. Europeans never achieved military integration outside NATO. They did move beyond the American framework in economic integration over the next half century, but the roots of European economic integration did not come out of the vision of European statesmen. What was achieved had its heritage in American vision and strategy. In the fog of history and myth, the American role in championing and underwriting European integration is frequently forgotten, along with the resistance of the Europeans.

Nationalism and European Integration

The one thing the Europeans were unwilling to do was give up national sovereignty to become part of an irrevocable and comprehensive federation. Certainly there were some individuals, many with influence, who imagined true federation, but they never had the political power to impose it. The desire for sovereignty was widespread, but it was most intense in Britain, which had, after all, won the war and didn't think of itself as another European nation. Even as it became obvious to the British that their empire would not survive, they still wanted to limit their involvement in Europe. The foundation of British foreign policy was that safety lay in balancing competing powers in Europe. Alternatively, they saw themselves as balancing between the two superpowers.

The French, meanwhile, were just as adamant on sovereignty, yet much more involved in Europe. As Europe stabilized and prosperity began reappearing, de Gaulle, who had left the leadership after World War II, took over the reins again in 1958. De Gaulle knew that France needed to lead a coalition in Europe if it was to have real power. That real power meant not depending on the Americans to deal with the Soviets but being able to manage the Soviets on their own. De Gaulle saw that the need for American economic help had passed. Europe, with its sophisticated population, had used the aid money well and European economies were reviving. Now the danger to Europe was the U.S.–Soviet confrontation. Decisions on war and peace were no longer being made in the European capitals, but in Moscow and Washington. De Gaulle, as the new head of France, wanted to recapture full sovereignty for Europe—with France at its head.

De Gaulle wanted to change the two-way struggle in Europe into a three-way game in which Europe was not neutral on the question of Soviet expansion, but not simply subservient to the United States, nor entirely dependent on the United States for defense. In particular, he didn't want Europe occupied by the Americans. Therefore he asked all NATO forces to leave French soil in 1958. He didn't leave NATO, although a few years later he would pull France out of the military committee. French cooperation with NATO continued and plans existed for French participation in case of war. But if there was war, he was determined that France and Europe would be making that decision, not just Washington and Moscow.

For this to happen, De Gaulle believed that two things were necessary. First, there had to be a European nuclear option. Since there was no united European plan to build one, de Gaulle insisted that France's small nuclear program be expanded. De Gaulle argued that under the current strategy, the only way to hold Europe against a conventional Soviet attack was with an American nuclear attack. He did not believe that the United States would lose Chicago on behalf of Europe, and more important, the Soviets also didn't believe they would. Therefore, the U.S. nuclear guarantee was not credible. A French nuclear force would be, because France, along with the rest of Europe, would be facing catastrophe. The Soviets had to know that it would very likely be used, and they would be much more cautious. As de Gaulle put it, France did not need to be able to destroy the Soviet Union, but only to tear off an arm. Therefore he insisted on an independent nuclear option for France.

The second thing that de Gaulle realized was the importance of European economic integration, and particularly a close binding of France and Germany. Germany was the strategic key in any war, since its territory needed to be defended, but de Gaulle's vision was that France and Germany together would defend Europe. They were by far the largest countries and had the most power. He was quite content to let the British stay outside the peninsula's politics. Britain's exclusion allowed France more room for maneuver. Binding Germany and France together forced the rest of Western Europe to align with this core group.

De Gaulle understood that France didn't have a competitive modern economy and that Germany was developing one. He was quite open about wanting the German economic miracle, as it was called, to transform the French economy. Economic integration would increase Europe's economic power and decrease dependence on the United States. It would create a coalition, not necessarily a transnational entity, and it would put the defense of Europe in European hands.

There was another vital part. France would become the dominant power in Europe, and Europe would join the ranks of superpowers. The Germans were forgiven under the concept of no collective guilt, the principle that Germany as a whole could not be held responsible for the crimes of the Nazis, but that only individuals who had committed the crimes could be. Nevertheless they remained stunned and ashamed by what they had done. This made it natural for the French to take the political lead. The Germans had no stomach for geopolitical leadership. No other nation could resist the Franco-German relationship, which offered vast economic advantages and a European-based defense system. The British were too deeply ambivalent, too deeply involved with the Americans, and ultimately too deeply committed to British national interests to try to undermine this coalition. France, having been defeated and occupied during World War II, would emerge the winner, leading a coalition of prosperous and militarily capable Europeans in defense of their global interests.

However, it did not work out quite as de Gaulle planned. The Germans were too exposed along their eastern flashpoint and too much under American influence to go beyond economic alignment. The smaller countries did not want to become satellites to the Franco-German bloc and saw the American role as more benign than the Franco-German one might be. And there were fundamental tensions between the creaking French and the roaring German economies. The vast Gaullist vision of a powerful independent Europe did not quite take off.

But, and this is vital, it was in Gaullism that the most ambitious and genuinely European vision of integration originated. De Gaulle believed that Europe must not simply be an American satellite. Germany and France must become indivisible in order to make Europe great and avoid the nationalism that had torn Europe apart since 1871. The Franco-German bloc must become the pivot around which a vast European coalition could revolve. For de Gaulle, of course, there was no economic coalition or integration without a military dimension. He wanted to redefine NATO as a European force with a diminished American presence. That's not what happened, and in that tale rests the underlying weakness of Europe.

The European Union

European integration formally began in 1957 with the signing of the Treaty of Rome. There had been precursors like the European Coal and Steel Community, created in 1951, but this treaty was much broader and deeper, and the ambitions behind it ultimately led to the formation of the European Union.

The treaty bound together six countries—France, Germany, the Netherlands, Belgium, Luxembourg, and Italy. The most important part was that it tied together Germany and France. Belgium, the Netherlands, and Luxembourg constituted the small borderland between the two.

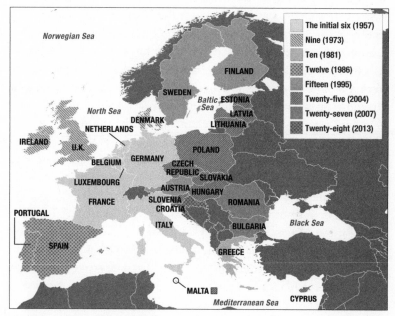

History of European Integration

For the Europeans, this represented an entente between Germany and France, whose hostilities along their borderland had defined Europe since 1871 and really since the Napoleonic Wars. The promise of the European Community, the next step toward the EU, was contained in the Treaty of Rome: peace and prosperity. What the Europeans wanted now was what my father wanted when he went to America: safety and the chance to make a living. But the treaty also had a more ambitious line: "an ever closer union between the peoples of Europe."

This was the nexus of the problem of the European Community and the European Union that followed. They were promised peace and prosperity, but in order to achieve peace there had to be an ever-closer union between the peoples. Since there was no mention of the limits, the idea of closer union ultimately challenged the principle of unique and distinct nations. But without closer unions, how could France and Germany, with their history, guarantee peace and prosperity? From the beginning, this would be the issue that Europe couldn't resolve.

The EC was also an instrument of the Cold War. It bound France and Germany together within NATO, with Germany on the front line protecting the northern European Plain, and France as the rear area where U.S. reinforcements would land and move forward. The inclusion of Italy rounded out the picture. Italy had been less involved in drafting the treaty than the others. But it was critical because it held NATO's southern flank and except for formally neutral Switzerland and Austria, Italy's inclusion created a line across the entire European peninsula.

The British remained outside the EC. They wanted to maintain control over their economy even though they needed a free-trade zone. They feared that a continental free-trade zone would reduce British exports. During the mid-1950s Britain created an alternative to the EC, called the European Free Trade Association, formally established in 1960, consisting of Britain, Austria, Denmark, Sweden, Norway, Finland, Switzerland, Liechtenstein, and Portugal. The distinction is clear. First, the EFTA had only one major country in it, Britain. Second, it consisted of the periphery of Europe, and mostly countries off the peninsula altogether. It was Britain's response to its historic fear of being drawn into the peninsula and desire to control its economic policies by dominating its partners.

In the end the EFTA failed. Among the major reasons was American opposition to it and support for the EC. The United States did not want Europe fragmented. It favored the technical structure of the EC and its trade policies over the EFTA and, most important, the geography of the EC. It served American strategic interests. The EFTA was an attempt to create an alternative to the process under way in the European peninsula. In the end it could not be sustained.

The EFTA really marked the last attempt by Britain to try to be a leader of Europe. It was losing its empire, and it simply lacked the economic and political weight to claim a leadership role. The British were so diminished that the countries it could rally for its free-trade zone had a combined population of only 52 million people, to Britain's 94 million. Although these countries would eventually abandon the EFTA (though Norway, Iceland, Switzerland, and Liechtenstein are still members, proving that international organizations never die) and align with the EC and EU, the EFTA established the principle of British unease with the EC, EU, and excessive involvement in the Continent. But history was not on Britain's side, and the EC expanded and changed into the EU.

The EC members developed closer and more complex relations, but the organization did not expand until 1973, when Britain finally joined, along with Denmark and Ireland. It slowly expanded until in 1991 it consisted of twelve countries, having added Spain, Portugal, and Greece. The EC had grown slowly and carefully, trying to make sure that its members were viable and appropriate. It did not ask enormous amounts from them, nor give them much more than a stable trade zone in which to enhance their prosperity and their peace. Behind this was a complexity that tore at the fabric of Europe, a complexity that was political, historical, and geographical. Yet over time, the plans increased in ambition.

In 1991 the underlying radicalism of the project emerged formally at the same time that the Cold War ended and the American hand that had shaped the EC's development, particularly at its inception, was no longer significant. That was the year that the Maastricht Treaty was drafted and the structure of the modern European Union was born.

Maastricht is a town at the southern end of the Netherlands, right on the border with Belgium. It is on the edge of the Ardennes forest, where World War I began and World War II, on the Western Front at least, really ended. It is very close to Aachen, which was the seat of Charlemagne's power, and perhaps an hour's drive from Trier, where Constantine established his first capital. This is the heartland of the European peninsula, where the idea of Europe was in many ways created.

It is also in the heart of borderland between France and Germany, as are most of the European Union's main institutions. (The European Parliament has its official seat in Strasbourg in French Alsace near the Rhine. The European Council is in Brussels.) It is now peaceful to look at, but it was a churning cauldron for over a century. But if there were to be peace and prosperity in Europe, it would have to begin here. No one doubted that this was the heart of the matter, and that this was where the EU lived. Maastricht symbolized the founding of the EU. It was, not incidentally, at its geographical heart.

The Maastricht Treaty, as it is commonly called, or the Treaty on European Union, was the logical extension of the concept of "increased closeness of the people." Its intention went beyond the economic—although it brought radical extensions there too—to the social and political spheres. Ultimately, its moral intention was the most important. It wanted to create a union of Europeans, not just of European states, that would make a person's European identity at least as important as his or her national identity. It intended to create Europe not just as a geographic concept, but also as a cultural reality, binding together Europeans. It provided a European citizenship and European identity side by side with national citizenship and identity, trying to preserve national identity while overcoming it.

It came close to succeeding. The world has come to refer to Europe as if it had a political identity, rather than as a collection of sovereign states. But perhaps most important, while not abolishing national identity, it did create an overarching sense of European-ness and opened the door to Europeans thinking of themselves as having a shared fate. It sought to render national identity as an ethnic distinction within a common European culture. This was an enormous step.

Interestingly, this also happened in the American Civil War. Americans went into the war thinking of themselves in terms of their states and emerged a single nation, forged in blood. But that would be difficult to accomplish in Europe. First, nothing could be forged in blood in a continental union built on the idea of peace and prosperity. Second, the differences between American states had to do not with things that are difficult to change, like language or culture, but with issues that could be decided by war, such as the abolition of slavery and the structure of the economy.

There was resistance from the beginning. John Major, British prime minister at the time, objected to the term "federal goal" being included in the treaty. The chairman of the meeting changed it to "federal vocation." Major went ballistic. The British had no intention of joining a federation or an organization that appeared to be moving toward that goal. He was prepared to enter a treaty organization that benefited Britain, but he was not prepared to have Britain become a state in a united Europe, with power in the hands of the European Parliament rather than the British. Forging a multinational state out of the mélange of nation-states was beyond the ability of Europe at that time.

But what could not be reached directly might be reached through complexity. The more complicated the system of governance, the harder it was to use, but also to understand, and thus object to. Therefore the compromise position on governance was a system of enormous complexity with a rotating president, a parliament with vague powers, a court whose power, like that of the U.S. Supreme Court, would emerge over time. Most important, the EU would have a system of decision making that required unanimity in some cases but a majority in others, and was not a fixed but a deliberately evolving system. In addition there was a bureaucracy that could stealthily impose Europe-wide solutions without even a vote. The inability to craft a system that preserved sovereignty while guaranteeing unity required a solution so complex that its management was difficult to comprehend, and thereby it could be managed by mere managers.

The Maastricht Treaty created one element that was undoubtedly a challenge to sovereignty: the euro. It was a currency that lacked a face. When you look at the currency in most countries, you will see on it the faces of historical figures from politics and culture. There are no faces on the euro because the Europeans could not reach any agreement on who should be there. The coins seemed to matter less, so there were faces there. There is common agreement that Washington, Lincoln, Jackson, Franklin, and other famous Americans ought to be on the American currency. But the United States has a shared history. Europe does not. Nor does one country necessarily celebrate the heroes of another. Napoleon might be a French hero, but it is doubtful that Spaniards would celebrate him.

The euro is certainly a usurpation of national sovereignty. A nation has a degree of control over the value of its currency. Using a currency that belongs to a group of countries means that a crucial economic decision is in the hands of another entity. More than that, it means that one entity, the European Central Bank, manages the euro's valuation internally and externally. Another entity, the nation-state, determines tax policy, public spending, and other aspects of fiscal policy.

There are currently eighteen countries in the EU using the euro.

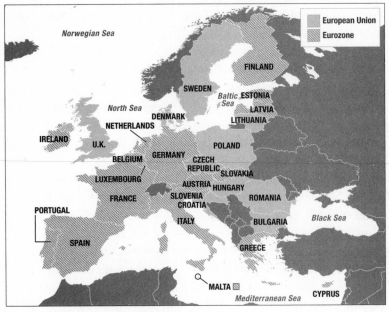

EU Member Countries Using the Euro

The euro is concentrated in the western part of the European peninsula, with the first two tiers of the peninsula generally excluded. But there is a tremendous difference in the level of economic development and the social conditions even among these countries. So, for example, a mature country that is a net creditor on international markets wants a stable currency to protect the value of its loans. A poorer developing country might want a weaker currency to reduce the cost of its exports, or inflation to reduce the value of the loans outstanding. Currencies are an important tool in managing economies, allowing countries to tilt the table in their favor occasionally. And in a massive economic crisis, the ability to devalue the currency increases exports and stabilizes the economy.

It is difficult to fully understand the reasons why the EU expanded the euro to the south and east, and why the countries there accepted. This can only be explained in terms of reckless optimism and the European dream. The optimism was based on the belief that Europe had somehow abolished economic crises and would never face difficult decisions about who should bear the burden of austerity. There was the complementary belief that by being part of the EU and the euro zone, you would become European. By this I mean that they believed they would become Western European, with Western values, wealth, and culture—all without abandoning their own culture and way of life. It followed from this optimism that the pitfalls of membership were ignored. Nations that would find it difficult to survive in a crisis clamored for membership and were admitted.

With one currency being used for all these countries a major problem was created. Germany and Greece, for example, needed different monetary policies. They were at different stages of development, had different economic problems, and had different tax policies. Germany was far more influential in the ECB, which was built around the German Bundesbank's concept that it was there primarily to fight inflation. Germany was the largest economy in Europe and its health was vital. Greece's health was less vital. The ECB inevitably created monetary policies that were optimal for Germany and less so for Greece. Multiply this by all the variations in Europe, and the core problem begins to emerge.

After World War II Europe boiled down all its dreams to safety and wealth. The secular vision of the Enlightenment, grounded in the notion of the passion to live and the passion for pleasure, had transcended such concerns in its desire that reason touch the heavens. The Europeans had had enough of transcendent visions. They cut off the Enlightenment's arms and kept its legs. What else could they do?

Europe's anthem is the "Ode to Joy" from Beethoven's Ninth Symphony, whose lyrics come from the German poet Schiller. It opens:

Joy, beautiful sparkle of the gods,
Daughter of Elysium,
We enter, fire-drunk,
Heavenly one, your shrine.
Your magic binds again
What custom has strictly parted.
All men become brothers
Where your tender wing lingers.

It is about the joy of joining men into a single brotherhood, overcoming the divisions of mere custom. Then there would be joy.

Brotherhood means shared fate. If all that binds you is peace and prosperity, then that must never depart. If some become poor and others rich, if some go to war and others don't, then where is the shared fate? Therefore it was vital to the European project that fate bind the nations together rather than separate them. There should always be peace and prosperity so that hard questions of national identity and fate would not arise.

Europe promised its people only good things. The United States understood that peace was not an end in itself, and that society could not promise prosperity. But it was held together by the idea of a "more perfect union" and of "certain inalienable rights." America forged a nation out of diverse peoples by organizing them around a transcendent set of principles. The United States never promised peace or prosperity, only their possibility.

The problem with the EU was that the Europeans had nothing to offer but peace and prosperity—an Ode to Joy. But what would happen if the joy failed, if either peace or prosperity evaporated? Then what would hold men together in brotherhood, and what would hold the European Union together?

7

Crisis and Division

The Soviet Union collapsed the same month the Maastricht Treaty's draft was completed. All the Soviet republics became independent. For the first time in centuries all the European peninsula countries were free from the Russian mainland. And for the most part, every language now had its own nation. As important, for the first time in almost exactly five hundred years, no European power was a real global power. Europe was a place of small sovereign countries crammed into a very small space.

After the Maastricht Treaty was signed, Europe developed as expected. It developed new European political structures, a more powerful bureaucracy, and a new currency. Europe's economy became increasingly integrated and there was talk of a United States of Europe. For a while in the 2000s it appeared possible.

There was great optimism. The Soviet Union had collapsed, and the countries to the east of the EU, freed of Soviet domination, were eager to join the EU. Europe was experiencing a period of prosperity. All of Europe didn't prosper equally, but all of Europe prospered. European nations were still sovereign. They would not give up the ultimate power to control their destiny. There was no integrated defense or foreign policy and the only real unity was economic. But that didn't seem to matter. The need for defense appeared archaic, and the distinction between foreign policy and trade policy seemed academic. Economics was what mattered, and Europe was, as the EU had promised, peaceful and prosperous.

From its founding until 2008, the EU flourished. Then in six weeks all the self-confident certainties of Europe began to unravel. Prosperity shattered, and Europe fell into an existential crisis. How would the European Union hold together when it must offer pain and sacrifice along with the pleasures of membership?

First, on August 7, Russia went to war with Georgia. Then on September 15, Lehman Brothers went bankrupt. The two events seemed completely unrelated, and certainly no one saw them as marking the end of an era. But they were enormously significant, and they did end an era. The first event changed the relationship between Europe and Russia, ending Russia's long period of irrelevance. It also ended the illusion that war between nations was impossible in Europe. The second event resulted in the first financial panic that the EU had to deal with and eventually undermined the European economic system, ultimately breaking the fine balance between union and sovereignty. Together they set in motion processes that led to an insoluble crisis and challenged Europe's peace and prosperity. We are still living in the shadow of these twin events. The conflict in Ukraine in 2014 and the slow growth of Europe are intimately bound up with these events. They define our generation.

At the heart of all this there was a contradiction. Europe had feared nationalism. With the collapse of the Soviet empire, new nations were spawned and old nations were freed. At the same time that the EU feared nationalism, it celebrated these new nations with their complex, not fully defined interests. The newly emerged nations weren't yet included in either NATO or the European Union. Most of the countries of Eastern Europe and even the former Soviet Union wanted to join NATO and the EU because they believed that this would guarantee their security, prosperity, and a liberal polity based on European values. Of course they also wanted to retain their newfound sovereignty. There were multiple contradictions developing, but they did not deter the Europeans.

The existing members saw expansion to the east as a guarantee of European peace, both by locking out Russia and building a strong barrier against its reemergence, and by creating prosperity and liberalism throughout non-Russian Europe. Some even thought of including Russia in the EU in due course. The desire to expand and the desire to join were driven by the same assumption: prosperity meant peace and the

European Union guaranteed prosperity. The precise meaning of sovereignty was left hanging, not demanding a definitive solution.

The European Union didn't create a European defense policy. NATO continued to exist even though the Cold War was gone. But it was an odd organization because its historical purpose was to deal with an enemy that had collapsed. The United States was a member, and where European nations were militarily weak, the United States was strong, and engaged in wars in Afghanistan and Iraq. The American presence was disruptive, dividing NATO between those collaborating with the United States and those refusing to, and those engaged in one war and not the other. The ability of NATO to function as an institution was limited, but it still incorporated most of Europe, even if it wasn't strictly European.

By 2008, NATO and the EU had expanded eastward dramatically. They shared one mission: the integration of the newly liberated states of Eastern Europe, and potentially the former Soviet Union, into the West. This wasn't meant to be only a defense or economic integration. It was meant to be a moral and cultural one. Membership in either meant to the West that the new member was going to enter secular, multinational, peaceful Europe. It meant for the entering member that it would share in the economic prosperity and enjoy the peace and culture of Europe.

The European Union looked remarkably like NATO, excepting the United States. The biggest difference was that Turkey was a member of NATO but not of the EU, and there were differences in Scandinavia. Other than that the two organizations were remarkably similar. As their boundaries moved east, they left out Russia and the borderland of Belarus and Ukraine. And the excluded and dismissed Russia returned unexpectedly to history.

The Georgian Crisis

The 1990s had been a disaster for Russia economically and geopolitically. The economy was shattered by the fall of communism, and Russia's vast influence had disappeared. Vladimir Putin came to power because he represented one of the few functioning institutions in Russia—the secret police. This had been the foundation of both the czarist and the com-

munist regime. It held the country together, and while many of its operatives had participated in the chaotic looting of the Russian economy in
the 1990s, they now had to protect what they and their collaborators had
stolen. Putin and the FSB (Federal Security Service) apparatus came to
power. The regime that he created still defines Russia and affects everything it touches.

Putin and the FSB were committed to protecting the national interests of Russia. Russia had contracted, but the fear was that it would disintegrate further. Putin set about not only stabilizing the economy and
society, but also re-creating Russian power to protect its geopolitical
interests. In doing this, Russia preserved its borders, and NATO and the
EU, which had expanded to include the Baltic states, went no further.

During the early 2000s, the inclination to expand NATO and the
EU further eastward continued. The United States and some European countries sought to create a pro-Western government in Ukraine.
If Ukraine were a member of NATO, and if NATO ever resurrected its
military power, Russia would be wide open to invasion. Russia was not
about to dismiss this possibility. When the United States began supporting political groups in Ukraine that were pro-democracy in the eyes of
the Americans and Europeans, the Russians saw this as an attempt to seat
an anti-Russian government in Kiev and pave the way for the breakup
of the Russian Federation. In 2004, the Orange Revolution brought just
that type of government to power.

Ukraine's Orange Revolution transformed Russia's view of the
United States and Europe as well. The Orange Revolution occurred at a
time when the United States was bogged down in Iraq and Afghanistan,
and the Europeans were militarily weak. The Russians needed to deliver
a message, not so much to the United States as to the Ukrainians and
other countries in the former Soviet empire. They chose to deliver it in
Georgia, an American ally in the Caucasus. The circumstances of the
war were complex, and the Russians did not perform brilliantly, but they
didn't need to. They performed well enough. They defeated the Georgians and thus delivered this message.

Ukraine and the former satellites heard the message. Georgia looked
to NATO for support. None was forthcoming. NATO had become a
paper organization, whose weakness was masked by the fact that no one

would challenge it. When Russia did and no one came to Georgia's aid, a founding premise of European unification—that the EU would take care of the economy while NATO would take care of security—became more uncertain. True, Georgia wasn't part of NATO, but the United States and key NATO partners like Britain had been dueling with Russia over Ukraine and were supporting Georgia. Weakness was weakness and it showed. All this helped set up the Ukrainian crisis of 2014.

For the new members of NATO, who had assumed that Russia would never dare challenge NATO interests or the interests of NATO's leading members, the events in Georgia were a shock. The shock deepened when France negotiated a cease-fire, and the Russians violated it to demonstrate that they could—and there was no response. There had been an assumption that Russia was shattered and unwilling to take risks. That assumption, as well as the assumption that NATO would be effective, fell apart in August 2008. It was a shock, but a greater one was coming.

The Russo-Georgian war revealed the impotence of NATO, changed the strategic dynamic of the former Soviet Union, and posed long-term challenges to the West. But what happened next had both an immediate effect on how Europeans lived and on what European integration meant. Together the two blows ended the post–Cold War world and took everyone into a new and yet unnamed place. When, on September 15, Lehman Brothers went bankrupt and was unable to honor its debts, it threw the global financial system into disarray.

The Financial Crisis

The financial crisis began when a completely safe investment turned out to be incredibly risky. Prices of residential housing had risen continually since World War II. Americans believed that this would go on forever and that buying houses was a way to build equity. They also believed that lending money to home buyers was a risk-free investment.

However, over time, a dramatic change occurred in how mortgage lending took place. Money used to be lent by a bank, and the bank was repaid. It was the bank's responsibility to make sure that borrowers could repay the loan or it was stuck with the house. But the system evolved to the point where bankers didn't make money from the loan, but from the transaction itself. They took the loan and sold it to other institutions. Since the lenders, the mortgage brokers, and everyone else took a chunk of cash for closing the deal, none of them was worried about being repaid. Under this system the more loans they made, the more money they earned. Since they weren't worried about being repaid and they wanted to make all the loans they could, they didn't worry about creditworthiness, terms, or the rest. Lenders and their brokers wound up making loans with nothing down and almost no interest for five years against houses worth less than the loan. Buyers were being pulled into the market, and the price of houses soared.

The loans themselves were sold off to large, conservative investors in huge bundles. No one examined too carefully what was in the bundle because they believed there was no risk. Since financial institutions made money on each transaction, they invented new ways to take advantage of mortgages that were so complicated few understood them. But since everyone believed housing prices were going to continue rising, there was no risk. And since there was no risk, investment bankers and pension funds not only sold these, but bought them as well. So people who couldn't afford houses were getting mortgages, while investors who had no idea of the risk simply waited for the payments to roll in.

By September 15, 2008, three things that were inevitable had happened. First, the price of houses fell. Second, masses of unqualified buyers facing massive balloon payments defaulted. Third, the markets suddenly realized that they had no idea of the values of their mortgage holdings. Lehman Brothers, a huge investment banker, held a great deal of this paper and was no longer able to borrow against it for short-term transactions. The government refused to bail out Lehman Brothers, and it went bankrupt. It didn't pay any of its debts, and a tidal wave swept outward, with no one lending and many defaulting.

This was a very old story. In 1637 the price of tulip bulbs rose to a point where tulips were selling for astronomical amounts, trading on tulip bulb exchanges. People became obsessed with buying them, and as the price went up many became rich. Everyone was convinced that tulip bulb prices could only go up. Some people made fortunes; others were ruined when the prices came crashing down. So what happened in the subprime markets is an old story.

It was an old story in the United States as well. This was the fourth time since World War II that the country had a "can't lose" class of assets collapse in price, creating a financial crisis. In the 1970s, municipal bonds sold by cities and states were in danger of default because a recession cut tax receipts. The assumption had been that a government would never default. In the 1980s there was the third-world debt crisis. With energy and mineral prices soaring, investments surged into third-world countries to fund governments and businesses developing resources. The belief was that you couldn't lose, because prices could only rise. They fell, and the third world defaulted. Also in the 1980s there was the savings and loan crisis, when these banks were permitted to invest in commercial real estate that was a safe bet, until it collapsed, taking the banks with them.

The federal government handled each of these in the same way. It printed money and refinanced the system. It was painful, messy, and inefficient, but it worked. When the 2008 crisis came it had a model for dealing with these things, and the government and the Federal Reserve Bank collaborated in dealing with the crisis. Each crisis is different and each looked apocalyptic, but there is a road map, both political and technical, that is used. That's what happened after Lehman Brothers failed. The government and the Fed brought together the major bank CEOs and invented a solution. Its virtue was that the Fed could address the financial problem, while a political solution could be aligned with it. Everyone was moving in the same chaotic direction.

The Europeans had their own housing crisis, and they had also bought U.S. bundled mortgages. What they didn't have was a road map. The European Union had never faced a financial crisis of this magnitude. The European Central Bank was less than a decade old, and it had to align its policies with multiple governments. Its decision-making process was slow and complex, and the political reality was that it served sovereign states with very different interests.

The EU did not include all of Europe, and not all the members used the euro. Those that used the euro were as different as Greece and Germany. A coherent solution was impossible because the EU did not govern. This is where the contradiction of the EU was revealed. Nations retained ultimate authority; the EU controlled the central bank, or at least some nations had influence over it. The nations' unwillingness to abandon sovereignty to the European Union meant that those with authority could not speak for all of Europe, while those who spoke for Europe had little real authority.

The center and anchor of the EU was the Franco-German relationship. But it was no longer an equal partnership. Germany was by far the strongest economic power in Europe, and since the EU was primarily about economics, it was Europe's greatest power. France, on the other hand, not only lagged behind Germany, but differences within France made it difficult for the French to speak with one voice. Germany had the loudest voice in Europe, but its chancellor did not speak for Europe, and Germany's interests were not the same as the interests of the rest of Europe.

Germany currently exports the equivalent of 35–40 percent of its GDP. That is an enormous amount. The United States, by comparison, exports less than 10 percent of its GDP. China exports about 30 percent of its GDP. There are small countries that export a larger percentage of GDP than Germany, but no major power that does. Germany is both an extremely efficient producer and heavily dependent on its customers for its economic well-being. Germany's production outstrips its ability to consume what it produces by a huge margin. If it can't export, if its customers can't or won't buy, Germany faces economic crisis. Understanding this is the key to understanding everything else that happened in Europe.

Half of all German exports are sold in the European Union free-trade zone. For Germany, the free-trade zone made prosperity possible. No matter how efficiently it produces, unless markets aren't protected by tariffs, Germany can't maintain its domestic economy, and unemployment will rise. Therefore, Germany needs the European Union more than other members with lower export dependency. Germany, as the largest economy and lender of last resort, has a disproportionate influence on EU policies. It influences the ECBs monetary policy to support its needs and can influence European regulations as well.

After the financial crisis hit Europe, the Germans did not want to excessively underwrite the banking system. It was managing its own situation well enough. The problems were in other countries. Voters in other countries did not elect the German chancellor. She needed to respond to her voters, who didn't necessarily understand the degree to which their welfare and jobs depended on the rest of Europe's ability to buy Germany's products. From the German point of view, the problems in the rest of Europe were the result of laziness and self-indulgence. From the point of view of some in the rest of Europe, the problem originated in Germany rigging the system in its favor. This framed the current issue in Europe, which increasingly divides Germany from other members of the EU.

The mortgage problem turned into a sovereign debt crisis. Austerity measures used to stabilize the banks created a slowdown in Europe's economy. Cuts in government spending meant cuts in government employment and government purchases. This slowed the economy further. Tax receipts declined, and some of Europe's governments found it difficult to pay their debts. This created a new banking crisis, since European banks had bought European debt as a "can't lose" investment. If countries like Greece or Spain defaulted, the banks would fail and then the entire financial system would collapse.

There were three strategies. In one, the wealthier countries of Europe, Germany in particular, would cover Greece's debts and those of other southern European debtors. At the other extreme, Greece would pay off its debts by dramatic cuts in government spending. The third was that the banks would absorb the loans and swallow any bad loan. The third option was taken off the table. European banks would be severely damaged or destroyed if they had to pay for their mistakes. Germany liked the second plan. Greece liked the first. As you'd expect, a sort of compromise was reached. The banks would forgive some of Greece's debts, more of them would be covered by money coming from the EU, European Central Bank, and IMF, and Greece would cut expenses, creating a more austere environment.

It seemed reasonable. But the impact on Greece of government cuts was far greater than expected. Like many European countries, the Greeks ran many economic activities, including medicine and other essential services, through the state, making physicians and other health-care professionals government employees. When cuts were made in public-sector pay and employment, it deeply affected the professional and middle classes.

Over the course of several years, unemployment in Greece rose to over 25 percent. This was higher than unemployment in the United

States during the Depression. Some said that Greece's black economy was making up the difference and things weren't that bad. That was true to some extent but not nearly as much as people thought, since the black economy was simply an extension of the rest of the economy, and business was bad everywhere. In fact the situation was worse than it appeared to be, since there were many government workers who were still employed but had had their wages cut drastically, many by as much as two-thirds.

The Greek story was repeated in Spain and, to a somewhat lesser extent, in Portugal, southern France, and southern Italy. Mediterranean Europe had entered the European Union with the expectation that membership would raise their living standards to the level of northern Europe. The sovereign debt crisis hit them particularly hard because in the free-trade zone this region had found it difficult to develop its economies, as they would have normally. Therefore, the first economic crisis devastated them.

The crisis divided Europe dramatically. The integration that had

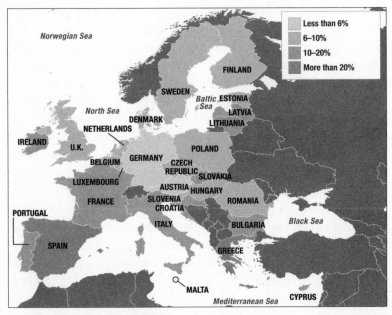

Unemployment in Europe 2013

seemed so promising during the years after Maastricht had encountered its first financial crisis, and the most important thing the crisis broke was European unity. What was in the interests of the Germans was not in the interests of the Spaniards, and vice versa. It became very much a German issue, as the Germans were the largest economy in Europe, the largest exporter in Europe, and the most adamant that austerity was the only way to solve Europe's problems. But it was an austerity that would not be borne by the Germans. It would be borne by the Mediterranean countries to varying degrees.

This had implications that went much deeper than the financial crisis. It meant breaking the basic social contract of the European Union. First, the promise of prosperity, the expectation that being part of Europe meant that there was a level of assurance on this score, was shattered. Second, any notion of shared fates was gone. What happened in Greece at one extreme and in Austria at the other were wildly different. The implicit and explicit promise of the EU was being lost on a molecular level, in household after household.

Consider a family with a breadwinner in his forties who was a professional, owned a home, cars, perhaps a small summer cottage. They took vacations and lived the life of the upper middle class. Suddenly the breadwinner was unemployed, unable to pay his mortgage and car loans, living in a small apartment, and trying to survive with dwindling savings. If he had children, his plans of providing them with a good education and future were gone. What was sensed but not yet clearly understood was that the problem would not go away quickly. The global depression of the 1920s and 1930s was solved by fascism and war. It took ten or fifteen years to deal with it. A man who was forty-five might not yet realize that he would live the rest of his life, in effect, in the penury into which he had fallen.

The poor are poor and it is usually difficult to make them poorer, but if that happens it's not a radical change, and often it's what they expect from life. But a professional in his forties or fifties is facing a crisis that he never expected, did not cause, and that has changed his sense of self profoundly. He has lost not only his wealth, earned by labor, but his sense of self. Who is he if not a lawyer or doctor or shopkeeper? When the middle classes fall into the ranks of the unemployed poor, and when that fall is inexplicable and, worse, something from which there would appear to be no chance to recover, that is where political instability begins.

The need to explain what happened to him, in a world that is incomprehensible, causes him to invent explanations or to be open to those who claim to know not only the answer, but also how to remedy the situation. In the 1920s and 1930s, during the global depression, Roosevelt said that we have nothing to fear but fear itself. This was not mere rhetoric. He understood that a very real catastrophe without clear explanation or justification, and apparently without end, creates a fear that craves understanding. The words of the ECB were neither comprehensible nor persuasive. In the 1920s and 1930s the explanation was that the capitalists caused this because of their greed, or that the Jews did this because that is what Jews do. There was no clear explanation, even a mistaken one, as to why this happened. In a world that has become incomprehensible, that which can be understood is seized on even if it is preposterous.

In both Greece and Spain, unemployment of those under age twenty-five hovered between 50 and 60 percent. Over half of all young people had no jobs and very little hope of getting one. In France it was much better. Only 25 percent of those under twenty-five were unemployed. Unemployed youth are dangerous. They become thieves or gravitate to extremist organizations. But by themselves, they lack the weight to pose a political threat. But combine them with a shattered, older middle class, and you have both the gravitas and energy needed to threaten the status quo.

In the current crisis two things kept this in check. The first was the continued belief that all this was temporary, that this was a technical glitch and not a massive system failure and the bad dream would go away if only they were patient. There was a deep trust in elites, a European idea that the authorities know what they are doing. It was sometimes mingled with distrust, yet on balance, that trust was still there and the people waited.

The second was the sense among the technocrats running the EU that the situation was not only going to be under control soon, but was already under control by 2010. And from the point of view of the technocrats, the problem was solved. The banks were solvent and stable, the financial system operating. In a strange lack of understanding redolent of the European aristocracy in the past, the technocrats could not grasp the significance of the unemployment, so fixated were they on the health of the financial system. In an odd way, this helped stabilize the political response to the system. The self-confidence of the elite helped reinforce the idea that they knew what they were doing.

Austerity was making recovery impossible. For an economy to function, infrastructure and organization are needed. Assume that the government wants to fund a project to build a bridge. That takes the technology, workforce, and management of a construction company, whether state owned or private. In the worst-hit countries, construction companies were driven out of business. The capacity to build had contracted, and whether the company has been dissolved because of budget cuts or bankruptcy makes little difference. The usual solution to a downturn is to stimulate the economy by pumping money into new demand with projects, grants, or tax cuts. But if the economy has been so badly hurt that the production system is no longer there, at least in some critical areas, then all the stimulus in the world can't help.

What had happened in Europe is that Germany had regained its preeminent position on the peninsula. It became the arbiter of how to handle the crisis because it had become the lender of last resort. And Germany was opposed to stimuli even if they might have worked. It wanted to preserve its resources in case it had problems of its own with unemployment. Reunited Germany, along with Austria, had the lowest unemployment rates in Europe, and they quite reasonably intended to preserve them.

The Franco-German relationship frayed as well. France, with much higher unemployment, wanted a stimulus package. Germany opposed it. This was the worst-case scenario of 1947: Germany was reemerging as the great power of Europe and the bond between France and Germany breaking. Of course this didn't mean war. Germany had no desire for war or even domination. But independently from what it wanted, Germany was dominating Europe, and the friction was intense. There were four regions in Europe: Germany-Austria, Northern Europe, Southern Europe, and Eastern Europe. Each had different interests from the others, and within each bloc there were frictions between nations.

The EU still existed, but no one was speaking for it. Each nation was calculating its own interests and forming coalitions independent of the EU. The central bureaucracy was no longer making the important decisions. Rather, national leaders were making decisions in the interest of their own nations. Europe had returned to the nation-state. In fact, there were more nation-states, more intensely treasured, after 1992 than before. The crisis revived distrust and dread, more in some countries than others. But they all knew that something had gone terribly wrong, and as time went on a suspicion was born that whatever the EU would become, it would not be able to solve its own problems.

We need to raise these questions. Is it possible that Europe will return to its old condition? What would happen if the EU wasn't there, or simply became a paralyzed arena of conflict like the UN? What would happen if the eastern countries lost all confidence in NATO and felt they had to make their peace with a rising Russia? Before 2008 these would have been fanciful questions.

Some say that Europe realized in 1945 that nationalism had destroyed it and would never let that happen again. Others say that Europe is too exhausted, too bereft of belief in anything, for conflict to occur. Perhaps. But Germany has reemerged as the leading and resented power on the peninsula, and Russia is drawing the mainland back together again. Simply considering that gives us a sense of the distance we have traveled in a very short time.

The intensity of nationalistic feelings has diminished over time. But they have not gone away and can reignite. Stripped of ideology and religion, the national fear and malice are still there. Sit down with a Pole and ask him about his family's experience with the Germans and Russians. Talk to a Scottish nationalist and hear the litany of charges against Britain. Talk to a Bosnian about the Serbs. The idea that national resentment isn't there will fast disappear. Historical memory in Europe lives outside time. Things that happened long ago are more real than things that are here now. Those memories are reemerging. They have not become as virulent as before, but they can become powerful.

The European sensibility is not that of an American. Americans are obsessed with the future. The past appears trivial. The battle site where the Civil War began is in Manassas, Virginia. There is now a shopping mall there. Things are remembered in America, but not with the anguish and pride with which Europeans remember things. Since 1945 they have tried to achieve a collective amnesia. It worked for a while, but memory is reemerging.

The place you see this most clearly is in the borderlands. A borderland is a region, not a line. It is the place where countries meet and blend. Europe has many borderlands. The EU tried to make them antiques. It was as if the distinctions between nations had been abolished. But the old customs sheds are still there on the roads at the old borders. It is easy to miss them. It would not be hard to reopen them. On a continent where German power is surging, this time in the form of exports, how long will it be before the customs sheds are reopened? And what of the borders between countries inside and outside the EU, such as Slovakia and Ukraine?

I crossed the border there one day in September 2011. It took hours to enter from the Ukrainian side. The Slovakian guards were particularly suspicious of Ukrainians entering the EU. The guards were as gruff as in the Cold War. There was no bathroom at the crossing. But a man has to go when a man has to go. I went off to a building that sold Johnnie Walker Black but had no restroom, a government store. I went behind the building. A female guard (of course) rushed up to put a stop to this breech of Ukrainian dignity. I waved an American passport. She quieted down and left. I felt like it was 1975 again, when an American passport either got you arrested or got you the royal treatment.

The people waiting to cross were speaking in all tongues. One group of Hungarians was standing by their cars eating peanuts. They threw the shells on the ground. The same border guard rushed up to them yelling, apparently demanding they pick up the shells. Obviously there was history here, but I didn't want to know it. But the Hungarians spoke Ukrainian and vice versa. Some Romanians got into the fun, and they were understood as well. I spoke to the Hungarians in Hungarian. They regularly deliver goods from the EU to Ukraine via the trunk of their car. They have "made arrangements," and I suspect the border guard had known them in various capacities, hence the rage over the peanuts.

Each knew the other. They all understood each other's languages. They all conspired to ignore the border. And there was history. Not just the personal kind over peanuts. But the mixture of Slovaks, Hungarians, Romanians, and Ukrainians, given circumstance and need, could become explosive. It had before. This was history of a deeper kind. It had been there for centuries and hadn't gone away.

It takes a long time for a borderland to disappear. This is the underlying problem of the EU. You can try to forget it's there. You can forgive, you can pretend to forget, but the memory, fear, and malice never quite go away. And when things get tough, as they do everywhere at some time, the memories emerge, along with the fear and malice. The Europeans think that can't happen again. They try to forget Yugoslavia and the Caucasus. They dismiss Ukraine. But old habits are hard to overcome.

Part Three

FLASHPOINTS

8

The Wars of Maastricht

The drafting, signing, and implementation of the Maastricht Treaty was intended to usher in a time of peace in Europe. It is ironic, therefore, that the creation of the European Union coincided with the start of major European wars in both the Balkans and Caucasus. In the Balkans, there were about a quarter of a million casualties in the 1990s. In the Caucasus the Armenia–Azerbaijani war cost about 115,000 casualties, and hundreds of thousands were displaced. Maastricht did not cause these wars, and the warring parties were not part of the European Union. Nevertheless, it is a fact that the time when the EU was created was also a time of war. In fact, since the EU was created, there have been more wars in Europe than between 1945 and 1992.

Many Europeans evade this fact. They regard Yugoslavia as unique and not reflective of modern Europe, and the Caucasus wars as not really European. History had left Europe with a hunger for pride, a wish to demonstrate that there was something extraordinary about Europe other than imperialism or mass murder. A belief had developed that the Europeans had learned the lesson that war doesn't pay and had devised a society that had put war behind it. They thought they had something important to teach the world. As prosperity returned to Europe, the persistence of peace became a key part of the story of their resurrection. It was important for the Europeans to deny that these wars were European. Yet they were, and they spoke to the fragility of peace.

Another kind of evasion is possible as well. When NATO attacked Serbia in the war over Kosovo, the United States did the heavy lifting in the war, accompanied by some NATO allies. Very quickly, the war turned, psychologically, into an American war from the viewpoint of many Europeans. Denial can take the form of insisting on collective security, yet regarding the actual acts of war as belonging to someone else, in this case the United States.

The Balkans and the Caucasus are borderlands, and within these borderlands more borderlands are nested like Russian matrushka dolls, one inside the other. Each is smaller than the last, and they continually surprise you when one more borderland, ever smaller, appears. Finally you are left with tiny villages divided into factions of families or parts of families, each hardened by history and conflict, never forgetting, rarely forgiving.

It is not surprising that the two wars took place in mountainous regions. Small nations survive in mountains despite wars and conquest. The mountains shield them and provide refuge. But mountains also make it difficult to create nations. The mountains fragment as well as shield, and in the mountains families and clans can be more real than nations. Mountains frequently hide what might be called proto-nations, premodern entities linking clans with common languages and religions with each other.

Mountains are often lawless places. If conquerors can't root out the small, fragmentary nations, then they can hardly be expected to enforce laws. And it's those who retain their independence who enforce the law, which in the mountains means it's the families and clans who enforce the customs that constitute the laws. In times of trouble there was no one else to call on but allies in the next valley. This insularity bred hard people, able to suffer and able to fight. It also created regions where the broad geopolitical forces of rising and falling empires could have an impact, but never obliterate these small realities. The mountains were therefore filled with small, fierce, and fragmented ethnic groups, and when the pressure on them to keep their tensions in check eased, they exploded.

There was another characteristic to these post-Soviet, post-Maastricht wars. They occurred in the borderlands of Europe where Christianity and Islam mixed. Bosnia, Albania, and Kosovo were Muslim regions. Serbia and Croatia were Christian. Azerbaijan was Muslim, Armenia and Georgia Christian. The first wars after the collapse of communism were Christian–Muslim wars. They were the first harbingers of a resurrected issue—Islam within Europe. The conflicts were more ethnic than religious, but still they were not new wars so much as the renewal of an older one. They were flashpoints come back to life.

The Balkan explosion was bloodier and more visible to the world. After World War I the western part of the peninsula was named Yugoslavia. It combined nations divided by ethnicity, religion, and a history of hostility, much as the rest of Europe had been. To solve the problem, these nations were gathered together into a single federation by the victors on the theory that conflict could be overcome. It failed in the same year that the Maastricht Treaty was signed, 1991, and when it failed, it revealed a side of Europe that Europeans wanted to believe had disappeared. To many people the Balkans are not really part of Europe, and what happens there can't be taken as representative of Europe. Reading the Balkans out of Europe is a comforting notion but not an accurate one. They are not only part of Europe, but important to its history. We should remember what Bismarck said in 1888: "If there is ever another war in Europe, it will come out of some damned silly thing in the Balkans."

Balkan Wars

My father used to tell me to stay out of the Balkans. It was, he said, a dark place where you could be killed for the change in your pocket or a careless glance. In France before World War II the word *Balkan* was associated with violence and with being uncivilized—as in calling a thug "Balkan." I felt that things had improved. During the Cold War Yugoslavia was considered enlightened compared to other communist countries. Then the 1990s came, and the Balkans, at least the Yugoslavian region, started living up to their old reputation.

The Balkans are a fragmented region caught between three great powers: Turkey to the southeast, Russia to the east and northeast, and the Germanic countries to the northwest. Great European empires met and dueled here. Historically, none of these great powers stayed in the Balkans. Each was on its way to somewhere else, somewhere more important. The Balkans were a defensive bulwark or a springboard rather than a destination. In the fourteenth century the Ottomans transited on their way to great prizes to the north. The Hapsburgs came through, pushing the Ottomans back. In the twentieth century the Soviets hoped to get ports on the Adriatic but were blocked by the Yugoslav communists, who turned on the Soviets. The Soviets had to settle for Romania and Bulgaria.

In passing through, they all left tracks: Muslims here, Catholics there, Orthodox elsewhere, in a religious and ethnic hodgepodge. New conquerors left their imprint but did not have the strength or interest to wipe out the old imprints that were embedded in valleys. Consequently, successive conquerors left the geopolitics of many small and angry ethnic groups relatively undisturbed. These groups grew hard and tough.

The Balkans

The more they were conquered the harder they became, until uprooting them became too difficult to achieve and too much trouble to try.

It was during one of those rare times when the pressure was off that the Balkans exploded. The Soviets had collapsed, the Americans were not very concerned, the Germans were busy integrating east with west, and the Turks were still inward looking. The Balkans were not under pressure, and Yugoslavia had more freedom than it had had since its creation. There was a connection between the absence of external pressure and an internal explosion. During the Cold War, NATO and the Warsaw Pact held Yugoslavia in their force field. Yugoslavia feared Soviet domination. NATO counterbalanced the Soviets, but Yugoslavia had to be held together internally with an iron grip. Once the Soviet Union collapsed, NATO had lost interest and Tito was ten years dead. The suppressed antagonism reemerged and Yugoslavia exploded.

Yugoslavia was a country of internal borderlands where virtually everything had multiple meanings depending on who you were. Even a small bridge could be a borderland. Ivo Andrić, a Bosnian, won the Nobel Prize in Literature for his book *The Bridge on the Drina*. It uses a bridge to capture the lives of Muslims and Christians in Bosnia:

> On the Bridge and its *kapia* [a widened area halfway across where people could gather], about it or in connection with it, flowed and developed, as we shall see, the life of the townsmen. . . . The Christian children, born on the left bank of the Drina, crossed the bridge at once on the first days of their lives, for they were always taken across in their first week to be christened. But all other children, those who were born on the right bank and the Moslem children who were not christened at all, passed, as had once their fathers and grandfathers, the main part of their childhood on or around the bridge.

Andrić conveyed a sense of order and peace deliberately and ironically. He understood the distinctions between the two groups, and the anger and blood they share. A borderland can be a frightening place. A borderland within a borderland is even more so, because escaping one confrontation simply takes you to another dangerous place. People cling together out of the fear of losing what they know and love, and that fear causes them to turn on those on the other side of the bridge. It is an irrational fear only to people far away who have other fears but not this fear, or who are so safe or powerful that they fear nothing. In the borderlands of the world, life isn't that casual and the fears are not unreasonable.

As we have seen multiple times, the consequences of these hatreds and fears can resonate in Europe. In 1912, Serbia and Montenegro allied with Greece and attacked the Ottomans, who still hung on to parts of the Balkans. The war ended quickly with the Ottomans continuing their century-long retreat. In 1913 the war broke out again. This time, Bulgaria, dissatisfied with the spoils of an earlier war, attacked Macedonia. Greece, allied with Bulgaria, also attacked Macedonia. Romania and the Ottomans jumped in against Bulgaria. Small countries and fragments within these countries formed a swirling kaleidoscope of shifting alliances. Each mistrusted the other and feared its intentions. When Gavrilo Princip, a member of "Unification or Death," a Serbian group, assassinated Archduke Ferdinand and his wife in Sarajevo in 1914, it set in motion a European war. Each feared the other and planned for the worst. This fear was not irrational.

After World War I, the victors decided that what was needed in the western Balkans was a multinational state. Catholic Slovenia and Croatia, Orthodox Serbia and Macedonia, and Bosnia-Herzegovina (thought of as Muslim but with a large Serbian Orthodox population) joined together in a nation whose unifying principle was discord. None of these countries was ethnically pure. Each was filled with enclaves of other nationalities and religions. And each of these was divided against itself.

Europe's solution to the problem of the Balkans was to create a union, hopefully overcoming Bismarck's prophecy. Founded in 1918, it was originally called the Kingdom of Serbs, Croats, and Slovenes, which gives a sense of how divided it was. (And how odd, in an age when kings were losing power, to decide to put the Serbian king on the throne over all these divided countries.) King Alexander held it together in a dictatorship until the Germans invaded in 1941. Then the union fragmented under the pressure, and all the underlying hatreds emerged, some groups siding with the Germans, others fighting them, others ignoring the Germans and fighting each other.

After World War II, unity was restored, and the conflict was suppressed by another dictatorship. A communist state headed by Marshal Josip Broz Tito suppressed internal conflict with an iron hand and careful concessions to the constituent republics. He also preserved Yugoslavia from Soviet domination. Following a somewhat more liberal economic policy than other communist countries, Yugoslavia had the most vibrant economy in the communist world in the 1960s. Perhaps that wasn't saying much.

However, when I visited Belgrade, Zagreb, and Ljubljana in 1974, the contrast with Warsaw or Prague was striking—and the contrast to Soviet cities even more so. Within the constraints of geography and ideology, they were doing well. I remember visiting Bled, a small and beautiful town in the Julian Alps. There was a graciousness there that you could not find in the rest of Eastern Europe. Strolling around the lake and eating in restaurants overlooking it, restaurants I couldn't afford, were what I guessed was the Yugoslav elite. When I talked to them, they turned out to be mid-level bureaucrats and small businessmen. I stayed at a small, cheap pension, with a feather bed and beautiful windows. The owners lived elsewhere. They owned several buildings. Austria was just on the other side of a mountain. There were endless unmapped trails that could take you there. The Yugoslavs didn't care who left; the Austrians worried about who came in. In 1974 in a communist country with a ubiquitous red star, this was all startling.

When Tito died in 1980 Yugoslavia started to shatter. The republics decided not to replace Tito but to create a rotating presidency of eight. It was the only compromise that everyone could agree to, and it eliminated the monarchy and dictatorship that had held Yugoslavia together from its founding. The existing national distinctions were now institutionalized.

When the Soviet Union's power in Eastern Europe collapsed in 1989, it released a force field that had frozen Yugoslavia in its position. The collapse of communism took all moral authority from the regime. What remained were constituent states, hostile communities within states, and the weapons that were in many homes. In the 1970s I stood in a train station in Zagreb, the capital of Croatia, and saw soldiers on leave, carrying their weapons home. Postwar Yugoslavia had been a partisan state, founded by guerrillas, and that ethic survived in the military. It also fueled the fire. Between slivovitz, a strong plum brandy that is the regional beverage and will rip your guts out, and machine pistols stored in the hall closet, very real tensions could turn to violence very quickly.

War broke out between Croatia and Serbia, old enemies, in 1991, transforming a relatively peaceful federation of nations into a small holocaust. Animosities between the two nations can be traced back a long way. During World War II, Croatia was relatively friendly to the Nazis, while Serbia had been a center of resistance. Catholic Croatia had long had an affinity with the European peninsula—with Italy, Austria, Hungary, and Germany. Part of it was cultural and part came from the fact that Croatia feared the much larger Serbia and needed allies. The Serbs were Orthodox, and even the communists saw some connection between themselves and the Russian Orthodox. The communists tried to transcend nationalism. The Ustashi, Croatian irregulars, hunted the communist partisans, many but far from all Serbian, and helped the Nazis. Many unforgiveable things took place between Serbs and Croats. This never was settled and it never went away.

In the early 1970s I once spent an evening with some Marxists in Zagreb, near the university. They were not Stalinist but part of the New Left—part of what had been called the Praxis Group, for very obscure reasons. These were educated men and women, learned in philosophy, who clearly regarded themselves as heirs to the Enlightenment. They saw their task as bringing a new form of socialism to Yugoslavia, one that would be more humane than what they currently had, though even that was liberal compared to Romania, Czechoslovakia, or the Soviet Union at the time.

The slivovitz flowed freely, and I turned the discussion to people I had met in Belgrade. Not quickly, but surely, the mood shifted. The evening ended with a fairly eminent philosopher spitting on the floor and cursing the city, the country, and its animals—he was very insistent on cursing Serbia's animals. This was a man who I could easily envision at an American university, but when he drank enough brandy and the night moved into those hours where truths are uttered, he was simply a Croat neither able to forgive nor forget what had happened to his nation at the hands of the Serbs. After midnight, the Enlightenment was far away.

You can probe as deeply as you like for the reason behind his hatred, but in the end, he loved his own and that is who he was. His grand-father's memories were his memories. For all the corrosive power of the Enlightenment, this was the one thing that could not be corroded. And in the Balkans, as in much of Europe, the memories were bad ones, bringing forth rage and malice. They could be suppressed by dictator-ship, appeased by prosperity, and rendered unacceptable by enlightened thought, but as these withered, the old memories reappeared.

The war devolved into endless multilateral battles and maneuvers so complicated that even the chess that the Yugoslavs all play couldn't begin to teach you how to cope with it. It ended not merely in battle but in concentration camps, different from the German camps in terms of industrial efficiency, but not hunger and violence. Bosnia had Muslim, Croatian, and Serbian communities that all went to war with each other. But the northern part of Bosnia, which was Serbian, was the strongest. The Serbians went south to Sarajevo and laid siege to the Muslim capital, creating a situation that was almost medieval, except for the artillery fire.

I visited Banja Luka about fourteen years after the siege ended. The capital of the Srpska Republika, Banja Luka is peaceful and prosper-ous looking. A Sunday afternoon stroll on streets around the city center reveals a fairly genteel life. In a park, two players move huge chess pieces around, with a dozen or more absorbed onlookers. The ice cream was good, and the hotel's café was filled with young people dressed well. I wandered up one leafy street and saw a building with a KPMG sign. In the capital of the outlaw republic that still flies its own flag and not Bos-nia's, the ultimate sign of modern civilization can be seen: the name of a major American accounting and consulting firm.

I was startled to realize I was not at all surprised that the vast major-ity of signs are either in English or have English words in them. When I was young, the second language in Bosnia was German. At the seat of a rebellion that the Americans fought to repress, all outward signs indi-cated that the residents were enthusiastically letting bygones be bygones.

The road south from Banja Luka is only two lanes wide but well paved, with lots of construction taking place along the hilly road. Obvi-ously someone thinks that business on the road between Banja Luka and Sarajevo will be good. As you approach Sarajevo, the development of highways and construction of office buildings is substantial. On the main road into town the traffic is heavy even in mid-afternoon, moving alongside a river that flows to the old city. There the buildings are quaint, the streets crooked, and in the summer evening, below the hills where people live, the night is lively with food and music.

A little more than a decade ago, Banja Luka was the seat of power for Ratko Mladic, the leader of the Srpska Republika. Back then the road south was filled with military vehicles and artillery that, when it arrived at Sarajevo, conducted a brutal shelling of the city. This was far from the worst hell Europe had seen, but it was the worst hell between 1945 and today.

I was amazed at how well Bosnia had reconstructed itself. It was more than just cleaning up the debris, it had also rehabilitated its people. The term *war torn* is widely—perhaps too widely—used for places, but it is best applied to people. People who have recently been through wars look war torn. The people in Banja Luka and Sarajevo do not. And the road that had carried all the military traffic was . . . just a road. But as much as they cleaned up, the men praying in the evening in the mosque in Sarajevo, indistinguishable otherwise from other Europeans, and the men playing chess in Banja Luka had not forgotten and had not forgiven. For them, events five hundred years before, or in 1995, are as if they had happened yesterday. There is a willful desire to appear to forget. But there is no real amnesia here.

Europe looked at Yugoslavia as atavistic, as some sort of prehistoric being that had nothing to do with Europe. Europe no longer waged vicious wars between multiple nations. Europe no longer sent people to concentration camps because of their ethnicity. Europe no longer was an abomination before the world. Therefore, since Yugoslavs had done all these things in 1995 they were in some way not really European. It was not obvious who they were, but they were clearly completely opposed to the European spirit. On the other hand, when the Balkan wars erupted in 1912 the same thing could have been said, and what followed in the rest of Europe was much worse than what happened in the Balkans.

We stayed in Sarajevo in a small hotel owned by an older, cultured woman, short and a bit stout, who reminded me intensely of my aunts, bustling about to make us comfortable. After some prodding and hesitation she spoke quietly about the days under bombardment from the men from Banja Luka. I told her that there is now a KPMG office in Banja Luka, a sign that it can't happen again. She smiled sadly and assured me that in this place matters of war and peace don't depend on money. The wars would be back, she said, but "for now I have a hotel." Her delight was not that there was peace, but that for the moment there was enough peace to enjoy her hotel. Her modest expectations became her but are a warning about realities.

The details of this round of the Balkan wars are not important. Getting a sense of the aftermath is more important. They happened, men and women died, some horribly, and it ended when the Americans negotiated a peace and finally went to war with Serbia over the predominantly Albanian and Muslim province of Kosovo, which the Serbs see as essential to their national identity. After all, the battle of Kosovo, fought in 1389, could not be forgotten. It means as much today as six hundred years ago.

The Europeans couldn't prevent the war, nor stop it. When it was over they patrolled it. But more than anything it was the exhaustion of all sides, physical and emotional, that ended the war. But as before, nothing is settled. The idea that Yugoslavia would abandon the bloodshed of 1912 and 1913 was an illusion. Enemies are enemies, no matter what flag they must live under. There is the belief of many that if only they were admitted to the European Union, all this would end. It isn't clear why they believe this, but some believe it passionately. Others know that another round is coming. The advocates of the EU were more enthusiastic. The people I spoke to who expected war were more grim and determined. I took them more seriously.

Caucasus Wars

The western Balkans are a flashpoint in their own right. They are also a flashpoint because the Turks are rising again and the Russians have reemerged as a regional power, and because Europe is weak and unsettled, with a very powerful Germany in danger of being decoupled from a multinational Europe. Nothing has been settled within the former Yugoslavia, and the incentives to keep the peace are withering. We must

carefully consider the reemergence of forgotten great powers that look
at the region as a road to commerce, and later, perhaps, as a road to war.
And recall that the United States sent troops to Bosnia and Kosovo, and
they were there for years.

The Caucasus Mountains are on the land bridge between the Black
Sea and the Caspian. The bridge connects the European mainland with
the Anatolian Peninsula and Persia.

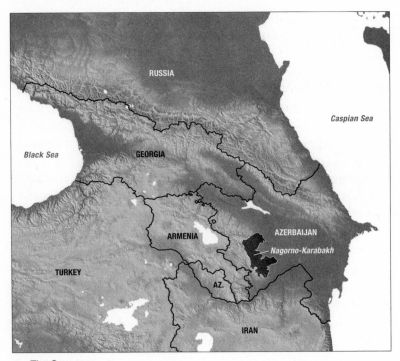

The Caucasus

The Caucasus consists of two mountain ranges. To the north is the
High Caucasus, containing some of the highest and most rugged mountains in Europe, Mount Elbrus being the highest at 18,510 feet. To the
south are the Lesser Caucasus, lower and similar to the ranges in the
Balkans—rugged and inaccessible. Between the two ranges is a plain,
hilly in the west and becoming increasingly flat to the east. The plain is
created by the Kura River, which starts in the mountains of eastern Turkey, and flows east into the Caspian. The plain extends west to the Black

Sea, where the coastal plain creates the western extension. Two of the Caucasus nations, Georgia and Azerbaijan, are on this plain. Armenia, the third, is for the most part in the southern mountain range.

The Caucasus is surrounded by three great powers, two of them also on the periphery of the Balkans: Turkey to the southwest, Iran to the southeast, and Russia to the north. Each of them has at varying times tried to take control of the Caucasus. Most often it was shared between the three. The mountains protect each from the other. It almost didn't matter where the line was drawn, so long as each had a foothold. The mountains, even the Lesser Caucasus, were so rugged that it was almost impossible for an army to pass all the way through. For the Russians, the High Caucasus was essential. To their north is a flat plain, difficult to defend, that is the end of the European Plain. Penetrating that far would open the door to the Russian heartland. Even after the fall of the Soviet Union, this was a region the Russians would not retreat from, even in the face of Muslim resistance to their presence in Chechnya and Dagestan.

The Russians needed, in fact, to move as far south as possible to discourage any attack. In the nineteenth century, given the weakness of the Ottomans and Persians, the Russians were able to push through the Kura valley to the Lesser Caucasus, in the process absorbing Georgia, Armenia, and Azerbaijan. After the Russian Revolution, these countries temporarily gained independence, but the Soviets returned to their old line and integrated these countries into the Soviet Union. Turkey was weak, as was Iran, and that meant no one could do anything about it.

This gave the Soviets three things. First, it guaranteed they would not lose control over the High Caucasus. Second, they established a line through the Lesser Caucasus that was particularly important during the early Cold War when the Soviets feared American attack from Turkey and Iran. Finally, and perhaps most important, it gave the Soviets Europe's greatest source of oil—Baku, the capital of Azerbaijan. This drove Soviet industrialization. Without Baku's oil I doubt the Soviets would have survived World War II. Certainly Hitler believed that if he could take Baku, he would win the war. The entire point of the battle of Stalingrad was to open the door to Baku. The Germans were stopped by the Soviets and the mountains and lost the war, to a great extent, because the High Caucasus defeated them.

The fall of the Soviet Union actually began in the Caucasus. Haydar

Aliyev was a member of the Soviet politburo. He had been head of the KGB in Azerbaijan. Forced out by Mikhail Gorbachev, he returned to Azerbaijan, convinced that the Soviet Union would not survive under Gorbachev. He returned to Azerbaijan to both bide his time and build a political base that would allow Azerbaijan to withdraw from the Soviet Union and remain intact.

At about the same time, a dramatic but little noticed event took place. The provincial parliament of a region of Azerbaijan asked Moscow for permission to leave Azerbaijan and join Armenia. Gorbachev objected, fearing that this would trigger other demands for border shifts in the Soviet Union. Since Stalin in particular had been casual about moving historic borders, and since many borders were unclear anyway, he was afraid this would become a destabilizing force in the Soviet Union as a whole.

The problem was rooted in Soviet policy. The Soviets had reshaped borders of their constituent republics, moved populations around, and sometimes deported masses of people, depending on their political and strategic needs. Azeris had been deported to Central Asia during World War II, and populations had shifted around within the Caucasus. Armenians were permitted to move in large numbers into a region of Azerbaijan known as Nagorno-Karabakh. Over the years, what had been Azeri was settled by Armenians.

As the Soviet Union weakened and collapsed, Gorbachev's objection to the Armenian demand that Azerbaijan transfer control over Nagorno-Karabakh became meaningless. As Armenia and Azerbaijan became sovereign republics, tensions between them rose. Azeris died in Armenia and Armenians died in Azerbaijan. By the winter of 1992, at about the same time that war was breaking out in the Balkans, Armenia attacked Nagorno-Karabakh, and the two sides, using Soviet military equipment, went to war. Over 800,000 Azeris and about 250,000 Armenians became refugees. About 30,000 Azeris and 6,000 Armenians were killed. The war was halted in 1994, but it was never settled and the conflict continues to fester. Snipers are still active along the border, and UN resolutions are ignored.

When I first visited Azerbaijan more than a decade after the war ended, I was greeted by a government official and immediately taken to a memorial for those killed establishing an independent Azerbaijan, where I was to lay flowers. A group of TV reporters with their cameras were waiting to interview me. The first question they asked was about my position on the Nagorno-Karabakh issue. It was my first visit, and while I was aware of the issue I was unaware of the passions it stirred. It is hard to understand these things unless you are there. My answer was noncommittal, but I agreed that the UN resolution had to be honored. I was frankly wondering why anyone would care what my opinion was.

That interview and others I did were posted on the Internet. I was quickly attacked by the Armenians as being in the pay of the Azerbaijanis because I had gone to Azerbaijan in the first place, and had said approving things about Baku, which is in fact a very attractive city. That statement was taken to mean that I was bought and paid for by the Azeris. Both sides demand that the United States solve the problem, but in the end, it is a problem that will be solved by those directly involved.

It is very easy to regard the political passions of others as irrational and misguided. We fully understand our own loves and hates, so we take them seriously, but regard those of others as frivolous, and even pathological. The fact is that we all have memories, and all but the most powerful nations feel victimized by some wrong that cannot be made right. This is true in the Balkans, and this is certainly true in the Caucasus. Failure to understand the passions of others can lead you into grave political error. What the other person cares about never quite makes sense. In the Caucasus I was taught what memory and passion mean. And for the record, I did not take money from the Azeris.

Conclusion

The Balkans and the Caucasus defy the European narrative of the new Europe. The wars there, including the Russian war with Georgia in 2008, raged as the European Union was institutionalizing itself. The kinds of passions that had defined Europe prior to 1945 were alive and well, not within the EU, perhaps, but in Europe, and in the case of the Balkans, on the European peninsula.

Some Europeans have dismissed these conflicts as occurring in primitive parts of Europe (the Balkans) or not really in Europe (the Caucasus). However, primitive or not, we should remember that the Balkans are where the First World War began, and the High Caucasus, Chechnya and Dagestan, is where Russia is currently fighting a counterinsurgency against Islamists. To dismiss all these conflicts requires constant redefinition of Europe. In the end it has to be said that the European wars did not end with the fall of the Soviet Union and the rise of the EU.

What can be said is that in the part of Europe inside the EU, there were no wars. This is a powerful point supporting the argument that the EU can moderate Europe's appetite for conflict successfully. But that raises another question. What happens to Europe if the EU fails, fragments, or simply ceases to function effectively? If it is the structure of the EU that pacifies Europe, and the structure slips or fails, what will restrain Europe?

I have made the argument that the EU is facing a crisis it cannot easily deal with. The EU is failing, and the question is whether it can regain its balance. I am arguing that it cannot because its problems are structural and will lead to failure. If it is true that it is the integration of Europe that has abolished conflict, and that without the EU conflict will return, as it did in the Balkans and Caucasus, then Europe's future is very different from what most are expecting.

Since that is my assertion, what comes next is an analysis of the various potential flashpoints. Europe has old traditions, and one of them is the recurrence of conflicts in certain places.

9

The German Question Once More

The question of Europe now is again the question of Germany, of what it wants, what it fears, what it will and won't do. This is the old question of Europe. It goes along with the oldest question in Europe: When will the next war start and where will it be fought? The unification of Germany led to the thirty-one years. For forty-five years Germany was divided and there was peace. Now Germany is united again and is unquestionably the leading power of Europe. If the European Union fails and its collaborative structure breaks, then the question is whether the Europe that tore itself apart will return to its prior structure.

In 1945 it was assumed that Germany was finished as a great power. It has reemerged as the leading, if not dominant, power of the European peninsula. The question is what this means for Europe and the world. Germany today is certainly not in any way the Germany of Adolf Hitler. It has limited military force, and its internal set of beliefs and principles is deeply constitutional and democratic. However, this doesn't change the fact that Germany is the most powerful country in Europe today, and that the decisions it makes and the actions it takes have much greater effect on the European peninsula and beyond than those of other countries.

This is not a new position for Germany to be in. Its unification in 1871 changed the way Europe worked, creating a massive, creative, and insecure power in the center of the European Plain. Indeed, going back to the beginning of Europe, the presence of Germanic tribes east of the Rhine River defined the limits of the Roman Empire. These tribes, north of the Alps, east of the Rhine, and with an indeterminate border in the east, could not be ignored.

In 1871, with Prussia at its core, Germany became a modern nation-state, and not just a nation with dozens of states. Three times since then Germany has reemerged as a very powerful entity, politically and economically. In 1871 its unification and defeat of France in war redefined Europe. In 1918, having been defeated in World War I, it began the process of reemergence that culminated in Nazi Germany. In 1945 it began reemerging again, culminating in the reunification of East and West Germany in 1990. Germany originated from fragmentation, was repeatedly crushed and reshaped, and continually reemerged, not merely as a country, but as the leading country in Europe.

Part of this simply has to do with geography. Any country located in the middle of the northern plain of Europe will be important, whether fragmented, as it was during the Holy Roman Empire, or united. But its repeated reemergence as the leading power in Europe is a more complex matter. In 1945 very few would have imagined the Germany of the twenty-first century, and those who did would have been terrified.

Yet we are again talking about Germany, the essential country of Europe, about the problems it creates and solves, about its leadership and the resentment of that leadership. Before we even begin thinking about what this means, we have to consider why this is so, and particularly why this has been so ever since 1871 in spite of the catastrophes through which Germany has passed.

It is interesting to think of Japan, sitting on the other side of Russia from Germany. At about the time Germany was unifying and beginning its upward surge, Japan was also unifying and beginning its surge. Japan was even poorer in natural resources and even less schooled in the modern arts of warfare. It needed the British to build it a fleet and the Germans to build it an army. Amazingly, by 1905 it had defeated the Russian navy and by World War II it had become East Asia's leading economic and military power. Like Germany, Japan had developed extraordinarily rapidly under pressure—indeed from a far lower base. Like Germany, it had resorted to war to redress imbalances, and like Germany it was devastated in the war, with no apparent chance that it would recover. But Japan, in parallel with Germany, also surged back and today ranks ahead of it as the third leading economic power in the world. Russia, Britain, and France were far less damaged during World War II and were ultimately victorious, but they have not done nearly as well since then.

So rather than ask the question "Why Germany?," let's expand that to ask, "Why Germany and Japan?" Germany wasn't unique. It was part of the class of countries that achieved unification relatively late. It also industrialized later than other countries. Late in the nineteenth century both Japan and Germany unified and then surged economically. Both needed access to raw materials in order to feed their new industrial machine. Both were blocked by stronger powers that had unified and industrialized earlier. Both resorted to war as a means of ensuring access to raw materials and markets. Both were ultimately severely beaten yet within a generation reemerged economically, but with weak militaries. Interestingly, Italy, which unified at about the same time, had a less intense industrialization process, suffered less in its wars, and never gained the importance of the other two.

The industrial revolutions in both Germany and Japan were encouraged and even imposed by the state. These were both outward-looking powers. The Prussians wanted unification in order to compete with Britain and France. Rapid industrialization was central. When the Japanese encountered the Americans and watched the British in China, they realized that without unification and industrialization they would meet China's fate. In 1868 the Meiji Restoration re-created the unified government that had been missing in Japan for centuries. That unified government forced industrialization both for economic and military reasons.

These actions led not to state ownership, but to state policy shaping industrial policy. Both countries had an aristocracy that helped implement the policy, aware of their responsibility for the fate of their country and prepared to lead industrialization for their self-interest. Unlike the Italians, who did not face the dire geopolitical threats of Germany and Japan and whose aristocracy was not highly disciplined for collective action, the Germans and the Japanese were able to act.

Industrialism, unification, and military power were intertwined. Each supported the other. As a result both Germany and Japan developed militaristic ideologies that presented the military as the embodiment of the nation, the aristocracy as the natural leaders of the military, and the general population as enthusiastic participants. Italians tried to invent a militaristic ideology under Mussolini, but the Fascist Party was built on a base of sand.

After World War II both Japan and Germany developed antimilitaristic ideologies. Japan became constitutionally pacifist. Germany resumed its military tradition in NATO but never regained any enthusiasm for the ideology. Nevertheless both countries developed rapidly economically. This development, which was necessary for recovery, created an alternative ideology to militarism, which we might call "economism"—the pursuit of the national interest primarily by an obsession with economic development. Economic development made militarism obsolete in their minds.

Japan and Germany shared another characteristic. Both were vital to the United States during the Cold War. The American economy produced about half the world's GDP in the postwar years. Having close economic relations with the United States was extremely beneficial, as it gave both countries access to the largest market in the world. The United States needed both Germany and Japan as part of its containment strategy for the Soviet Union. But it needed them prosperous. Therefore, the United States rapidly abandoned any idea of punishing them for the war and leaving them impoverished. Due to the postwar geopolitical situation, the economies of both nations had to be revived. Foreign aid and access to the American market—and allowing both to protect their own markets with tariffs—gave them the energy to begin recovery.

The social reality created by Germany's geopolitical situation had produced a population that, under orders, would do extraordinarily vicious things during a war. But this population would also do extraordinarily hard work after the war. Discipline in the face of economic deprivation was not alien to them. The Germans could face this in ways other populations couldn't and didn't. The contrast with Italy demonstrates this, but so does Germany rising out of nowhere to bypass Britain and France twice in a century.

Japan is the third-largest economy in the world. Germany is the fourth. Both have, until now, tried to become economic giants without becoming militarily powerful. Both exercise less international power than they could. Both have existed in the postwar world in the context of

American power. But neither exists in a stable environment. The United States is diverted, and regional issues have become uncertain. Both are weighing their options and hoping they will not have to exert themselves or take risks.

It is important to see Germany in the context of Japan because it allows us to avoid seeing Germany as a singular nation instead of in a more general context. Its unification and further development were not identical to Japan's, but the similarities are striking and instructive. Late unification and industrialization created a situation that countries like Italy could not fully manage, and that even for Germany and Japan led to national catastrophes from which they have emerged.

The basic social solidarity that held both countries together after unification is still in place, a solidarity that also helped them recover from defeat. This social discipline continues to exist in Germany. It may appear to be fraying on the edges culturally, but if so this isn't decisive. The differential between Germany's economic performance and that of the rest of Europe attests to its endurance. Although the generation that rebuilt Germany in the 1950s and 1960s is dying, its successor, apparently steeped in the radicalism of the 1960s and 1970s, does not appear markedly different.

What is different, of course, is its approach to militarism. The Cold War generation, reluctantly or not, was caught up in defending the homeland against a very real threat. The generation after the Cold War has little interest in the military. This is reasonable because circumstances are such that, as with the Weimar Republic, Germany does not face a military danger.

For the Germans, success and disaster are intimately linked, so they are simultaneously afraid of what they have achieved and tremendously proud of it. They fear that success will force them into a role they no longer want and fear will overwhelm them again. They do not aspire to lead a new Europe. They fear that they can't escape the role. The rest of Europe harbors suspicions that Germany's public fears and modesty are feigned, that in the end the old Germany has never died but has merely been asleep. There is no country in Europe that doesn't have bad memories of Germany. Even the Germans have bad memories of themselves.

Germans want to believe that the history that causes them to shudder is behind them. It is as if someone did something terrible and convinced himself that it was a dream, that it didn't happen, or that it happened in a different life. Over time the dream fades and he can pretend it is gone. But he has never really forgotten the truth. The dream is not a dream. It really happened. And his dread is that it will happen again. All those around him, who know it wasn't a dream, share the same fear. In a sense, the German sensibility is that of Europe as a whole.

With each of Germany's many successes, with every action designed to control or manage its neighbors, with every action that must in some small way decide the fate of a neighbor, the fear arises. What makes this time different for Germany is not success and power, or the need to act, but the fear attached to it. One can assume that the fear is a moderating force. On the other hand, knowing there is a madness within you doesn't guarantee that it won't take over your mind. Once you have done the kind of things the Germans did, you can never be at ease with yourself, and no one else is at ease with you.

For Germany, the only solution has been a meticulous innocuous-ness that includes very public soul-searching to demonstrate to the world that Germany takes what happened with the utmost seriousness. This takes place alongside a singularly ordinary life. In a way, German life resembles those of its victims—a constant introspection coupled with a desire to simply live. Of course, the parallels in how they live cannot hide who the victim and victimizer were.

It is interesting to watch the one place all this doesn't hold together: with the youth. A Saturday night in Berlin will introduce you to some of the more bizarre ways a human being can live. It reminds me of a Bertholt Brecht play gone mad, a study in the strange forms that human life can take, along with a deep philosophical gloss on the redemptive possibilities arising from the bizarre. Bohemianism has been a longtime tradition of German youth, and it is being maintained. Yet when I visit the young revolutionaries I knew in the 1970s, who are now in impor-tant positions at Siemens or Deutsche Bank, I realize that even this was simply a ritualized indulgence in preparation for the authority and the prosaic life they claimed to have hated when they were twenty.

The unconventionality and rebellion of the young, followed by a capitulation to life, are far from being uniquely German. Yet, on a Saturday night in Berlin you get the sense that the universal takes a particularly intense form here. During the 1970s, the European New Left was a widespread, university-based movement. Out of it came groups engaged in direct action—bombings, shootings, and kidnappings. In Germany, there was a group called the Baader-Meinhof Group, which later became the Red Army Faction. Its members were convicted of numerous acts of terrorism. Ulrike Meinhof committed suicide during her trial in 1976. Baader and others committed suicide on what they called a "death night" in 1977.

Youthful sensuality exists everywhere. Youthful ideological commitment exists in many places. Youthful terrorism, in the 1970s, existed in many countries. The death night of the German terrorists reflected a deeper darkness than elsewhere. I won't go so far as to speak of death worship, as I simply don't know their motives, but there is a saying about German philosophers: they go down deeper, stay down longer, and come up dirtier than any others. I am not altogether certain this applies to German philosophy, but it can reasonably be applied to the Red Army Faction. Almost all the other radicals went on to the ordinary life I spoke of. These few did not, but their twilight was striking. This was not about left or right. It was about being young, believing passionately, and making the unthinkable happen to others and yourself. There is no collective guilt, but culture is by its nature collective. When I heard of these deaths I thought of Heine and of German thunder, vastly diminished from the past, but still clearly heard.

These things happen in other countries too, but when they happen in Germany they take on a deeper meaning, fairly or unfairly. The Germans simply want to go on and hold things together, to maintain what has buffered them in the past. At the same time, they know they can't simply remain the same.

The Germans are caught between the ordinary and extraordinary. Their fear of the extraordinary is real and deep, and they take shelter not only in being ordinary but in being almost invisible. But the fourth-largest economy in the world, and the largest in Europe, can't stay invisible. They try to hold on to what has protected them from being extraordinary, yet still want to change things. They want to remain in NATO, but Afghanistan was their last, and fairly limited, attempt to do anything in it, they think. They want to remain in the European Union but want it to work for Germany's interests. But then they don't want to appear to have interests—interests are frightening to a country that went mad over its self-interest. Yet events are constantly forcing Germany out of its self-imposed cocoon.

Germany continues to be obsessed in a very nonmilitary way with foreign affairs. Germany exports the equivalent of about 40 percent of its GDP. Its industrial production is much greater than what it can consume domestically, so if it were to lose even part of its exports, the internal repercussions would be substantial. Germany cannot sustain full employment simply by exporting high-margin products. It needs a full-court press. The origin of this generation's export obsession was the United States, which encouraged Germany to grow fast and unevenly, with its industrial plant outstripping domestic demand and the United States and other countries buying up the surplus. But that was a long time ago, in the 1950s. Adjustments could have been made to this export obsession over the years, but instead German preoccupation with exports only expanded.

German intentions are to have an economic policy without political, and certainly without military, consequences. They intend to be the dominant power in Europe without imposing their will on anyone. Their intention is to exercise only one element of national power, the economic, and to exercise that without the brutal pursuit of self-interest. Germany wants to retain national sovereignty but only in the context of supranational institutions that respect all sovereignty. This is an understandable impulse. It is not clear that it is practical.

Europe is in an economic crisis. Germany is the wealthiest country in Europe and it benefits the most from Europe. However, the German public doesn't want to pay for what they see as Greek indolence and corruption. Thus, an old narrative is reemerging in Germany, in its mildest form. It juxtaposes hardworking, disciplined Germans with feckless and irresponsible southern Europeans. It is a narrative that has some truth to it, but as I've pointed out it tells only part of the story. What is important is that it is a narrative that is both persuasive and powerful.

The immediate point of this view is that Germany should not bear the burdens of southern European indebtedness. But there is also a deeper meaning. It is the argument that the northern Europeans, and Germany in particular, are at least culturally superior to southern Europeans. It may not be a matter of blood, but it is a matter of values. The southern Europeans cannot be trusted to successfully manage their affairs. Therefore, the more responsible northern Europeans need to take them in hand and impose on them discipline and hard work.

Ultimately, this is what the austerity argument is about. Who should bear the burden of the EU crisis? Germans think they are the victims of the crisis, their hard work and discipline in danger of being lost. The debts incurred by the southern Europeans must be paid, if not in full then certainly in large part. That is not only because it is owed, but in order to teach southern Europeans the consequence of irresponsibility, and to compel them through austerity to change their ways.

German policy and German public opinion are not divided on this. Where this becomes complex is when a purely economic discipline no longer works. The southern Europeans will resist the discipline, and they have the power of all debtors—default. There comes a moment when the price of paying a debt is higher than the cost of refusing to pay it. It is likely that no one will lend you money in the near future, but that is less painful than paying it back. As we can see with large corporations, bankruptcy doesn't cut off their credit anyway. Neither does it do so for nations.

The German plan of having an economic strategy only works if all the players are willing to play only the economic game. But once default takes place, the game is changed. How does Germany compel repayment of debts through purely economic means? The logic here leads to either capitulating economically, difficult for the Germans, or moving toward some sort of political option. There is in Germany's reality a slippery slope where the desire to work within the EU and the desire to work only from an economic standpoint become unsupportable, and Germany either accepts the consequences of defeat in the debt game or moves beyond economics.

Hannah Arendt, a postwar philosopher, once said that the most dangerous thing in the world is to be rich and weak. Wealth can only be protected by strength, as unlike the poor, the wealthy are envied and have things others want, and unlike the strong they are subject to power. My father used to say that the richest man in the world couldn't survive a cheap bullet. The same is true of nations. Wealth without strength is an invitation to disaster. It is good, as I have said, to be neither victim nor victimizer. Unfortunately, it is not possible.

What will happen in the part of Europe that is in depression, with over a quarter of their workforce unemployed, and where massive debts have to be repaid? Political movements will emerge that demand, first, that the debts not be repaid, second, that the scoundrels who created the debts be punished, and third, that what wealth there is be made available to the rest. There is a racial component to these parties. They oppose both immigration and the free movement of EU populations across borders. These issues are linked.

They see the EU as primarily benefiting the elite, and leaving the rest to struggle for jobs with migrants. The fallen middle class is particularly destabilized by personal disaster and a sense of being a stranger in their own countries. Just as migrants are changing the national character of these countries, the inability of Europe to culturally absorb immigrants, and the unwillingness of immigrants to be absorbed, mean that the national fabric is being transformed. Capital may have no country, as Marx argued, but the lower classes not only have countries but cling to them. Economic issues and cultural issues merge, fear of the outsider rises, and the result is political pressure from the Right. This is not confined only to the failing countries. It is there in northern European countries as well, even Germany. Or the United States. It is simply milder.

Not surprisingly we see these already existing. Look at Golden Dawn in Greece, Five Star in Italy, National Front in France, or Jobbik in Hungary. Virtually every European country has an emergent right-wing party, some having gained substantial strength. At this point they are just emerging, and they will develop and change. They may shout leftist or rightist slogans (rightist is more likely), but that doesn't really matter. What emerges will leave Germany stiffed on the debt, assert Germany and its German partners in their countries to be the guilty party, and seize and redistribute assets.

A desperate nation will take desperate action. When steps are taken against a rich and weak country, there is little risk. As anti-German, anti-austerity sentiment rises, Germany, with vital interests, investments, markets, and so on, will become a target, and attacks on its interests will escalate. Germany will have a choice of accepting the punishment or using its vast resources to transform wealth into power. Nations do not become strong because they feel like it but because they must. Germany will face stark choices, and increasing its strength in all dimensions will become more bearable than the alternatives.

Germany will therefore become a full-fledged power, first flexing its political muscles and in time its military ones as pressures develop. Economic, not military, considerations will be driving Germany. That time is not far off. It will be managing its fundamental problem, overdependence on exports, inability to increase demand within Germany, and the need to have a stable framework for its export-based economy. If the EU continues to destabilize or increase protectionism, Germany will need to create another collation of customers, which it is already trying to do.

Obviously, regardless of what happens to the EU, Germany will remain deeply embedded in Europe's attempt to integrate. But as the EU becomes increasingly nationalist in outlook, and as it seeks closer economic ties with Russia, or emerging economies in Latin America or Africa, Germany will encounter a difficult reality. While it is primarily interested in economics, its new partners link economics with national security. So, for example, if Germany deepens its relationships to Russia, it will have to deal with a country for which economic and national security issues are closely tied. Therefore, one of the conditions for Russia will be Germany accepting Russian preeminence in Ukraine and Belarus. That will, in the future, not be something the United States will want to see. Nor will Poland. A closer U.S. military relationship with Poland might emerge, triggering Russian alarm and forcing Germany to make decisions.

Nations do not choose to engage in an assertive foreign policy. Circumstances force them to do so. For the Germans this might be in concert with NATO or bilaterally with other countries. The point is that Germany was rearmed in the Cold War and remains rearmed, if not to its full capacity. Unlike Japan, Germany has nothing but psychological bars to rearming itself. But the truth is that no nation is fully sovereign without weapons, and whatever Germany's memories and nightmares, the idea of perpetual peace is a dream. A prosperous economic life without needing to protect it is not sustainable.

The fourth-largest economy in the world does not have the option of avoiding politics. Everything that happens in the world might affect its interests, and certainly everything that happens in Europe will affect Germany. It has the option of being passive and hoping for the best, but its internal politics, like those of any nation, don't permit that. Economic decline without action to defend German interests would create a political reaction in Germany that would overwhelm the political classes. Therefore, what is to be done?

The first obvious action is to attempt to maintain the European Union and the free-trade zone. This is not impossible, but it would require that Germany invest substantially in the effort, an investment that might not succeed. Solving the unemployment crisis in southern Europe and making certain that Eastern Europe remains committed to the EU will be a costly matter. Germany has to hedge its bets on the European Union. It has to remain overtly committed to a solution to the EU problems while examining new options.

Germany has to make two decisions, as it has always had to. The first is what to do with France and the second what to do with Russia. Sitting on the northern European Plain means that Germany is always making this calculus. German history since 1871 has been entirely about this, and the question keeps reemerging. Since World War II a close relationship to France has been fundamental to Germany, and Russia has been the threat, occupying half of Germany and threatening to seize the other half.

Germany is still deeply committed to its relationship with France, but their interests have diverged. France has high unemployment and wants to stimulate the economy even if it means inflation. Germany remains committed to a strategy of austerity. Russia is hardly the appropriate partner for Germany, yet it is one that in many ways fits most closely. Germany, like all nations, wants all things, and it is possible that the Germans might stabilize the EU, maintain the partnership with France, and reach an accommodation with Russia. But it is difficult to imagine policies that would achieve this and also satisfy German needs and its public's demands.

A more likely scenario is increasing economic tension with France, with France looking more and more to Africa and the Mediterranean, and an attempt to align with Russia. Where this all leads to is likely peaceful maneuvering among the great powers, but more serious tensions among the smaller powers caught in the borderland between Germany and Russia, and perhaps even in the borderland between France and Germany.

10

Mainland and Peninsula

My mother's father was born in Pressburg. His children were born in Pozsony. After World War I his family left Bratislava. They are all the same city. Its name changed depending on whether the Austrians, the Hungarians, or the Slovaks controlled it. In a borderland, a city might have three names in the lifetime of one man, though he might refer to it by only one, and not the current name at that. On the other hand, don't call it Pozsony when speaking to a Slovak, especially not after midnight in a bar. The borderland between Russia and the European peninsula is a place where names matter, and blood will be shed over the names. This is true of all borderlands. It is especially true here.

The peninsula is formed by the Mediterranean and Black Seas in the south, and by the North Sea and the Baltic Sea in the north. At the easternmost point of the Baltic Sea lies the city of St. Petersburg. The city of Rostov is at the easternmost point of the Black Sea. If you draw a line from St. Petersburg to Rostov, you have defined the base of the European peninsula. Everything to the west of the line is on the peninsula. Everything to the east is on the Eurasian mainland.

This line also roughly defines the western border of Russia. The Baltic states, Belarus, and Ukraine, formerly part of the Russian Empire and Soviet Union, are actually the eastern tier of nations on the peninsula and are both peninsular and mainland, Catholic and Orthodox. The borders of the Russian Empire have over the centuries moved back and forth, encompassing these countries and then releasing them. Sometimes Russia has moved deeper into the peninsula—during the Cold War to the center of Germany. But no country on the peninsula has per-

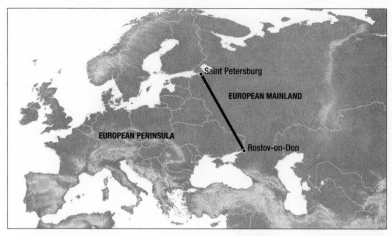

Borderlands Between Russia and the European Peninsula

manently held territory in Russia. Those who tried, like Napoleon and Hitler, were destroyed. Two tiers of countries—the Baltics to Ukraine and Poland to Bulgaria—represent the borderland between the fractious European peninsula and unified Russia.

The peninsula and the mainland are profoundly different. The peninsula is small, measuring only about 1,500 miles at its widest point, between northern Denmark and the tip of Italy. Tapering from east to west, it is only 300 miles wide at its narrowest point, in the Pyrenees. The European peninsula is the most crowded part of Europe, in terms of both population and number of nations.

Russia, on the other hand, is enormous. It measures 2,000 miles north to south and about 1,100 miles from the border with Belarus to the Urals. Obviously Russia also stretches thousands of miles to the east, through Siberia. But Siberia is more an adjunct to Russia than part of its core, and it is certainly not part of European Russia.

European Russia is for the most part a flat plain, unbroken by barriers other than rivers. Linguistically, religiously, and ethnically Russia is much more homogeneous than the peninsula. Where the peninsula has diversity that cannot be overcome, Russia has homogeneity that cannot be destroyed. While Russia has about one hundred ethnic groups, more than 80 percent of the population is Russian, with the Tatars, at 3.9 percent, being the next-largest group. That means that while there are numerous ethnic groups, no one group is particularly significant. Muslims in Chechnya may be violent, but they can't overthrow Moscow. Religion is important, but ethnicity is more important, particularly when language divides ethnic groups. Muslims are a very large group, but it would be a mistake to treat Muslims as a single group. In Russia they are divided by space and language, as well as varieties and intensity of Islam.

Russia is basically a landlocked country, with most of the population far from the sea. The sea surrounds the European peninsula and its economy, and its culture is built around maritime commerce. Thucydides pointed out that Sparta was landlocked and poor, while Athens was on the sea and rich. Athens traded with the world. Sparta had to live off what it could grow. Of course Thucydides also said that people who live near the sea are made soft by luxury, while those who live far from the sea can endure great hardship. When you think of the hardiness of the Russian soldier, you can see the point Thucydides was making.

As a result of geography, there is a huge difference between Russia and the European peninsula economically. There are today just over 500 million people living on the peninsula compared to a little more than 140 million living in all of mainland Russia. The peninsula's GDP is about $14 trillion, or $28,000 per capita. Russia's GDP is approximately $2 trillion, or $14,246 per capita. Citizens of the peninsula are more than twice as rich as Russians. Inequality in Russia is much deeper than on the peninsula.

Russia is insular. Living in a midsize Russian town is an utterly different experience from living in an equivalent town on the peninsula. In Russia there is much less of everything, from opportunity to life expectancy, and relative homogeneity has not translated into particularly happy lives. Solzhenitsyn makes the argument that the Russians, for all their poverty, are spiritually superior to the inhabitants of the peninsula as individuals. Perhaps this is true, but what is certain is that life in Russia is hard.

Besides the sea, the rivers of the European peninsula also made it wealthy. The largest of these, the Danube, provides a low-cost route from the eastern Alps to the Black Sea. The Rhine provides a route to the North Sea, the Rhone to the Mediterranean, the Dniester to the Black Sea. This means the interior of the peninsula could engage in global trade, not merely the port cities. There are rivers in Russia and they serve an important function, but they are far from much of Russia. What trade there is depends on land transportation.

The center of this borderland is the place where the eastern borders of Poland, Slovakia, Hungary, and Romania converge on the western borders of Ukraine. It is about sixty miles from Poland to Romania, and in those sixty miles five countries meet, five languages are spoken, and five histories are intertwined. This is the place my father's family called home. There is therefore a sixth history, or a ghost of a history here, that of the Jews.

This place is pivotal in another sense. It separates the northern and southern parts of the borderland. The northern part is the flat European Plain. The southern part is hilly, mountainous, and hard to traverse. The Europe of the plain and the Europe of the mountains are, in effect, two different Europes. The northern tip of the Carpathians, the most pivotal point, divides the two parts of the European peninsula.

Munkács, once Hungarian and now the Ukrainian city of Mukachevo, is right at this pivot point, in the foothills of the Carpathians. People in this town spoke more than one language, if not fluently, then well enough to be understood. And everyone knew the little paths that aren't on maps, and which goods cost more on the other side of a border. Everyone also knew the signs of war as readily as peasants could read the weather. It is a pressure cooker, and those who come from here know how to endure pressure.

This is fortunate because this is the place where the pressures of the European peninsula and the pressures of the European mainland converge, and at various times exert unbearable force. To the west are the remnants of the Austro-Hungarian Empire, now reunited in the European Union. To the northwest is Germany, also in the EU but a power in its own right. To the southwest are the Balkans. Beyond Ukraine is Russia, weakened but as always united and always a factor. People who live here understand that borders are agile.

This is also the point that U.S. foreign policy is focused now. During the Cold War, the flashpoint was the line down the center of Germany. Now it has moved east, into Ukraine, where Russia and the West are struggling for supremacy and for the safety of the Ukrainian buffer zone. If the West succeeds, the key borderland will be along the Ukrainian-Russian frontier. If Russia triumphs, the line will be here, in the borderlands that Russia and the peninsula have struggled over for centuries. The outcome of the Ukrainian struggle will likely determine where American soldiers will be based during the next generation. Maps change fast here.

Consider how the map can change in just three generations. Here is the map my father was born to.

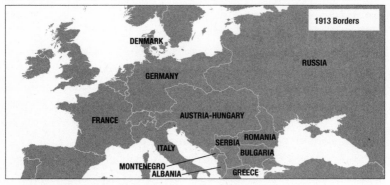

Mainland–Peninsula Borderlands: Pre–World War I

Poland, the Czech Republic, Slovakia, Hungary, the Baltic states, Belarus, and Ukraine didn't exist as independent nations. The borderland was divided between three great powers: Austria-Hungary, Russia, and Germany, which controlled a small bit in the north.

My borderland, the borderland of the Cold War, looked very different. Austria-Hungary had disappeared, Germany was divided, many new nations had been created, and the Russian Empire had moved far to the west.

Mainland–Peninsula Borderlands: Cold War

The border was farther to the west than ever before. But it was a different kind of border. It was no longer porous as it was for my father. For him, the border was an ambiguous place, subject to interpretation. For me it was a knife cutting Europe in half with precision. A foot on the wrong side might mean death. Somewhere in my soul, Warsaw will always be enemy territory.

My children see a very different Europe.

Mainland–Peninsula Borderlands: Post–Cold War

Russia has retreated to the borders it had before Peter the Great expanded the Russian Empire. Nations that haven't been independent in centuries are now sovereign. In a little more than fifty years, the boundary of Russian power has moved from the center of Germany to somewhere near Smolensk, once deep in the Russian Empire. For my children, Europe has become just another place, interesting to visit, but not the existential boundary between life and the apocalypse that it was for me.

It is difficult to describe such a broad area, but we can begin with a small sliver of it that contains all the complexity and ambiguity and danger that characterize the region. Moldova is an extreme example, but it helps you understand the nature of the borderland and how it works, and in fact how most borderlands work.

At various times since 1800, Moldova has been part of the Ottoman Empire, the Russian Empire, and the Soviet Union, part of Romania, and independent. If you don't like Moldova's position, wait a few years and it will change. Given its size it does not have great significance. However, it does have a strategic advantage: geography. The main language is Romanian, spoken in a distinct regional dialect. But Russian is used just as much.

Romanians, Russians, and Ukrainians mingle here. It used to be a center of Jewish settlement until the Germans came in World War II. It is famous in Jewish history for a pogrom that took place in 1903. A Christian woman died in a Jewish hospital in the capital, then Kishinev and now Chisinau. A Russian-language newspaper published a story claiming Jewish doctors had poisoned her. In retaliation, over fifty people were killed, and newspapers covered the pogrom internationally. The *New York Times* featured it on the front page. When I visited Chisinau I bore this in mind, but in an odd way. In 1903 the death of fifty Jews in an obscure place was still a noteworthy event. When you consider how many were killed there forty years later, there is something innocent about the Kishinev pogrom. There are borderlands in time as well as space.

Moldova may be obscure in the global mind, but it is important nevertheless. Moldova sits between two rivers: the Prut is its current border with Romania, and the Dniester River is roughly its border with Ukraine. Ukraine's chief port is Odessa, and it is also the city Russia uses to access the Black Sea and the Mediterranean. In the hands of enemies like Nazi Germany, Odessa is lost to the Russians, and with it Russia's access to the world. Ukrainians and Russians, united or divided, must care a great deal about Odessa. The Russians are now struggling to increase their influence there, while Romania, backed by the United States, is trying to restrain them. It is not a flashpoint in the sense of war breaking out, but a flashpoint in terms of potential internal strife.

Both Russia and Ukraine want the border of Ukraine to be the Prut because if it is the Dniester, the distance to Odessa is only fifty miles or so. If a foreign power controlled the west bank of the Dniester, it would be difficult to defend the city. Since the Dnieper also flows to the capital, Kiev's access to the sea could be lost. It matters who controls Moldova. For Russia and Ukraine, it is the path to the Carpathians and security. For a Western power it is a jumping-off point to the east. Not surprisingly, when the Hitler-Stalin pact was signed, a secret codicil gave the Soviets the right to seize Bessarabia, a part of Moldova. In 2014 a small number of U.S. marines conducted exercises in Moldova. No one is expecting imminent war, but all sides are watching Moldova, not because it itself is important, but because it is the key to important things.

Official statistics say that Moldova is the poorest country in Europe. When I visited, I was accompanied by my wife and a female member of my staff, both sober and serious people. However, as we walked down the streets of Chisinau, they spent their time estimating the price of the boots that young women were wearing. I learned that those boots were not cheap. In the poorest country in Europe, the women were wearing boots that cost impressive sums. I learned something about Moldova, as well as about my wife and staffer. Moldova is not as poor as I had thought, and my wife and staffer knew things I hadn't dreamed they knew.

Even more interesting was a town outside of Chisinau that we visited called Orhei. Though it is statistically poor, the streets were nevertheless lined with cars, quite a few of them BMWs. More significantly, they were lined with banks, including major international banks like Société Générale. BMWs, seven or eight banks, and well-dressed people were not what I expected to find.

As frequently happens, official statistics don't capture the reality. This is the borderland between Ukraine and Romania, which means between the Russian and the European Union spheres of influence. Romanian banks are European banks, and getting money into them allows it to be cleansed and transformed into European investment capital, moving about the world and increasing its value. Russians and Ukrainians want to get their money into Europe. Who, after all, knows what will be the fate of money east of the Dniester?

Trans-Dniester, the region east of the Dniester, is legally part of Moldova but effectively independent. Some have called it a Mafia state, which means that it is run by organized crime as a hub of illegal activities, from drugs to money laundering. It is dominated by Russian oligarchs even though the area would be Ukrainian if it weren't Moldovan. The fate of money from Trans-Dniester is, at the moment, not known. It moves west into the EU and disappears to reemerge clean. John le Carré, in his novel *A Most Wanted Man*, referred to this as Lipizzaner money. Lipizzaners are horses that are born black and then turn snow white. The alchemy of black to white is a major industry here. The future is unknown, and therefore it is the enemy. The money must be cleansed quickly.

Moldovans now have the right to get Romanian passports, a right granted by Romania and resisted, but not too strongly, by Ukraine and Russia. If you can get money into Moldova and into the hands of someone with a Romanian passport whom you trust—or better yet, who is afraid of you—you can move money into the EU, and into its sparkling-clean investment opportunities. The process is complex, but it explains the large number of banks, the expensive boots, and the BMWs.

As in all borderlands, smuggling is an essential service, and in this case the object of smuggling is money. This is very different from what was smuggled in the 1990s: women. It was said that a huge number of women in Europe's legal brothels were Moldovan, trying desperately to stay alive in a world that had collapsed around them. That trade seems to have subsided now, with the more lucrative trade in money.

The power of the European Union and NATO never stretched this far. There is talk of incorporating Moldova into Romania. The Europeans are not eager to see Moldova formally part of the EU, certainly not now, and at least some Moldovans make too much money from the country's position as a transshipment point between Russia and Europe to accept and actually enforce European regulations. It is partly for this reason that Romania has not been included in the Schengen Agreement, which allows all those with the passport of an EU country to pass unchallenged (and unsearched) into any other EU country. The Romanians are increasingly motivated in blocking this activity, but no matter how effective they become, smuggling is a way of life in the borderland. Moldova reflects tension between what the borderland is and what Romania intends to become. Romania's desires are genuine and plausible, but such desires challenge the borderland.

The important thing to remember is that this region, called by various names, has been serving this role, with different products, for centuries. Old mosques that are now churches, a mélange of languages, and taverns in which heavy, well-dressed, hard-eyed men speak quietly to each other tell that tale. So do the memories of the wars that have been fought here, particularly in the thirty-one years when the region was decimated by Soviet and Nazi troops, along with Romanians fighting on both sides. In a way, it is the story of Europe, dirty and messy, compared to the cleanliness of the European Union.

The borderland is again a vast, porous place, even more porous and filled with more trade and movement, both legal and illegal, than it was before World War I. It would appear that, as before, a large and powerful force from the peninsula has pushed eastward: the European Union, taking advantage of Russia's retreat. The issue is whether the EU is a great power or an optical illusion.

Of course, it is not clear how sparkling Europe is now. Particularly in the eastern regions, the old Eastern Europe, the situation is more than uncertain. Germany, the major power of Europe, has reemerged, the dynamics of Europe have shifted, and the United States is in one of its distant, contemplative phases, which means everyone is afraid it will do nothing. This leaves us with the question of whether this borderland, the arena of terrible conflict, has become quiet or whether the former Yugoslavia is somehow a model for what might happen in this region.

11

Russia and Its Borderlands

The collapse of the Soviet Union left Russia extremely vulnerable in its reduced size. Economically, Russia was in chaos, and that chaos was based not only on privatization. Russian industry was one or two generations behind the West's. It couldn't compete unless it had a captive and enclosed empire of similarly backward republics to trade with. The Soviet Union had provided that, and now it was lost.

Russia's industry couldn't compete, but Russian raw material was badly needed, particularly oil and natural gas. The European peninsula was badly in need of both, and the Russians used existing and new pipelines and shipping lanes to provide them.

The Russian economy depended on the peninsula buying its oil. Fortunately for Russia, the peninsula was eager to do so. But there were problems. First, Russia needed the price of energy to rise. Second, it had to make certain that alternative sources didn't become available. Finally, it had to be certain that the energy could get to the customer. All the existing and planned pipelines went through independent countries. They had to cross Belarus or Ukraine, then travel through Poland, Slovakia, or Hungary to get to the vital Austrian and German markets.

Russia must have access to Germany, and it must have access without other countries adding surcharges so high that Germany will look elsewhere for energy and force Russia to keep its prices steady and swallow the surcharges. This problem is political and not economic. From a purely economic point of view, surcharges make perfect sense. Russia needs to find a way to dissuade these countries from charging them. But

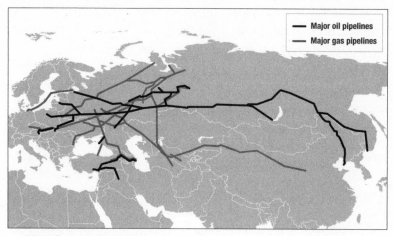

Major Eurasian Pipelines

another problem has to be faced. These countries can choose to block transit. There is no obvious reason for doing so, but the Russians can't simply hope for the best. That policy has often not worked in the past.

Russia must, therefore, achieve a degree of control over Belarus and Ukraine, a struggle that is under way now. It must then extend its control, to some degree, to Poland, Slovakia, Hungary, and Romania. The logic of Russia's post–Cold War economic strategy forces it westward, as it did in the past. While Russia currently has no intention of going to war, it can't simply leave the future of the borderland open. Its strategy has to first focus on Belarus and Ukraine. At the moment Belarus is not a problem. It is weak, has a leader who will bend to the Russians' will, and needs Russian investment. But even Belarus can't be taken for granted. Once the current leader, Lukashenko, leaves the scene, no one can predict the political evolution of the country. So the Russians must institutionalize their influence economically and through relations with the Belorussian intelligence services. The Russians must be constantly active in Belarus.

The more immediate problem is Ukraine. It is a story that goes back to a strategic decision made by the United States and the peninsula in the 1990s. There were two strategies they could follow. One was to allow a neutral buffer zone of former Soviet-dominated states to exist. The other was to incorporate as many of these states into NATO and the EU as possible. The Russians were not in a position to block this move east. They thought, or at least claimed to have been promised, that NATO would never advance into the former Soviet Union. When the Baltic states were admitted to NATO, that promise, whether real or not, was broken. NATO had moved more than five hundred miles east, toward Moscow, and it was now one hundred miles from St. Petersburg.

The first duel was over Ukraine, the key region for Russia. It wasn't only a matter of energy pipelines, but of the long-term physical security of Russia. The Ukrainian border with Russia is over seven hundred miles long. It is five hundred miles from Moscow over flat, open terrain. Odessa and Sevastopol, both in Ukraine, provide Russia with commercial and military access to the Black Sea and the Mediterranean. If Ukraine were to be integrated into NATO and the European Union, Russia would face a threat not only in the Baltics, but one from Ukraine. Loss of access to Ukrainian territory would be a blow to Russian economic strategy. A Ukrainian alliance with NATO would pose an unmistakable threat to Russian national security. Precisely that threat has resurfaced. The Ukrainian situation simply does not reach closure. Everything settled is reopened. Given its importance to Russia, this makes sense.

The word *Ukraine* means "on the edge." It is a vast borderland linking the mainland to the peninsula. The eastern part is heavily Russian, ethnically, and the native tongue is Russian. The western part is dominated by Ukrainians oriented to the peninsula. The farther west you go, the more western Ukraine becomes.

I was recently visiting Mukachevo, home of my ancestors. It was a Sunday morning, and there were many people driving and walking to church. Parking was a problem, so our driver said he'd drop us off and find a place to wait farther out from the town center. He was afraid to leave the car alone, he said (it had Polish license plates and was a fairly new car), for fear the tires would be removed by the time we returned. Or the car itself would have disappeared.

As we strolled we came to a street in the town where there were two good-sized churches, a Roman Catholic church and an Orthodox church, across the street from each other. It was a lovely fall day and both churches were overflowing with families standing around outside to listen to the services. The crowds flowed out into the street. As more people came to listen, we realized that the prayers in one church were competing with those of the other church. They were getting more intense and louder, and each church seemed to be trying to drown out the other. Suddenly the Catholic Church switched on a loudspeaker system, blasting its prayers into the street. The Orthodox didn't have amplification, but worshippers left their church and spilled out onto the street, lending their voices to their own side. We were a few miles from Catholic Slovakia, but at a place that had been Ukrainian since 1920. Clearly, the matter wasn't settled here either.

There is a fragility to Ukraine. In the east the Russian influence is heavy. Polish and Romanian influence dominates in the west, and Ukrainians as a whole are divided politically between those wanting to be part of the EU, those wanting to be close to Russia, and those who want a fully independent Ukraine. This makes the Russians even more uneasy. Divisions such as these make Ukraine fertile ground for manipulation by anyone interested in it. The Russians are very aware of this vulnerability because they themselves have been manipulating Ukraine for a long time. Because of this, the Russians will interpret outside involvement as manipulation, and potentially a threat to their overriding interests in Ukraine.

American and European policy toward the former Soviet Union consisted of trying to turn former Soviet Republics into constitutional democracies, under the prevailing theory that this would stabilize them and integrate them into the Western economic and political system. As a result, both these countries and the United States engaged in the funding of nongovernmental organizations (NGOs) they regarded as pro-democracy. The Russians saw funding of these groups as pro-Western and thus hostile to Russian interests. The same thing happened in Ukraine. Americans were oblivious to how Russians saw this interference. The Russians, on the other hand, did not believe the Westerners were that naive.

In the 1990s the Russians couldn't respond. They were too weak and fragmented themselves. The American and European view was that the Russians had nothing to respond to as NATO was obviously not a threat, and they would profit from close relations with the European Union. America and Europe took advantage of business opportunities in Russia, assuming that all tensions had been abolished. Along with this came NGOs, filled with good wishes and self-righteousness; they regarded those who distrusted them as archaic or corrupt. Their mind-set was that they intended good, so everyone of goodwill would see them as good.

By 2001, the United States was completely focused on the Islamic world, the European militaries were hollowed out, and NATO was barely functional. The idea that the Russians could feel threatened by support for democratic NGOs was dismissed as so implausible that the Russians couldn't possibly be serious. And to be frank, Europe and the Americans held Russia in contempt. It was weak and poor and the West would do what they wanted to do.

It was this attitude that helped create Vladimir Putin. His power originated in St. Petersburg, where his influence was enormous, but was forged in Kosovo, a province of Serbia. The Serbs had engaged in wars and war crimes in the former Yugoslavia. When conflict broke out between predominantly Albanian regions and the Serbian government in 1999, the West intervened and carried out a two-month-long bombing campaign against Serbia.

The Russians didn't want this to happen, but it did regardless of their desires. The Russians helped arrange the cease-fire and expected to participate in peacekeeping in Kosovo, but this didn't happen. The Russians felt that the West was treating them with contempt, though it was merely indifference. That indifference proved intolerable, and Vladimir Putin, who came to power intending to change the dynamic that had been in place since 1991, replaced Yeltsin.

Putin was a KGB man. He looked at the world in a certain way, with ruthless realism and little ideology. I doubt that the collapse of the Soviet Union surprised him. The KGB was the single institution in the Soviet Union that did not intentionally lie to itself. It had known, since the early 1980s under Yuri Andropov, the ultimate realist, that the Soviet Union was in deep trouble. It needed restructuring and openness to Western capital, and if geopolitical advantages had to be traded for that, then that was the price to be paid. Perestroika (restructuring) and glasnost (openness) were part of Gorbachev's plan to carry out Andropov's strategy for saving the state. It failed.

Putin, the supreme realist, understood immediately what failure meant. Privatization in Russia meant converting public assets into private property. In a country without laws, the property went to the strongest, and in the Soviet Union the best, the brightest, and the strongest were in the security apparatus. To a great extent they organized the creation of the oligarchy that followed. The Russian oligarchs, the Russian Mafia, and the former KGB were sometimes the same people and always linked. Putin built his power base in St. Petersburg on this foundation.

But as a KGB man, he also had a deep loyalty to the state and a commitment to his country. Intelligence people are cynical by nature and training, and they distrust declarations of loyalty. They understand that talk is cheap. But they have not taken civil service jobs with mediocre pay and, for some, potential personal risk because they see this as a path to wealth or glory. Wealth doesn't come with the job, and glory is rare in a life invisible to the world. Underneath everything is a patriotism coupled with a deep professional pride that makes losing unbearable.

Putin had been on the losing side and it hurt. Seeing his country impoverished and treated with indifference and contempt was unbearable. While he accumulated wealth and power, he also harbored a belief that he expressed publicly later in a political address: "Above all, we should acknowledge that the collapse of the Soviet Union was a major geopolitical catastrophe of the century." He now had the power to do something about it. In all his actions, Putin's personal pride at resurrecting a degree of Russian power can be seen. But so can love of his country, deeply buried beneath the requisite cynicism of an intelligence operative. The oath he took and the love of his own country burn in him.

Putin understood that the United States was far more powerful than Russia. He also understood that Washington could, in the long run, influence the European peninsula, particularly the countries in the borderland. But the United States was bogged down in the Middle East. Russia had a window of opportunity not only to reassert its military capability, but to reshape borderlands, particularly Ukraine, into something that would protect Russia. If he waited, the window would close. If he acted too early his military wouldn't be ready. But with the dependence of the peninsula on Russian energy, the situation was locked into place, and this was his opportunity.

The war with Georgia was designed to undermine the American

position in the borderlands, to undermine pro-U.S. and pro-European forces, and it succeeded. Clearly the United States would not intervene and Europe could not. The Russian-Georgian War changed the dynamic of the region.

Russia had struck in one direction, strengthening its position in the Caucasus and leveraging that to improve its position in Ukraine. Its approach in Georgia was direct military action; in Ukraine it was covert and overt political pressure in the face of internal Ukrainian unrest triggered by military action in the Balkans. For a time of peace, the tensions in the borderland were building. Economics mattered a great deal, but the old strategic realities were becoming as important.

Russia faces no military threat now, but it also knows that military threats emerge suddenly and unexpectedly from the peninsula. Given the uncertain future of Ukraine, that could come quickly. Russia doesn't have to use sudden military force to secure its interests, nor does it have that kind of force. But Russia would be reckless if it wasn't in the process of taking steps. This is the kind of thinking that seems archaic in today's Europe, but Vladimir Putin is a man trained not only in the permanence of geopolitical realities, but also in planning for the worst-case scenario. His statement that the fall of the Soviet Union was a geopolitical disaster for the Soviet Union is playing itself out here.

Russia has two strategies. One is to move as far west on the European Plain as possible, to create both strategic depth and industrial and technological resources. The other is to reach the Carpathian Mountains and use them as a barrier. Neither is currently a possibility. Assuming that Belarus remains in the Russian orbit, the Baltic states and Poland make a difficult barrier to expansion. Should something happen in Belarus, the line would move east. As for securing a foothold in the Carpathians to the south, the problem is not only Romania but Ukraine. Thus, underneath it all, the Russians face a serious strategic problem, and on the whole they face economic and strategic problems that they can't overcome.

But all such problems are relative to the capabilities of those you are facing. Russia is inherently more powerful than the countries that form the Baltic-Belarus-Ukraine line. Barring third-party intervention, they can force their way, or subvert their way, west. They also can assert tremendous and probably decisive power on the next tier of countries, the Poland-Romania line. What has thus far prevented this is the potential power of the EU and NATO if they choose to resist, and the fact that Russia benefits as much from a genuinely neutral buffer zone as from occupation. Russia is looking to secure itself, not expand.

When the former Soviet satellites joined NATO and the European Union they assumed three things. The first was that NATO would provide a military capability that would protect them from Russian power in the future. The second was that the European Union would provide them a degree of prosperity that would both satisfy political needs at home and integrate them into Europe's general prosperity. Finally, the feeling was that integration with these organizations would guarantee the permanence of constitutional liberalism in their countries. In other words, that they would become Western Europeans, banishing both authoritarianism and corruption.

The third wish depended on the first two coming true. But NATO is a shadow of its former self. Aside from the United States, and to a much lesser extent Britain and France, NATO's military capability is minimal. NATO really has capabilities only to the extent that the United States, a non-European power, participates. NATO also operates by consensus, so a single nation can block action. The European Union is in shambles, with no promise of regaining its prosperity. Therefore Eastern Europe has to recalculate its strategic position.

Life in Eastern Europe is not bad compared to what was there before, but it is nothing like what people expected when communism collapsed. Unemployment is high and the economies are flat. And they start at a lower level than the rest of Europe, so for them being flat is much more difficult than it is for others.

In Hungary hatred of the Russians runs deep. They still remember the 1956 revolution and Soviet tanks. Fear of the Russians is an anchor of Hungarian political culture. The other anchor was that membership in the EU would give them the good life of both constitutional democracy and prosperity. As in most things, life has proven more complex.

There is a shabbiness to Vaci Utca, Budapest's Fifth Avenue, that wasn't there ten years ago. Many of the top global brands have left, being replaced by lesser brands. I visited a jewelry store that had offered some expensive pieces of jewelry in 2005. Those weren't there now. Gundel is the finest, and certainly the most famous, restaurant in Budapest, but getting a reservation was no problem. It was half filled by an American Jewish tour, many dressed in sweat suits, and the violins played Jewish tunes rather than gypsy melodies. The lower-priced restaurants are filled with Hungarians.

Along the Danube and in the hills of Buda, the city remains gorgeous. The city was just subdued. Prior to 2008, Budapest had developed the tempo of a Western European city. There was bustle on the streets as people went about the urgent business of making money. In 2011 that urgency had declined. The streets were only occasionally congested, and crossing a street was not a problem.

It's critical to understand what the Hungarian government did in response to the European economic crisis. The prime minister of Hungary, Viktor Orbán, heads the center-right Fidesz Party, which governs with a substantial majority. Unlike most other prime ministers in this region, he can make decisions. When communism fell, Austrian and Italian banks moved into Hungary and other countries in the region and began offering mortgages. The Hungarians weren't part of the eurozone, the region that used the euro, and used their own currency, the forint. Mortgages denominated in forints carried a higher interest rate to compensate for the potential decline of the forint. So these banks lent money to Hungarians in euros, Swiss francs, and even yen. Because these currencies were assumed to carry a lower risk, the interest rates were lower.

Hungarians flocked to the lower interest rates just as Americans did. However, the forint did fall, and every month Hungarians had to pay more and more in forints in order to pay their mortgages. Eventually the Hungarians started defaulting. The banks were reluctant to foreclose and acknowledge the bad loans, but the borrowers were simply unable to pay them back. Orbán intervened, announcing that the loans would be repaid in forints, instead of the currency in which they were borrowed, and that only a certain percentage needed to be repaid.

While this decision protected Hungarians, it violated fundamental European Union understandings on how debts would be handled. A government claiming sovereign and unilateral authority over payments to the banks of other countries was not the way the game was to be played.

Nevertheless, and this is what matters, the banks and the EU swallowed it. The EU had threatened Orbán with sanctions, because Orbán had weakened Hungary's Constitutional Court, which affected the media and increased the likelihood that Orbán would hold on to power. After mild shifts in Orbán's position, the EU backed off on this threat. The EU was even less assertive over the loans. The banks basically capitulated, and the EU remained silent.

Two things were happening here. The first was that the European Union was struggling to hold Hungary and the rest of the Eastern European countries within its framework. The crisis in the eurozone forced policy makers in Brussels, Berlin, and Paris to focus on problems of the currency union, thus neglecting events in Eastern Europe. The benefits that Hungary had expected hadn't materialized, and Orbán was pursuing a nationalist position. His concern was not the EU, but Hungary and his position in it. And his protection of Hungarian debtors was obviously popular in Hungary. Amazingly the European Union did not challenge this move.

The European Union as an institution had little weight. It had lost its economic charm; it had no single foreign policy that all members followed and no defense policy. The European defense policy still ran through NATO, which was more American than European in terms of military power. The eastern part of the peninsula in 1991 saw a weak Russia and a strong Europe. Now the reverse was true. From Poland to Romania, there was disappointment in NATO, and in the EU, but more than that, a deep uncertainty about what would come next. This situation also had opened the door for the Russians to pursue their strategic interests.

Russia does not want to overtly dominate the region. But it does want to limit the power of NATO in the east. It also wishes to limit European integration, which could evolve into a strategic threat, by offering Eastern Europe economic alternatives. At a time when the Americans were uninterested and the Europeans incapable of massive economic involvement, Russia, even with limited resources, had the opportunity to spread its influence. This was particularly true in the Carpathian countries— Slovakia, Hungary, and Romania.

The Russians had two tools at their disposal. One I would call commercial geopolitics. Without dominating these countries, how did Russia prevent them from moving in directions it didn't want? As an incentive, the Russians offered investment in energy, minerals, and other enterprises. They did not try to take control of the economy or even of most of the businesses, but wanted just enough control so that business decisions could be influenced. They were interested in making money, and there was money to be made in this region.

More money might be made elsewhere, but the goal was geopolitical. The Russians created a network of dependency in various industries that exercised a degree of influence over political decisions. Alienating the Russians was not wise for countries that could not risk Russian hostility at a time when they were exposed, when European money was scarcer than it had been and American investment did not carry political protection with it. The investment in whatever industry was welcome, and the political price minimal. Increased integration into the EU was not happening, and cooperating with NATO was like cooperating with a ghost.

Second, and as important, the Russians had their intelligence service, and they had developed powerful relationships and sources in all these countries both during and after their occupation. They had files on everyone and knew all the things people might want to hide. The Russians did not have to be overt blackmailers. Things were much more subtle than that. The person knew what he had done and he knew Russian intelligence, and that it had a record of it. There was a kind of self-discipline imposed. This was not the case before 2008 and certainly not before 2001. There was a sense then that this was all in the past. But as Europe ceased to be a certainty, and as Russia played its hand very lightly, it was more prudent to cooperate. This did not affect the average person, but anyone who was involved in politics, labor, or business knew and it was enough to influence decisions.

The Russians had always looked at the Carpathians and the Hungarian plain with the Danube as an ideal buffer. But they did not need to occupy it. In fact the Russians had learned that occupation brought with it costly responsibilities that had played a role in hollowing out the Soviet Union and the Russian Empire before it. Putin approached the matter in a radically new way—enough control to protect Russia's most important interests, acquired as gently as possible.

What made Putin's approach particularly practical, of course, is that it suited both the commercial interests of businesses and the political interests of Russia. The growing sense that these countries of the former Soviet Union were on their own and no one else was in control caused some of them, like Hungary, to try taking control of their own destiny. And this meant that they needed to keep Russia happy while holding open the option of the European Union should it regain its balance.

Given the weakness of Russia and the uncertainty of the EU, everything was tentative in the borderland region, and stances were constantly shifting. During the interwar period, when the wind might blow from France, then the Soviet Union, then Germany, these countries had played similar games. But in those days the demands were harsher and more burdensome. Then it wasn't a casual affair but a shotgun marriage that was in the cards. Now there is no shotgun, only chocolates, and the wooing of a very reluctant bride—for the moment at least.

The situation north of the Carpathians is both simpler and more complex. The terrain is simpler: it's flat. That has historically made the stakes in the north higher. Russia only controlled the Carpathian countries during the Cold War. It wasn't the historical norm. In the north, Russian and German influence competed for over a century, with the border sliding back and forth along the plain, and Poland and the Baltic states usually disappearing under the tectonic plates.

It is the stakes that are higher. Germany is the world's fourth-largest economy. West of it on the plain is France, the fifth-largest economy. Combined they are the third-largest economy in the world, larger than Japan and just behind China and the United States. If we add in Poland, Russia, and smaller countries (Belgium, the Netherlands, Luxembourg, and the Baltic States), the economy of this region is larger than China's. The northern European Plain, taken together, is one of the wealthiest places on earth.

Because of the importance of this region any political fragmentation becomes much more significant and complicated. Germany and France were once intimate, but now there is more distance between them. Germany and Poland are close but have terrible memories, as does Poland with Russia and similarly the Baltic countries. This is the place whose soul was torn out in the thirty-one years between the start of World

War I and the end of World War II. Therefore, when we consider flash-points, this is the place that is always the most explosive.

Germany has returned to its prior position as the major European economy. It has not even tried to become a marginally significant military power. But that means little as such things change. It is Germany that is deciding the direction the EU will move in. It was German pressure that led to the austerity strategy. It was Germany that was decisive in negotiating terms for reducing debt. And it was Germany that had the greatest control over the value of the euro as managed by the Central Bank.

Once again Germany is greatly admired but also deeply resented. In southern and eastern Europe the view of Germany is that of an aggressive exporter insensitive to the needs of smaller countries. Regarded as the inevitable European power, it is once again feared. Germany's reemergence after 1945 is extraordinary. France's fear that Germany would become the dominant European country has materialized. As we have seen, the United States had a great deal to do with Germany's initial recovery, and also its longer-term recovery, as it could export to the United States. But those days of dependency, economic and military, are long gone. Germany is on its own, leading an exceedingly fractured Europe.

When it looks at Europe, Germany is also frightened because a crucial market for its goods is contracting due to recession, and in danger of fragmenting. It is also afraid of the rising nationalism in the region. That nationalism is generating hostility toward Germany and poses the danger of generating nationalism within Germany. There was deep resentment in Germany at what was regarded as Greek irresponsibility, and at the idea that Germany would be called on to bail out Greece and other European countries. There was a sense of satisfaction at Germany's economic vibrancy, and also a sense that Germany was being victimized by those who had run into trouble. The degree to which Germany had prospered at the expense of these nations was not factored in, but we are talking here about nationalism.

German leaders understand that there is a boundary that once crossed would return Germany to its past. The boundary consists of a sense of unjust victimization coupled with a military threat. While the sense of victimization is emerging, no foreign military threat is present. The only potential one, Russia, is no threat at the moment. And therefore Germany is not in danger of crossing that line.

The problem is that the Russians are inherently drawn west out of fear. It is difficult to defend Russia in the north, and Belarus is indispensable as a buffer. But the Russians have a significant fear of three small and weak countries: Lithuania, Estonia, and Latvia. It is not the countries themselves that are the problem. It is their geography. The Baltic states are a bayonet pointing at St. Petersburg. Another nation that is also a major power could use them as a base from which to attack Russia. In many ways these Baltic countries are more part of Scandinavia than of the European Plain. That they are on the plain is their historic tragedy.

The only conceivable threatening power is Germany, which has not the slightest intention of significantly rearming, let alone attacking Russia. But as I have said, intentions change with circumstances. In the long run the Russians cannot guarantee that the next generation of Germans will think as did the last. This is particularly the case with the uncertainty surrounding Europe's future and therefore Germany's position on the Continent. Russia needs buffers, and historically that is Poland. Poland was independent for about twenty years between World Wars I and II. It was then occupied and has been independent in a complete sense since 1989. Since then it has grown rapidly and has become a significant European power. But it is still between Russia and Germany, fears both, but must live with both.

The fundamental question is the relationship between Germany and Russia, and this is a question that will define Europe as a whole. It is the relationship between the mainland and the peninsula. Germany is the dominant peninsula economic power and Russia dominates the mainland. Between them they will shape, if not decide, the fate of the borderland.

Germany remains deeply committed to the European Union for all the reasons discussed before. Germany has a serious problem, however. If the European Union, for whatever reasons, fails and trade barriers reemerge, then Germany, with a massive dependency on exports, will face a profound economic problem. Germany certainly doesn't want the EU to fail but it may not be able to control that. And if the EU does fail or run into long-term difficulties, it must develop alternative economic relations. There are few available in the European peninsula. China is a competitive exporter. The United States, an importer, is constantly involved in conflicts and wants Germany involved as well, and is not shy in using leverage like trade to force allies into cooperation in these adventures.

Russia is the only substantial potential partner and is already essential to Germany as a source for energy. The problem is that the Russian economy is not fully symmetrical with the German. It is not large enough or rich enough to absorb German exports. Germany doesn't want to maintain its dependence on Russian energy but is searching for alternatives. And of course there are the historic bad memories on both sides.

There is a compensating aspect. Germany's population is declining rapidly, as is Russia's. But Russia still has surplus labor and substantial underemployment and poverty. Declining population might actually address some economic problems. Not so for Germany. Declines in German population mean economic decline, unless miraculous productivity devices emerge. Germany does not want any more immigrants. Muslim migration into Germany has been massive and, in the view of many Germans, already destabilized the country. Any way you look at it, increased immigration to compensate for population decline would have an overwhelming impact.

Germany has a classic quandary—it needs more workers for its economy, but it can't manage more immigrants. One solution is to ship factories to another country with a surplus workforce, like Russia, and get the benefits of more workers without the social costs. To some extent this is already under way. The issue for both is how dependent each wants to become on the other. Recall my argument that interdependence breeds friction. Neither the Germans nor the Russians want friction, but in the event of failure (or a feeling of failure) in the EU as a whole, Germany would need to realign, and that realignment would by default be with Russia.

This would not be the first time for such an alignment. In the mid-nineteenth century Russia supported German unification as a buffer against another attack from France. Between World Wars I and II there was an arrangement between Germany and the Soviet Union, called the Rapallo Agreement, that allowed cooperation between the two countries. It was abrogated with the rise of Hitler, and a new version implemented in 1939, as both countries cooperated to divide Poland. The fact is that when in the past such agreements were reached, they were tentative, short, and bracketed by conflict.

If Germany and Russia aligned, it would determine the fate of Poland, the Baltics, and Belarus. This is not to say they would be occupied militarily. It would mean, however, that with the two major continental powers cooperating with each other, these countries would be compelled to cooperate. Economically and politically they would have limited options. If the military factor were added, then the question would simply be where the line would be drawn.

Belarus would likely be content, or sufficiently nonresistant, to accept absorption by Russia. In fact some would welcome it. But this outcome would leave the Baltic states and Poland in their nightmare situation. Having achieved sovereignty after many years, they might retain it only to see their room for maneuver evaporate. For Poland, the country with weight, it could tolerate hostility between Russia and Germany far better than friendship and cooperation. For Poland, always balancing on the edge, this would be a return to a nightmare.

Indeed, Poland has just awakened over the past two decades from a long nightmare, of German occupation followed by Soviet occupation. It is amazing how well it has recovered. During the Cold War, Warsaw was a gloomy city, dark even during the day and sullen. It was a city waiting for something better, and fully expecting it not to come. The transformation is startling. The only word for its inner city is lovely. When you look at the Chopin Palace in a light snow, the only word that comes to mind is charming. When you drive south, toward Krakow and farther south, into the northern Carpathians, the sense you have is of a new Switzerland, with chalets being built everywhere. When you remember that Warsaw was destroyed by the Germans and looted by the Soviets, and that Krakow is very near the site of Auschwitz, the changes that have occurred in twenty years are staggering.

Poland is still not a lighthearted place by any means and it has yet to regain its bearings. In Krakow, tours are offered of Auschwitz. There are little jitneys with tops made of a blue material standing by to take the tourist there, and many do indeed go. I could not. The juxtaposition of the jitney with the reality of Auschwitz is too jarring. It is as if the Poles don't know what to make of it. Polish Catholics were killed there as well as Jews. But still it is a place to visit, a shrine to Europe's reality. People need a way to get there, and those that take them in jitneys must make a living. There is something inappropriate about this, yet I can't imagine what would be appropriate. Auschwitz happens to be in Poland, but it is not Polish. It is German and that has to be remembered.

The clearest place to see Poland's failure to recover is the roads between Warsaw and Brest, on the Belorussian border. About twenty miles outside the city you feel as though you've left the European peninsula. The buildings are reminders of the Soviet era, and some are damaged as if they had not been rebuilt since World War II. The roads and drivers are amazingly bad, and it is said that there are more highway deaths here than anywhere else in Europe. I don't know if that is true, as it is said with a kind of suicidal pride, but perhaps it is. The roundabouts that eastern Poland is full of are not raised platforms but merely notions, and drivers blithely drive through them while others circle around. The potential mayhem is of course immeasurable.

The land is flat, with old factories intermingled with farms. This is the area that Sholem Aleichem, the bard of Poland's Jews (from whose works the musical *Fiddler on the Roof* was taken), came from. The town of Chelm is just south of here. There are no Jews left; the land is poor and the people dress shabbily. If the Russians ever become sufficiently frightened, this is where they will cross the border, and how they will drive to Warsaw.

But as I said earlier, the Russians don't want to invade Poland, and neither do the Germans. They don't even necessarily want a deal with each other, although the more the EU languishes and the more demanding the Americans become, the more enticing is the possibility. And even if economic relations between Russia and Germany deepen, Poland will take part and may even profit. The danger doesn't come from cooperation but from fear, and for the Russians, fear comes from dependence on and from underestimating the peninsula and misreading its intentions.

This was Stalin's mistake. It was not so much dependence on Germany as German dependence on Russia for its wheat and raw materials. Stalin underestimated how much Hitler needed these and how much he hated being dependent on Stalin's goodwill. Stalin, who should have fully understood Hitler's mind, so close was it to his own, should have seen that Hitler needed Russia too much to leave it alone. He engaged in wishful thinking, and that cost the Soviet Union 20 million dead and nearly cost it its independent existence.

The United States never recovered psychologically from Pearl Harbor, the attack that came at the last place it was expected and at a time when the country was amazingly unprepared. It has spent the decades since then making sure it is never again taken by surprise. When 9/11 came, and the United States was again surprised, it threw the country into a frenzy. In the same way, the Russian mind is fixated on June 22, 1941, the day Germany invaded the Soviet Union. For them, all safety is illusory. So they must control Belarus. And they must be strong in Kaliningrad, the small enclave they hold on the Polish border, and in the Baltic states. And they must not take the Baltics as anything but a potential threat.

I've pointed out the geographic and potential military significance of the Baltics. These three countries, occupied by the Soviets for years, have two realities. One is that these are not really Slavic countries; they have much in common with Scandinavia and particularly Finland and owe much of their history to the Teutonic Knights. Soviet architecture impacts their cities, but the people are Nordic.

But each country contains a time bomb that the Russians could set off at any time. They all have significant minority Russian populations, and the Russians have made clear that no matter where they live, Russians are under their protection. It means little elsewhere, but it means a great deal here. The Russians are deeply concerned about the Baltic countries' membership in NATO and what it means for the future, and the Russian population of the Baltic states is disliked and feels discriminated against.

A simple scenario presents itself. Due to some incident, real or manufactured, Russians in a Baltic capital begin demonstrating, police use tear gas, and somewhere violence breaks out and Russians are killed. The Russian government demands the right to protect its citizens, the Baltic country rejects the demand. Violence mounts, and the Russians demand that NATO stop the fighting. The Baltic state insists it is an internal matter, claims that Russian intelligence caused the violence, and demands that Russian intelligence stop its intervention. A series of explosions kill a large number of Russians, and Russia occupies the country.

For now the Russians have other issues, but if anything goes wrong, the Baltic states will pose a significant threat to Russia. And in Russian thinking there is always something that will go wrong. Because of this fear, the Baltics are one place where the Russians can't relax. There are long-term flashpoints throughout the borderland, but this is the immediate flashpoint in the borderland between the peninsula and mainland.

12

France, Germany, and Their Ancient Borderlands

While visiting Luxembourg, my wife and I hired a guide so we could tour the city in detail. While walking among some modest but well-kept buildings, we saw a distinguished-looking older man taking bags out of his trunk. Our guide said a hearty hello and then mentioned that the man happened to be the prime minister, Jean-Claude Juncker. My wife decided to go chat with him. He stopped unloading the car and was happy to speak with her. I walked over, and he mentioned that he was going to a NATO and G8 conference in Chicago the next day. I responded that Putin was unlikely to be there—which seemed important that morning—and he told me he had spoken to Putin a few hours before and thought he might come.

It was a surreal moment made no less surreal when our guide, a Luxembourger tracing his lineage back centuries, said that he had gone to school with the prime minister and that he hoped Juncker would not be assassinated, since that would mean that Luxembourg would become like other countries, where security surrounded and isolated the political leaders. Luxembourg was unique in its openness and lack of security.

It was a moment where something extraordinarily out of time segued into a conversation that was strikingly contemporary. That seemed to sum up Luxembourg. It is a city I first visited in 1973 and keep coming back to because as clean and enchanting as it is, the remainders of its castles and fortresses remind me that it is a country deeply rooted in war. It is a city made for walking and exploring, and the gorge that cuts through it is a delightful park housing the remnants of buildings designed for war.

Part of the pleasure of Luxembourg is the surrounding countryside, filled with villages and castles. As you drive up Route A35 from Switzerland, through the Rhine Valley and Alsace, you are surrounded by voluptuously beautiful farmland. It is difficult to remember the battles between France and Germany over this land, now French, sometimes German, with both languages spoken and understood. As you drive into and through Luxembourg and head north, the terrain becomes hilly and thickly forested. When you walk along country lanes and see the thickly overgrown and wooded slopes, it is inconceivable that anyone could move through them, let alone fight.

Nevertheless, this is the Ardennes, where the Battle of the Bulge was fought in 1944. From Luxembourg General George Patton commanded the counterattack that rescued the 101st Airborne. Four years earlier Hitler had attacked France through the same hilly forest. He attacked here because the French believed, like me, that the terrain was impassable. The very first action in World War I was an attack by the Germans on Luxembourg to seize a needed rail line. About fifty miles to the west are Verdun and Sedan, scenes of some of the bloodiest battlefields of World War I.

Not only modern wars were fought in this area. About eighty miles north of Luxembourg is the city of Aachen. This was the seat of Charlemagne when he fought to create his empire. If you drive east about twenty miles, you come to the city of Trier, the place where Karl Marx was born, and where Constantine waged war. Constantine was the emperor who brought Christianity to Rome. The Porta Negra, a building that looks like a four- or five-story apartment house, still stands in the center of the town to remind you that the Romans were here and conquered. The building is as familiar as our own homes and at the same time as jarringly alien as a Martian's.

The prevalence of war can be blamed on the inability of the Roman armies to defeat the Germans at the Battle of the Totenberg Forest. Roman tactics weren't suited for fighting in thickly wooded forests, so when the Romans crossed the Rhine, having conquered Gaul—modern France—they were defeated by the Germans. They never attempted to cross the Rhine again, and Roman civilization never went beyond there. West of the Rhine there developed a shifting mixture of Germanic-speaking (including Dutch) areas and French ones. This arrangement was designed for conflict, as the two civilizations fought and attempts were made to conquer and combine them.

The Mediterranean coast remains Latin. But when you travel up the Rhone Valley, following the path Julius Caesar took when he conquered Gaul and the American Fifth Army took in World War II, you enter a different world as you pass the Alps to the east. There in Switzerland, French, German, and Italian mix. From there to the North Sea, the history of the French and the Germans is complex. Drive up the E25 from Basel, through Strasbourg, Luxembourg, Liège, and then Amsterdam, and you will experience directly the ancient borderland that defined Rome and modern Europe. You can see it most easily in Luxembourg.

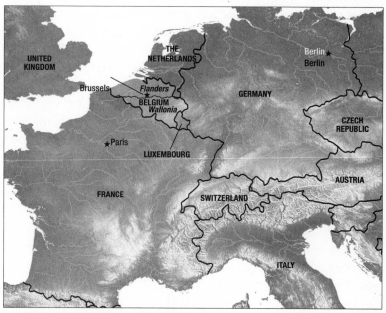

Belgium, Luxembourg, and the Netherlands

Luxembourg today is filled with European institutions, particularly financial ones. When you drive north of Luxembourg you quickly reach Maastricht, the town where the treaty creating the modern European Union was signed. Northwest from there is The Hague, where the International Court of Justice resides. Go back to Strasbourg, and you have traveled the borderland of France and Germany, traced wars going back millennia, and passed the institutions of the EU that are designed to prevent all future war. It wasn't an accident that this line contains so many critical institutions. When the EU was conceived, it was the border of France and Germany that concerned everyone. The placement of institutions was symbolic. It turned the borderland between the two countries into a place of peace instead of war.

If the mainland–peninsula borderland is the main split in Europe, then the Franco-German borderland is the main split within the peninsula. Wars can occur anywhere on the peninsula, but when this borderland is peaceful, general wars in Europe are difficult to envision. The geography of the peninsula contains and restrains wars, and there are no two other powers so strong that a war would draw in everybody. The Alps divide north and south, so the various peninsulas are to some degree self-contained. But if France and Germany are engaged, the war can spread south and east, and all of Europe can become involved. Keeping the peace here has been important since before Napoleon's time.

The fortification walls surrounding Luxembourg were dismantled in the 1860s following a diplomatic settlement between France and some German states. Several Luxembourgers told me that the fortifications were torn down because the treaty had made them unnecessary. It was decided that there would no longer be wars. From that point on, Luxembourg would be a peaceful city focusing only on commerce and trade. This was meant to give me a sense of the Luxembourgers' genuine commitment to peace and their commitment to the Maastricht Treaty. It was odd that they couldn't see how futile the act had been. Wars raged in and around Luxembourg for the next eighty years. If the Luxembourgers seriously expected fortifications to no longer be necessary in the nineteenth century, they were obviously wrong. The question is whether their current confidence is misplaced as well. The great question of Europe, of course, is whether after 1945 and the creation of the EU any war is possible, and most of all, a general war.

Belgium is a country that poses the problem to which Luxembourg thinks it has found the solution. Historically, the region was called the "battleground of Europe" because it was a key point at which the Germanic (including Dutch) and French worlds collided. The region was shaped into an independent country in 1830 to serve as a neutral border-land between Britain and France. Britain wanted to make certain that its great ports, particularly Antwerp, did not fall into French hands and serve as a potential base for challenging Britain. It was intended to be neither French nor Dutch, but a neutral borderland between Britain and the peninsula.

Belgium was created out of parts of the Netherlands and France. One part of Belgium, the Dutch, speaks Flemish. Another part, the Walloons, who live in a region called Wallonia, speaks French. The tension between the two is intense and has sometimes burst into riots. At one point the Walloons were better off than the Flemish. Today the reverse is true. The Germanic portion is much better off than the French. In that sense, Belgium is the borderland in microcosm, and the resulting friction there might be instructive as to the future relationship between France and Germany. For now it is enough to point out that in spite of almost two centuries of unification, the Dutch are still the Dutch and the French are still the French, and they still know it. It is an object lesson in community.

There has been serious talk in recent years of separation, and of the two regions reuniting with France and the Netherlands. Britain is no longer a decisive force and no longer gets to demand neutrality in the eastern exit to the English Channel. Therefore, the dissolution of Belgium is not outside the realm of possibility. Although there have been riots and incendiary speeches, there has not yet been separation. But it is not impossible to imagine this happening. This would be the test case assessing the stability of the borderland. If Belgium can't hold together, there is no reason for confidence.

The French-Dutch tension in Belgium is not universal in the border-land at this point. It is a peaceful place, but not for the first time. The question is whether it will remain peaceful, and that question depends on Germany and France and how permanent their current amiable rela-tionship is. I've discussed Germany at length. Let's consider France.

France was the glittering center of the European enlightenment. It was, in the eighteenth century, the center of the intellectual world, and until the first part of the twentieth century French was the language of civilized discourse, the language that all educated people spoke. In a sense it had replaced Latin as the language of intellectual life in the same way that the Enlightenment had elbowed its way in next to Christianity.

My first encounter with France was as a graduate student in political philosophy, grappling with Descartes and Pascal. They were both great mathematicians and philosophers, and utterly different from each other. Descartes was a systematic thinker. Everything fit together. Pascal gave you tiny prisms, short aphorisms, through which to view the world. With Descartes you could not understand the parts of his thinking without understanding the whole. With Pascal there was no whole except what you imposed on it. As different as they were, there were two things they had in common. One was Catholicism, which they embraced while logically skewering it. The other was a sense that they would skew their thinking in order to be witty. At the time I regarded this as their weakness.

As I got older I realized that a line from Rousseau explained the inconsistency that I thought to be his failure: "I have seen these contradictions and they have not rebuffed me." When you are young you wonder how this could possibly be true. As you get older you realize that the most elegant solution is likely to be wrong. Neither nature nor man is so orderly as to be explicable without recourse to contradiction. Descartes and Pascal had to be Catholics to be faithful to their past. They had to undermine the Church to be faithful to their future, and both understood they had to live with the contradiction between past and future.

Sitting in cafés on the Boulevard du Saint Germain, at a time when students could still afford to sit there, I took part in intense arguments that veered from subject to subject with an underlying theme that no one could remember. I recall how a confident one-liner and a Gallic expression would overwhelm my American logic on a topic I was still discussing while everyone had long since gone on to something seemingly disconnected.

I used to find this singularly unfair. I then learned that in human discourse, even for a Cartesian, pure logic was not the full measure of a human being; it was merely one part of being human. My French friends understood that what was critical was not winning the argument, but arguing in a human way, with a style and wisdom that went deeper than logic and displayed a different and more important dimension of humanity. If life is a set of contradictions, then to the French, the contradictions had to be crossed if not bridged. Self-confidence, style, and a sharp eye and tongue did what reason could not. I hated losing, especially when my argument seemed more disciplined to me. Yet I lost time and time again. As when I have argued with my wife, victory can quickly turn into defeat. And for the French, defeat can be turned into victory.

At about the time I was there in the 1970s and 1980s, Paris had become a gathering place for various terrorist groups, Arab and European. It was also a gathering place for their enemies—American, Israeli, British, and the rest. For the Americans, the terrorists needed to be identified and destroyed. The French didn't want a war in their streets, but they also saw the issue as more complex. There was a time and a place for everything. Some things had to be destroyed, other things preserved. Their goals were constantly shifting. Each group had to be seen in its own right, while remembering that the groups were also similar to each other in many ways. The French perfected the art of doing as little as possible, and, at times, seeming to protect the terrorists. Though there was no question that they were part of the antiterrorist coalition, there was no doubt that they saw the terrorists in a different light than their allies did.

In the words of Rousseau, the contradictions had not rebuffed the French. They saw the battle of Europe, as it was sometimes grandiosely called, as too important simply to be won. It had to be subtly managed to reach an acceptable outcome, not a solution. That acceptable outcome could not be simply defined, but would emerge over time. Simply killing everyone you thought was a terrorist would kill only those you knew of, not those you didn't. Watching and identifying the terrorists was like collecting stamps, as one person said to me. You do it slowly and carefully, focusing on different types, in no rush to buy or sell. It is a quiet, contemplative activity. The goal for the French was not to fight the battle in France and certainly not in Paris. That would attract others. As I was told, "We are too small to fight for the world. We fight for Paris, to keep it peaceful. You Americans can fight for the world, but not in Paris."

I was young and enraged by French perfidy. It seemed like contradictory nonsense. But then so did French philosophy, until I understood what I was being told: We would like to eliminate all terrorists, but we don't know how to do that. The trains run to Paris and more will arrive. We do not know how to eliminate terrorism in the world. But if we can get the terrorists not to kill too many in Paris, we will have done something. And if in the course of this we do things that baffle our allies, then it is something we French will have to endure, and we will, because we are French. For the French, their lives are not shaped by career plans, but by events—chance meetings, unplanned insights into themselves, casual affairs. Each of these creates the unexpected opportunity, the point of contemplation, the love of your life. Or not.

In the meantime you have your family, your blood, and the things you were born to. Whatever else happens, your family are the ones who will take you in. The contradiction between the cosmopolitan intellectual without a home and the Frenchman who always visits the family in the Vosges for the summer is startling, but I learned not to be rebuffed by it. I remember a woman of great brilliance and beauty who chose to befriend me. She lived an utterly bohemian life but went home each night to her room with her parents.

The French are so subtle they would confuse themselves, save they are so subtle they do not become confused. The dissonance of the world is something they simply wait out. They wait for what comes next. To understand the French and even the EU, keep in mind that they are rebuffed neither by contradiction nor by defeat or decline.

France's decline began in the early nineteenth century with Napoleon's defeat, but it was confirmed later in that century when Germany surged past it economically. France found itself caught between two extraordinarily successful industrial powers: Britain to the west, across a narrow channel, and Germany to the east across the Rhine. By the end of the nineteenth century, both of these countries towered over France.

The reason for this has been hotly debated. Max Weber, in *The Protestant Ethic and the Spirit of Capitalism*, argued that Protestantism provides a more powerful basis for economic development than Catholicism. That was persuasive but it ignored the fact that Bavaria and the Rhineland, both strongly Catholic, were part of Germany, and the Rhineland was Germany's industrial heartland. Others have argued that the French peasantry resisted industrialization. There are many other reasons, many of them undoubtedly having a great deal of truth to them, but none fully satisfying.

The explanation I favor is this. After Napoleon the British dominated the world's oceans and created a sparkling empire built around

India. They were able to create a massive empire that excluded others and allowed the British a tremendous trade advantage. The French had an empire, but in many ways it was an empire of the leftovers and far inferior to the British. It didn't offer the kind of self-contained trading system that Britain exploited.

Another difference was the British relationship with America. Though defeated in the American Revolution, the British maintained close trade relations with the United States, in particular the cornucopia of food that came pouring out of the Mississippi River basin. The British used this to lower food costs and drive farmers into urban factories. The French, supporting their farmers, made less use of American food products. This limited the workforce available for French industrialization and increased the cost of food in the cities. The British were more ruthless toward their farmers, and therefore more successful.

Meanwhile the Germans industrialized without an empire but with a tremendous advantage in Europe: a dominant economic position in the Austro-Hungarian and Russian Empires due to their proximity to the Rhine, the Elbe, and especially the Danube, Europe's main river for transport. Whatever the reason, France was left behind—not to the extent of simply being excluded from the ranks of Europe's most advanced states, and certainly not lacking substantial industry, but never quite in the first rank. Britain and Germany occupied that position.

The French had struggled with the British for centuries. Northwestern France—Brittany and Normandy—had been dominated by the British or fought over by the French and British. The French blamed the British for the defeat of Napoleon, both because the British defeated the French fleet at Trafalgar and, more important, because the British blockade starved the French of supplies. In France's view, Britain supported France's enemies and strangled French access to the oceans, without exposing itself to serious risk. The term "perfidious Albion" (treacherous England) long defined the French view. Bishop Bousset, a seventeenth-century French cleric, said:

> England, oh, treacherous England,
> that the ramparts of her seas made inaccessible to the Romans,
> there also the faith of Christ has landed.

France's history with Britain was not good. The feeling of treachery was reinforced in World War II, when—according to the French view—Britain abandoned France in its hour of need, withdrawing its forces. France's historical relationship with Britain, which had been instrumental in crushing Napoleon at Waterloo, was frequently poisonous.

Nor did France have a good history with the Germans. Prussian troops had also been critical in defeating Napoleon at Waterloo. As soon as Germany united, France and Germany fought a war that Germany won. In addition to seizing part of the borderland that had been French—Alsace and Lorraine—the Germans insisted on staging a parade in Paris. They did that to humiliate the French and because they could. Obviously when you include the two world wars, the history of French relations with Germany was worse than even the history of its relations with England.

France was caught between two historic enemies and constant irritants. As Germany rose in power, the French and the British allied and ultimately included Russia in that alliance, all designed to contain the most powerful country in Europe. But France's underlying tension with Britain had a long history, and good reasons. The British used the French to contain Germany so that Germany couldn't build fleets to challenge Britain. France had no choice but to play its role. It feared Germany too much. Even when aided by the British, the French felt trapped to play the role Britain and geography had designed for it.

After World War II, when there was discussion of European integration, one of the reasons de Gaulle was interested in it was because of his profound dislike and distrust of the British, something with a long history but in his case honed to a fine point by his experience in Britain during World War II. De Gaulle didn't want Britain in the European Community, as it was called then. He saw a reformed Germany in France's grip as preferable to Britain. In addition, he saw the British, now in decline, as a tool of the United States to deprive France of her sovereignty.

Therefore one of the things to bear in mind is that France's relationship to Germany is partly conditioned by its relationship to Britain within the European context, and with another player, the United States, in the broader context. France can resist Germany, assuming it wants to, only if Britain and the United States are prepared to support France. I'm not talking about war here, but rather about simply redefining economic and political relations. If France is alone, it must follow the German line. If France has support, it can consider alternatives. In the end, it is the odd inability to keep up with others, now Germany and the United States, that has made this support necessary. France can't do it alone.

Britain is drawing back from the European Union. It is not abandoning it, but it is not joining the euro and it is not participating in several of the European projects. As they have for centuries, the British have an interest in the European peninsula, and will get deeply involved when they must, but only if they must. Short of that it is involvement while maintaining other interests. It used to be the Empire that interested Britain. It is now a relationship with the United States that counterbalances its relationship with Europe.

The American position at the moment is to disengage from the Islamic world and avoid undertaking other commitments overseas. The United States views Europe as something that cannot be worked out using American resources, and any involvement in European economic affairs, beyond maintaining trade, would be dangerous. It has involved itself with two French military adventures. The first was the bombing of Libya in 2011, where the United States chose to support French calls for action, and while initially hanging back, wound up assuming the major load. Similarly, when the French sent troops to stabilize Mali in 2013, the United States backed France to the extent of providing logistical support.

It is vital to note that in neither case did the Germans get involved. This indicates a fundamental dynamic that is under way in Franco-German relations. In two instances where the French felt that fundamental national interests were at stake, the Germans refused to support them militarily, while the United States did support them. This happened at the same time that French economic interests diverged from German. French unemployment was about 12 percent. German unemployment was below 6 percent. The French wanted an EU policy that addressed unemployment whereas the Germans wanted an EU policy that increased fiscal responsibility.

These tensions didn't tear France and Germany apart. The French understood the historical and political limits facing the Germans on military intervention. They also were eager to bridge the gap on economic issues. The Germans certainly wanted to maintain a close relationship. The problem, of course, was not what the leadership wanted but what they might be forced to do by national interest and internal political issues.

The insoluble issue has been economic. Both Germany and France are more fragile than they look. Germany's dependence on exports makes them hostage to the appetite of their customers. France's economic weaknesses showed themselves after 2008. If the economic weakness that has been visible in France since then continues, as it has over the past two centuries, France will become increasingly noncompetitive in Europe, particularly compared to Germany. This would force France to follow different economic policies than Germany's, and that will be difficult within the current framework of the EU.

The French have no desire to break with the Germans but want them to moderate their policies. The Germans have no desire to break with the French but want them to moderate their policies. It is difficult to imagine the intimate relationship forged out of the Marshall Plan leading to hostilities. There is little to fight about. But between total integration and war there are many states in which two nations can exist. They can continue to have good relations but go on different paths.

Germany's strategic policy was built around economic relations with the largest group of countries possible in order to facilitate its exports. In this sense Germany had a global view, since it had global customers. But Germany was in no position to compel these to be customers by any but economic means. They neither depended on Germany nor felt compelled to deal with Germany. The instruments set up by the EU were the only means for Germany to control the EU members who consumed half of all Germany's exports.

Ironically, however, the more Germany used these EU levers, such as free trade, regulations, the euro's value, and the banking system, the more it shaped the system to take care of Germany's needs and inevitably repelled the rest of Europe, particularly France, which was strong enough to chart its own course. The Germans wanted the main focus of the European Central Bank to be inflation. France wanted it to address employment. The former was the German problem. The latter was the French.

The Germans won that fight, but it is a fight France can't abandon. When Germany demanded austerity, it was addressing its own needs and constraints, and alienating those who would bear the burden. Consequently, France would demand policies Germany couldn't provide, and the European Union would become an arena of tension rather than the peace and prosperity that it had dreamed of.

France will not leave the EU, but nor can it simply remain there. It will have to establish its own tax policy and run its own deficits, and its leaders will seek to suppress unemployment by policies that might not work in the long run but would work long enough for them to be reelected. Any alternative strategy would have to include something else. The question is what the alternative might be, and how to make it compatible with France's relationship with Germany and the European Union. Add to this the intense pressure in France for protectionism. A range of groups, from farmers to the right-wing National Front, want to see a France less dependent on the outside world. However impractical this might be, it is a serious political tendency that has to be taken into account by the French government.

The French think in three directions: the European Plain and Germany; the English Channel and the British; and the Mediterranean and Africa. The Mediterranean Union idea, launched in July 2008, came from deep within French geography. France was a northern European power. It was also a Mediterranean power. The idea was to organize the countries of the Mediterranean basin into an alternative economic union. From Gibraltar to the Bosporus, all countries, including the Europeans, North Africans, and the Israelis, would create a free-trade zone in which France could compete, and dominate.

France's strategy was to compensate for its economic weakness with close relations with former colonies in Africa, and to strengthen their position in the Middle East and in the Mediterranean. The French proposed a union of Mediterranean countries that would be separate from but linked to the European Union. It went nowhere. But an older Union of the Mediterranean exists. It has forty-three members, twenty-eight of them with overlapping memberships in the EU. The presidency of the Union of the Mediterranean rotates every two years between an EU member and a non-EU member, and decisions are made at the annual conference of foreign affairs ministers and the biennial summit of heads of state. It is an idea with an organization but no reality. It is not clear how this could possibly work. Could Syria and Israel both be members? Can the rules be harmonized with the EU? It is a brilliant concept that has profound contradictions in it. But the French have seen these contradictions and have not rebuffed them.

There is nothing defined in this Union, save that there might be some sort of trade zone. And its French champions try to breathe life into it. This shows us something of France's economic and political geography. It is finding it hard to reconcile its interests with those of Germany, yet badly wants to find a basis for maintaining the post-1945 European order. France sees Britain as not fully relevant to its problem or a solution, continuing to lump the "Anglo-Saxon" countries (a very archaic concept when you think of it) together. But France is not just a northern European country. It is also a southern European and Mediterranean country, and in that arena, it is the major power. That arena is also a fractured region. But France must explore this as one of its alternatives.

France maintained much closer relations with its African colonies than the British did with their Commonwealth. The French were a constant and frequently decisive presence, intervening militarily with some frequency. The French had left behind colonies far less ready for independence than those of the British, and then compensated by continuing to treat them in semicolonial ways.

In the Middle East, the French had relations with both Lebanon and Syria, and didn't intervene in Syria only because the United States refused to join them in that adventure. Lebanon and Syria had become French protectorates after World War I, and French interests in North Africa were powerful and continuing. The idea of a Mediterranean Union was not insane because to some extent, commerce in the Mediterranean centered on France already.

The idea of Israel joining such a community, assuming the Muslim powers would permit it, is certainly appealing to them. Turkey, rejected by the European Union, might also join. In an odd way, what appears at first preposterous begins to make sense, and it begins to explain why the Europeans are talking about it. The Mediterranean was, before the northern European industrial revolution, one of the wealthiest regions in the world. Divisions between Muslim North Africa and Christian southern Europe were contained, if not always peacefully.

The French have little to lose and a great deal to gain if they can create a supplement to their European relationships. How much there is to gain depends on how much wealth can be generated by an organization with France at its center. That is simply not clear. But if France could draw developed countries like Turkey, Italy, and France into a coalition with energy-wealthy Algeria and Libya, the possibilities would be substantial. And it would give France the shot at regional leadership that it lost to Germany in the EU.

The probability of a full membership on the order of the EU is unlikely. That some would be interested in such an entity is not. How it would be held together and how it would benefit its members, especially the French, are unclear. It is also unclear whether such an entity could exist without conflict, as many of the members are hostile to each other.

As unlikely as this is, it is the only route open to the French unless they can become more competitive with the Germans by increasing productivity and profitability. But given the policies their government will be forced to follow by an electorate overwhelmed by unemployment, it is difficult to imagine how France will maintain anything close to parity with the Germans. The structural inefficiencies that haunted France from the beginning of the industrial revolution are still there. Inside the EU, France will only lose ground. Alone, it is simply an isolated country with few options. The Mediterranean strategy is not clearly a viable alternative, but it *is* an alternative.

That means that the borderland between France and Germany will likely remain peaceful, although relations between the two countries may not be nearly as pleasant. A good model is Belgium, where French and Dutch were fused together in an artificial state designed to soothe British concerns. The Dutch have become wealthier, and the French have become poorer. The tensions between the Flemish and the Walloons are deep, and it is genuinely unclear whether Belgium can survive. It may, but the fact that its survival is not certain is important in a Europe that abhors such crises.

Belgium should be thought of as a metaphor for the relationship of the French and Germanic nations, although not a perfect one, as neither the French nor Germans want a divorce, whereas many in Belgium do. Germany is getting wealthier and France is getting poorer. The Germans don't want to be burdened with the French, nor do they want to let go of the psychological and political security the French offer. The French do not want to give up their place in Europe, but at the same time they cannot endure economic decline indefinitely.

The Germans will be looking east toward Russia and other places that want to buy their products. The French will be looking south to the Mediterranean. As with a marriage in decline, there is little thought of divorce, but the things that bound them together passionately are no longer there. Germany is not seeking redemption. France is not seeking to dominate an integrated Europe. They do, however, have neighbors who appear attractive and are flirting. The divorce can be amiable. Route E25 will be as peaceful as ever. But what will happen to the south of France will be another matter.

13

Mediterranean Europe Between Islam and Germany

The Mediterranean is the southern border of the European peninsula. It is an enclosed body of water from which you can reach the global oceans in only two ways. One is from the west, through the Strait of Gibraltar. The other is through the man-made Suez Canal in the east. There are other enclosed seas in the world, but few have as little access to the rest of the world. Fewer still are as large. None have shaped global history to the extent the Mediterranean has. The Mediterranean basin gave rise to Judaism and Christianity and became a center of Islamic life. It was the center of Alexandrian, Roman, and Egyptian history. The basin linked Europe to Africa and both to Asia. Columbus's voyage in 1492 originated in the Mediterranean and was shaped by its politics. Having this body of water as the southern frontier of Europe ensures both turbulence and remarkable influences.

The northern side of the Mediterranean is historically and generally Christian today, with exceptions in Turkey and the Balkans. The southern side, North Africa, is historically and overwhelmingly Muslim. The eastern side, the Levant, is a mixture of religions and sects, Christian, Muslim, Jewish, and all varieties of each. These are the remnants of historic wars and migrations that continue today.

The Mediterranean forms a single entity. It is a little over two thousand miles long, less than one hundred miles wide at its narrowest point, and a bit more than five hundred miles at its widest point. The two shores come closest at Gibraltar and meet in the Levant. What happens anywhere along the Mediterranean's shore has the potential to influence and shape events on any shore.

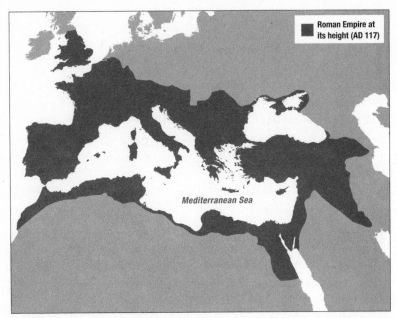

The Roman Empire AD 117

This was the case for the Romans. They named the Mediterranean the Middle Sea, or Mare Nostrum ("Our Sea"). It was the center of gravity of their imperial system. Efficient trade, such as getting grain from Egypt to Rome, required ships and a navy to protect the ships from pirates. More than the army, it was trade and the navy that tied the Roman Empire together, and that was made possible by the narrowness of the sea. The Romans bound the two shores together, and that bond still exists. The interaction between Rome and Egypt, as well as the Levant, created not a single system of thought but a system of linked cultures and economies that allowed Rome to maintain its system.

It is remarkable how beautiful the Mediterranean can be. Sitting on a cliff overlooking the volcanic island of Santorini at the edge of the Eurasian tectonic plate, I was able to look over a still, profoundly blue sea, out to the horizon that hid Crete. But closer in, forming an imperfect but still profoundly blue circle, was the caldera of a volcano that exploded some 2,500 years ago, tearing the island apart, destroying the Minoan civilization, possibly generating the story of Atlantis, and certainly changing the weather around the world for years. It is hard to imagine a more beautiful place than Santorini (its original name was Thera). It is also impossible to imagine a more violent place.

Shakespeare, in his last play, *The Tempest*, wrote of a shipwreck on a Mediterranean island, an island filled with sorcery and magic. Most see the beauty. Sebastian senses the corruption. Vincent van Gogh said, "The Mediterranean has the color of mackerel, changeable, I mean. You don't always know if it is green or violet, you can't even say it's blue, because the next moment the changing reflection has taken on a tinge of rose or gray." Homer speaks of the wine-dark seas, something I was never able to understand until I read van Gogh's description of its colors. Homer was struggling to describe the indescribable and changeable colors of the sea.

We all know of the Mediterranean climate with its mild temperatures, sun-drenched summers, and mild and wet winters. The Mediterranean seems benign, and on the surface it is, to the casual visitor. Those who live there, and understand its history, know that it is sensual and seductive. But beneath its surface it is a violent place. European civilizations like Venice and Britain, North African civilizations, powers from the Black Sea Basin, powers from the east like Babylon and Persia, all converge on the Mediterranean. Violent wars are waged along its shores—in Yugoslavia, Lebanon, Israel, Egypt, Libya, and Algeria just since World War II, many in the past few years. We think of indolence when we think of the Mediterranean. War is as reasonable a thought.

It is also a place of dramatic contrasts and contradictions. To see this contrast, simply think of the northern and southern shores a few hundred miles apart, one Christian, the other Muslim. On the surface, there are many similarities between these two religions. Each appears different depending on how you view it, the direction you face, and the amount of time you devote. Like the colors van Gogh describes, each changes. In that way they are similar. And they are similar in the view each has of the other. They are enemies and inexorably linked to each other. Think of the sands of the Sahara and the lush hills of southern Europe. They are parts of a single entity, never more than five hundred miles apart, sharing their history, and utterly different.

We've spoken of borderlands, and how they are both linked and divided. Here is a border sea, differing in many ways but sharing the basic characteristic of the borderland. Proximity separates as much as it divides. It facilitates trade, but also war. For Europe, this is another frontier both familiar and profoundly alien.

Islam invaded Europe twice from the Mediterranean, first in Iberia, the second time in southeastern Europe, as well as nibbling at Sicily and elsewhere. Christianity invaded Islam multiple times, the first time in the Crusades and in the battle to expel the Muslims from Iberia. Then it forced the Turks back from Central Europe. The Christians finally crossed the Mediterranean in the nineteenth century, taking control of large parts of North Africa. Each of these two religions wanted to dominate the other. Each seemed close to its goal. Neither was successful. What remains true is that Islam and Christianity were obsessed with each other from the first encounter. Like Rome and Egypt, they traded with each other and made war on each other.

The Europeans conquered North Africa in the late eighteenth century during their drive for global domination. Napoleon made his initial reputation in command of French forces in Egypt. The Sphinx, perhaps one of the greatest and most mysterious edifices in the world, has no nose. A French artillery officer shot it off for no apparent reason other than to show that he could. The occupation of North Africa gave Europeans dominion over the Mediterranean. The French and British competed for it. The British won and completed the Suez Canal that the French had begun. This gave Britain maritime access to the Red Sea and the Indian Ocean, and hence to India. It bound together Britain's global empire. It also made North Africa a battleground between Germany and Britain, with the canal as the prize. Britain won, but as its navy melted away, it was replaced by the U.S. Navy's Sixth Fleet, which dominated the ocean but never the shore.

The European conquest of North Africa led to the North African revolt against Europe. In Egypt, the British-selected King Farouk was overthrown, and the Suez Canal seized by the new government. Britain, France, and Israel invaded to retake the canal and hopefully overthrow the new regime. They failed. In Algeria, a bloody uprising occurred in the 1950s as the French sought to preserve their hold and the Algerian Muslims fought to overthrow them and expel the French settlers. The

Europeans were forced back to the northern shore of the Mediterranean, for the most part relieved to have left, and focusing on rebuilding after World War II.

That rebuilding forced another encounter with North Africa, and the Islamic world in general. As Europe's economies grew they needed additional labor. The nearest source of that labor was the Muslim world. Millions of Muslims came to Europe to earn money. This did not transform Europe, but it did change it. Belgium, for example, is now about 10 percent Muslim. Britain is just under 5 percent. Germany is 5 percent Muslim. The numbers in the cities are more startling. Paris is between 10 and 15 percent, and Brussels is one-third Muslim.

There have always been Muslims on the north shore of the Mediterranean. Turkey and Bosnia are obvious examples, and Bulgaria has had a substantial Muslim minority. There are three things that are different about this migration. The first is the number of migrants. The second is the scope of their settlement. Cities like Marseille and Barcelona have long had Muslim settlement. But what is different is that this time Muslims (and not all from the Mediterranean by any means) migrated to London, Brussels, Frankfurt, and other northern European cities that hadn't seen such migration before. The third difference is the speed with which this migration took place. It really began in the 1960s.

As important, the migration took place in societies that weren't very good at absorbing large-scale immigration. The inability of certain European nations to handle masses of immigrants goes back to the nature of their regimes. As discussed earlier, the foundation of European nation-states was a sense of shared fate, derived from common history, language, and culture. You were born a Hungarian or a Spaniard. You could acquire citizenship, but naturalization, turning into a Hungarian or Spaniard in a full sense through a legal process, went against the concept of nation as shared blood or at least common birth.

The Europeans tried to solve this problem through multiculturalism. Being unable to turn a new citizen into a German or Swede, and being strongly unwilling to return to racism, Europe attempted to accept immigrants as citizens while acknowledging that they could not share the culture. But under the doctrine of multiculturalism not only could they remain different, but that difference was officially declared to be equal to the native culture. Of course the difference between declaring something to be true and having it practiced by the majority is a difficult and complex matter.

Multiculturalism and the entire immigrant enterprise faced another challenge. Europe was crowded. Unlike the United States it didn't have the room to incorporate millions of immigrants, certainly not on a permanent basis. Even with population numbers slowly declining, the increase in population, particularly in the more prosperous countries, was difficult to manage. The doctrine of multiculturalism naturally encouraged a degree of separatism. Culture implies a desire to live with your own people. Given the economic status of immigrants the world over, the inevitable exclusion perhaps unintentionally incorporated in multiculturalism, and the desire of like to live with like, the Muslims found themselves living in extraordinarily crowded and squalid conditions. All around Paris there are high-rise apartment buildings housing and separating Muslims from the French, who live elsewhere.

This is not entirely different from the United States by any means, save for one thing. In the United States you are free to keep your cultural distinctness, but the failure to adopt American norms of language and culture to some degree will exclude you. Adopting these norms allows you to enter American life at the price of giving up the native culture, save for a special dish on the holidays. It is a high price, but entry to being American is not barred. It is more complex in Europe. The culture is richer and more complex—and older—than in the United States. It makes becoming French more difficult.

My parents loved Hungary before the war, but it was never clear, in the end, that they were Hungarians. They were Jews, after all, and however much they became Hungarian that distinction mattered. When we came to the United States, I was determined to be an American. The issue barring me was that I threw a baseball like a little girl, to quote the kids in the schoolyard. I worked hard to manage the smooth overhand. Having achieved it, I was welcomed. When I went to Cornell to go to graduate school, what barred me was not that I was a Jew. There were many at Cornell. It was my thick Bronx-gutter accent and the fact that my behavior was more appropriate on a Bronx schoolyard. These were correctable defects. By then there were plenty of newer immigrants to look down on. There was anti-Semitism in the United States, but it was minor and fundamentally different than in Europe, where the stranger remains the stranger because of where he was born, not because of bad manners.

Nazi anti-Semitism was the reductio ad absurdum of Europe—birth turned to blood, and blood to disease. Still, Europe never welcomed the outsider as one of its own. The Muslims are now experiencing what the Jews experienced. Europe can cope with outsiders in small numbers. It could not cope with the *Ostjuden*, the Jews from the East who flocked to Europe en masse in the nineteenth century. Nor can they cope with the Muslims who have flowed in more recently. This is not the problem of the wealthier Europeans, who can insulate themselves from all of Europe's lower class. It is the problem of the lower middle class and the poor, who cannot ignore the foreigners' presence and resent the pressure they place on their own lives. This is where the tension arises. Multiculturalism allows the distinction between immigrant and native to be institutionalized. But the radical cultural distinctions that result are felt by the most insecure of Europeans, while liberality of identity and diversity have been granted by those least likely to experience these distinctions close up.

A more honest representation of the European vision is found in the City Museum in Trier in Germany. There is a small selection devoted to the cosmopolitanism of the city, showing all the different nationalities who lived there. Sharing a small case are displays of Jewish and Muslim artifacts. The presence of Russians or Italians in Trier is one matter, and they are addressed differently in the museum. But to the curator, and I am certain that it was not done maliciously, the presences of Jews and Muslims in Trier's life share a common point. Trier is a Catholic city and deeply religious, more so than other parts of Germany. Posters on walls and in windows advertise and celebrate religious events and festivals. Quite correctly, Trier understands that Jews and Muslims are not Christians, that they have that in common, and that this fact differentiates them from others in cosmopolitan Trier. That they lived there at different times and endured different fates is not a prime distinguisher.

Modern Europe has become increasingly secular. Attendance at churches of all faiths has declined in most countries, and polls show that

Europeans tend to be indifferent to religion, if not hostile. Jews were part of that secularism prior to World War II. That at least was not a point of contention. Muslims, on the other hand, are religious. Perhaps this is not universally the case, but it is sufficiently true to put them at odds with the secularism of Europe. France, for example, banned the use of the veil in public by Muslim women. It was presented as a security matter, but it resonated as an attempt to control not so much Muslims, but the public presentation of their religion.

The Europeans had more than a slight problem with the movement of Muslims north across the Mediterranean, as well as those arriving into Britain from Pakistan, or into the Netherlands from Indonesia. Residents of Europe's former colonies were given the right to migrate following their independence, which meant those countries with former empires had unique migrations in addition to the kind of economic migration Germany encouraged.

Taken together, there was a substantial shift in the makeup of European societies. Differences in culture and religion, openly shown by dress and manners, destabilized some countries or cities disproportionately. The immigrants were badly needed during the period of postwar expansion. But they also failed to integrate into society. First, the societies were not shaped to support elective citizenship en masse. Second, many of the Muslims wanted to remain separate in order to preserve their own distinct culture. They were there to make a living, not abandon their way of life. They needed to work, not to build European societies.

Two things exacerbated the situation. The first was terrorism. Europe did not experience an attack on the scale of 9/11, but both Spain and Britain have been attacked. There was also the case of a Danish cartoonist who sketched what was seen as an insulting portrait of the Prophet Muhammad in 2006. Attempts were made on his life, thousands demonstrated against him, and so on. The sense grew in some countries that the accommodation of Muslims required a transformation of the host culture's commitment to free expression. Danish prime minister Rasmussen called this event the most dangerous crisis in Denmark since World War II, which may not have been true but is a measure of the anxiety at that time.

The second factor was the global financial crisis. Prior to 2008 Europe needed workers and was prepared to tolerate their perceived eccentricities. Low unemployment meant that people might be culturally threatened by immigrants, but not economically at risk. After the financial crisis came, and particularly when the unemployment rates soared, the Muslims were seen not simply as a cultural threat, but also as an economic one. This raised anti-Muslim feeling to higher levels in countries where the Muslim presence was more highly concentrated in certain areas, even if not greater nationally, and, most important, in countries that were under greater economic pressure. It did not always, or even usually, turn into a racial matter, but it was certainly a point of friction.

If anti-Muslim feeling was present throughout Europe, anti-European feeling had also risen in the Muslim community. There were extensive riots in Paris, for example, by Muslims protesting their treatment. But the issue there was primarily social: the tensions created in European states by foreigners. But it was in the south that the anti-immigrant, anti-Muslim sentiment would merge with the social crisis and lead Europe to a deeper crisis. About one-third of the population of Marseille and Barcelona is Muslim. These are extreme cases, but they are also in the area that has been the hardest hit by economic depression. As jobs are lost, and people seen as foreigners compete for them, the tension inevitably increases. The same Muslim population in Germany, where unemployment is below 6 percent, causes very different problems than in Barcelona, where unemployment is over 20 percent.

The global economic crisis created a massive split in Europe. Southern Europe experienced the economic crisis much more intensely than the north. But then southern Europe already experienced life differently than the north. The experience of being on the Mediterranean shaped southern Europe. But the south also differed from northern Europe in other ways. Southern Europe is hilly and more rugged than northern Europe, which makes travel more difficult, and it is harder for armies to scour the countryside for enemies. Clans can survive invaders, and the family, understood as widely extended, is more real than the abstract notions of the nation-state. Rome is far from Sicily, and Macedonia is far from Athens, but those you love are near at hand. Where the northern plain denied people a place to hide, the south is full of nooks and crannies. Southern Europe has nation-states and has a deep commitment to nationalism, but it is in some ways softer and less absolute than in the north. The difference between Fascist Italy and Nazi Germany provides a sense of this. The Fascists were more operatic, but more flexible than the Nazis.

I am not the first one to note these differences between north and south, but they are nonetheless true and important. The industrial revolution took place in the north, and what had previously been the wealthier part of Europe, right on the Mediterranean Sea trade routes, became the poorer. Southern Europe has consistently lagged behind the north. I would argue, along with many others, that the south had both a different sense of existence and was less hardened by nature. It is not that they don't work hard—anyone who has watched a Greek fisherman or a Spanish farmer at work knows that isn't true. However, their lives are not quite as filled with urgency as in the north. Winter's coming doesn't mean death if you are unprepared, and the disciplines of industrialism seem less important. We can make too much of this and romanticize it, but the simple fact is that the south behaves differently than the north.

Perhaps the difference in behavior and lifestyle in southern Europe was a matter of indolence induced by the climate, as the Germans seemed to feel. Or perhaps it was a matter of terrain, or of the disadvantages of the southern countries not having their own empires. There are many possible reasons, but southern Europe experienced 2008 in a different way than the north. And it was not just Europe as a whole, but even individual countries were split between north and south in their reaction to the financial crisis. As French president François Hollande stated, "Is France a northern European export powerhouse, or a Mediterranean indebted and dependent economy? Yes to both." ·

The ambivalence of France is the reality of the south. Perhaps the best place to focus in discussing both the Mediterranean region and the effect of the EU crisis is on Cyprus, an island not far from the coasts of Lebanon and Israel, which in microcosm illustrates some of the crises of southern Europe today. The extreme case sometimes makes it easier to see things clearly.

Cyprus is an island in the eastern Mediterranean, and probably the most extreme example of how southern Europe has been impacted by the financial crisis. It had been a colony of Britain until granted independence in 1960. About one-quarter of Cyprus's population is Turkish and

Muslim. The rest are Greeks and Orthodox Christians. Between 1960 and 1974 the island was ruled jointly. In 1974, Greek nationalists, wanting to merge with Greece, staged a coup. Turkey responded by invading the northern region, which was predominantly Turkish, and effectively partitioned the island.

Most countries did not recognize the division, but it was a reality. The southern part, the Republic of Cyprus, which officially is the only Cyprus, was admitted to the European Union in 2004. The reasons for admitting it included the desires of the Greek government, an expansionary vision of the EU, in which it was believed that any country admitted would benefit and grow, and problems with Turkey. Turkey wanted to enter the European Union, but in an organization that operates by consensus, the Greeks could block it. In addition, the Europeans weren't eager to have a large Muslim country in the EU, as it raised the possibility of uncontrolled Muslim Turkish immigration into the European peninsula. The Europeans did not want to state this as a reason, but the Turkish occupation of northern Cyprus was a reasonable justification for refusing to move forward on membership, and therefore the admission of the Greek portion of the island, and the official government, was meant as a signal to the Turks. The European-Turkish interplay had many dimensions, as did the European-Muslim interplay, and in Cyprus it played out in its most extreme form.

Historically, the Turkish part of Cyprus was poorer than the Greek part. There has now been somewhat of a reversal of fortunes. The economic crisis in Mediterranean Europe hurt Greek Cyprus intensely. Turkish Cyprus, linked to the healthier Turkish economy, did fairly well. The distinction between the two zones is very real. You can readily cross from one to the other, but not with a rental car, and when you cross, the differences are real. The two zones have existed for a long time. Cyprus was a borderland between Turkey and Greece, two countries hostile to each other for a long time. While that hostility is milder now, at times in the past it has become intense.

When you arrive in Cyprus and drive along the southern coast, you feel like you might be in any part of southern Europe. There is no sense of tension over partition and no signs of poverty. But there are oddities that very quickly stand out.

On one of our trips there we had booked reservations at the Four

Seasons in Limassol, figuring that you can't go wrong with the Four Seasons. The first thing we discovered was that while it was a nice luxury hotel, it wasn't part of *the* Four Seasons chain. I'm sure that by using the name they could charge higher prices and get tourists to go there. In other places trademarks matter. In Cyprus things were more casual. The second thing we noticed was that the dominant language being used among guests wasn't Greek or English but Russian. Eavesdropping on a conversation in an outdoor bar, I heard two Russians talking about a deal worth $75 million. All around, men were sitting with their heads inches apart, very focused.

We chartered a boat to take us offshore, past the huge British air base west of Limassol and around part of the island to Latchi. This was at the time in September 2013 when there were threats of U.S. and British intervention in Syria, and I was interested to see if there was any activity at the base. On our return we were nearing Limassol when one of the boat's two engines failed. This happens, and we were not perturbed, but controlling the boat was difficult on one engine with the stiff breeze, so the captain tried to contact the Limassol harbor patrol and the coast guard. Neither answered repeated calls on the emergency channel. Our captain said this was routine and that "they probably went out to have coffee." It was then I realized that in some fundamental ways, this was the third world. When the coast guard on an island surrounded by sea traffic takes a break from listening for Mayday calls, you aren't in Europe anymore.

This raises the important question of why Cyprus is in the European Union. Part of the reason is that the Europeans were accepting just about everybody into the EU before 2008—except the fastest-growing economy in Europe at the time, Turkey. Another part of the answer is that the Greeks wanted Cyprus in. We should not forget the fact that for a while Cyprus wanted to be the next Switzerland, and the Europeans took this seriously.

Cyprus was perfectly located for that purpose. It was just off the coasts of Israel, Lebanon, and Syria and close to North Africa, Turkey, the Balkans, and Italy. Anyone could come there if they had money, and over the years it was a notorious place for intelligence operatives to spy on each other. It was also a crossroads for money: Arab, Russian, Iranian, Israeli. Spies and money mingle well.

Cyprus tried to create a banking and corporate system modeled on Switzerland's and Liechtenstein's. Secret bank accounts were available for sizable deposits, and there were also corporations whose owners couldn't be traced. That's why a lot of Russians were there. They were visiting their money. Obviously, this drove the development of tourism, as well as other things, like the shipping of oil to places like Syria before the civil war.

The decision of the Cypriots to join the EU always puzzled me. Obviously the EU was going to shut down the secret banking and corporate operations. This is one of the reasons that Switzerland avoided the EU. Even though they had scaled back their operations dramatically, they still did not want to be subject to Brussels. In talking to Cypriots, it seems they simply believed in the glitter of the EU. Joining in 2004, and adopting the euro in 2008, Cyprus obviously thought that giving up control of its banking system was worth the economic benefits of membership. Switzerland couldn't be Switzerland if it joined the EU. Cyprus couldn't become another Switzerland if it joined. But the excitement of being a member seemed to have swept away all logic.

Unraveling secret corporations and banking was difficult. Bankers and lawyers liked the business, and depositors frequently had no other place to move the money. It was therefore true in 2008 that there was still some shady business going on in Cyprus. But there was also a developing economy that was increasingly defining banking. Then, along with others in Europe, Cyprus went into a financial crisis in which it was unable to service its sovereign debt. There were, as always, two choices. One was to help the Cypriots pay. The other was to force them to pay.

The Germans opted for the second one, but in the case of Cyprus, unlike the Greeks and others, the Germans meant it. The government didn't have the money. The EU forced the Cypriot government to freeze all bank accounts and seize assets worth more than 100,000 euros in individual accounts. Just under half the money seized was never returned, but was converted to shares in banks that were nearly insolvent.

Like all countries, Cyprus had its criminals, and the EU knew perfectly well that its financial system was a haven for them. The Germans hinted that they were in favor of confiscating deposits from the Russian Mafia. According to one estimate, illegal funds made up about a third of the confiscated money. But two-thirds of the deposits were by Cypriot businesses and individuals. While 100,000 euros is a lot of money, it is not so much that a private citizen couldn't have saved it for retirement or sold a house and deposited the proceeds. In reality the EU was seizing money from ordinary citizens, from many local Cypriot and Greek businesses, along with foreign money, much of it legitimate. The Cyprus government used the money to pay European banks holding Cypriot paper.

This action unleashed chaos in Cyprus. Companies couldn't meet payrolls, people's retirement plans were ruined, and businesses pulled money out of Cyprus to prevent further loss. Tourism, on which the country depended, was hit hard as hotels and restaurants lost their capital. We heard of one case where a hotel lost 6 million euros that have not been recovered. For weeks while the accounts were frozen the staff were not paid, and then received only 75 percent of their salaries. The European banks got paid, but at the cost of severely damaging the Cypriot economy and smashing the lives of ordinary Cypriots. To date, much of the confiscations have not been rescinded.

The Germans pressed the confiscation because they needed to send a message about the dangers of defaulting, but without actually hurting a major European country. They couldn't do this to Spain or Greece or Hungary because those countries would refuse to cooperate, and the Germans couldn't afford a threat to the free-trade zone. Cyprus was not only marginal to the EU, but also tied up in the complex politics of partition with Turkey, with a large Russian presence and a significant level of corruption and inefficiency. Like the rest of southern Europe it had a high unemployment rate, approaching 15 percent at the time of the crisis and later rising to 20 percent, and a shadow economy not producing tax revenue, with black money circulating. Cyprus was southern Europe in its most extreme form. It was weak, and it couldn't resist. Through Cyprus the EU delivered a message, demonstrating its ability to compel actions that ran against the obvious interest of the country.

An interesting dimension of this was the willingness of the Cypriot political leadership to comply with the basic EU demand that Cyprus choose bone-breaking austerity over default. Its leaders were eager to remain part of the European Union, to the point where they both agreed to the confiscation of bank deposits and implemented the decisions. This cooperation was the most important thing socially and politically.

The political and economic elites' interest in remaining part of the EU overrode everything else.

The fact is, most of the elites did not have their net worth in savings accounts. The impact of their decisions was greater on the middle class and small businesses that had a large part of their net worth in banks. The EU's strategy was to make not Cyprus but the middle class pay those debts. The government complied because on the whole remaining in the EU made sense. But while it might have made sense on the whole, looking at GDP figures without differentiating by class, it made little sense to the middle class, whose interests were overridden.

Cyprus represented the dynamic of the Mediterranean region as a whole. Germany insisted that the debtor solve its sovereign debt problem, and the debtor's only option was transferring assets to northern European banks. The political and economic elite in Cyprus wanted to remain within the EU structure, and was therefore prepared to enforce the agreements, resulting in tension between the elite and the masses, and a massive decline in confidence both in the EU and their own government. And as part of the backstory, there was tension between Greek Cypriots and Muslims. Many Cypriot businesses, particularly in the service industry, have adopted a policy of hiring only Cypriot workers, thus forcing the large number of foreigners (many of them Muslims from non-EU countries) trying to live and work in Cyprus into either poverty, crime, or having to leave the island.

The same pattern repeated itself through Mediterranean Europe, from Spain to Greece. Very different countries faced the same problem: a debt crisis, austerity demanded by the outside and enforced by their own governments, and the emergence of anti-EU, anti-immigrant parties that saw their own government as the problem. It extended beyond Muslims. In Spain there was a secessionist movement in Catalonia. In Italy, France, and Greece there were right-wing political parties emerging. In all these countries, the immigrants—who happened to be Muslims this time around—were seen as threats to national identity and to scarce jobs. The Roma were also hated, not because they were taking jobs but because they were seen as an uncontrollable criminal element.

Tension in Europe between north and south is not new. There is a profound difference, and the tension between them is played out in financial crises. But it is not something that leads to war between the north and south. The geography for war isn't there, and the Mediterranean region can't engage the north in war. Nevertheless, the south can't avoid significant instability internally. When your unemployment rate is over 25 percent, not including those whose wages have been slashed but still have their jobs, you have created a situation where middle-class professionals like physicians or engineers who work for the state have their lives ruined. That has consequences.

The first is the increased rift within the EU between north and south. Second are the growing tensions between the pro-EU elite and the broader masses that range from those dubious about the EU to those who are outright hostile. Northern Europe has two relationships with the south: one with the political and economic elites, and one with the masses. But in the end, no matter what the elites want, their room for maneuvering will contract.

Because of the economic situation, the wild card in the south will be Muslim immigrants. The tensions underlying the European idea of the nation-state will be tremendously exacerbated by unemployment. There will also be increased tension between radical political parties and mainstream parties. Some of these radical parties will be on the Left, but the most powerful ones will be on the Right because they will exploit anti-immigrant feeling. In Europe, when class and racial tensions coincide, instability results.

It is not that southern Europe is more sensitive to immigrants than the north. It is probably less sensitive. Denmark is probably more uncomfortable with immigrants and Muslims than any Mediterranean country. Indeed, the Mediterranean countries are a borderland between Europe and the Islamic world and are in many ways more comfortable with the current movement north. But their economic condition is extreme, and more moderate views of immigration will tend to erode.

The instability that will result here may spread north if the economic problems spread. They will not result in war between nations, but war within nations, between mass and elite, and between ethnic groups. Mediterranean politics has always had a softness to it. Part of it came from a culture, if not of toleration, then of inaction. There is a willingness to endure things that would be unendurable in the north. Consider our need for the Cyprus coast guard and the soft response of our boat captain. When I asked him if he would report the infraction, he shrugged, not helplessly, but indulgently. They needed coffee. He understood.

Some of this comes from being on the edge of Europe. Those in the south are European, but they are outsiders in some ways. The maniacal efficiency of northern Europeans, the culture of work as life, is not compatible with those of their Arab neighbors across the Mediterranean, with whom they have fought and traded for millennia. This is a trading culture, not an industrial one, and a trading culture has a profoundly different tempo. When you bargain in southern Europe, it is a social event that can take a day, with both parties enjoying the experience. In the north, the price is posted and nonnegotiable.

But a trading culture, like Venice in the sixteenth century, can be fabulously wealthy. That is not the case right now with Mediterranean Europe. Here, more than elsewhere in Europe, the idea of peace and prosperity is in danger. Peace depends on prosperity, and that prosperity is waning. And another power from outside the European Union is both emerging and facing uncertain times: Turkey.

14

Turkey on the Edge

Many people don't think of Turkey as European, but as the western extension of Asia. This is a mistake. Apart from geology—Turkey is on the European tectonic plate—Turkey, or its predecessor the Ottoman Empire, has been deeply involved in Europe for centuries. The empire extended deep into the European peninsula and shaped European history as much as any European power did. It was the enemy of some powers in Europe, an ally of others. Its history was as much European as anyone else's.

Europeans have viewed the Turks as alien for two reasons. First, they were primarily Muslim rather than Christian, and therefore not fully European. Second, it was the Ottoman Empire that destroyed Byzantium, the successor to the Eastern Roman Empire that Constantine founded. When the Turks seized Constantinople in 1453, they appeared to the Europeans as a threat to its civilization, much as the barbarian hordes threatened and brought down the Roman Empire. They were dangerous outsiders to Europe. Being Muslim and having smashed into European history have rendered them alien in European minds to this day.

Yet not all of Europe regarded them as unwelcome intruders, even in 1453. European Christianity was split between the Western Catholic Church and the Eastern Orthodox Churches. The dispute was bitter and deeply political. The Ottomans had a tradition of religious tolerance, if not as a moral principle, then as a political one. Building an empire involved more than defeating enemy armies. It involved governing, and the Ottomans understood that governing allies was easier than govern-

ing enemies. After the fall of Constantinople they granted the Orthodox religious freedom and allowed their institutions to continue. There
was no forced conversion. The Catholics were horrified at the barbaric
Ottomans sweeping into Europe, and concerned about the possibility of
increasing Orthodox influence sponsored by the Ottomans. The Orthodox adapted. The Catholics recoiled. The Orthodox and Muslims had
theological issues, but dealt with each other in a far more pragmatic way.

The Ottoman penetration of Europe, and the entire region, needs to
be understood and appreciated.

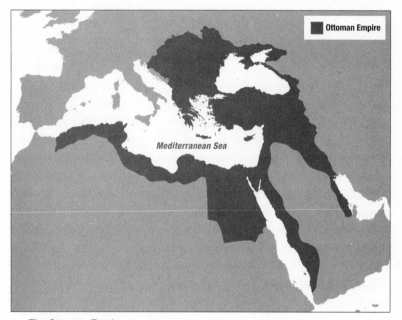

The Ottoman Empire

At the height of their empire, Ottomans controlled North Africa, the
Nile basin, the Red Sea, and the lands west of Persia. They had also penetrated deeply into Europe, beyond Budapest and nearly to Vienna and
Krakow. This was partly by conquest, but also by engaging in regional
politics with allies. But for a century, Budapest was an Ottoman city.

There is a synagogue in Budapest two blocks from where I was born
called the Dohany Utca Templom—Tobacco Street Synagogue. It is the

largest in Europe. *Dohany* is the Turkish word for tobacco. The Hungarians borrowed that from the Turks as well as much of the architecture of the synagogue, which is an amalgam of styles from various conquerors of Hungary. The style is a mixture of Turkish (called, for obvious reasons, Byzantine), Moorish, Gothic, and other things. It is a hodgepodge of styles, but when looked at, it is more Turkish than anything else. Although it was built in the nineteenth century, the synagogue reflects the fact that Budapest was conquered by the Ottomans in 1541 and remained in their hands for more than a century. The Ottomans tolerated the Jews and the synagogue's architecture was a reflection of that.

There is a prayer from the fifteenth century: God save us from the Devil, the Turk, and the comet. The devil is understandable, and a great comet terrified Europe in the fifteenth century. The Turks terrified them even more. They threatened to conquer far more than they already had. The Catholics were terrified, and this was a Catholic prayer. But even that is too simple. In seeking to dominate the Mediterranean, they became allied with the great naval power of the time, Venice. Venice was Catholic and the Ottomans were Muslim, yet strategy was strategy and business was business. Both managed to swallow their religious scruples. And as you will recall, it was Ottoman control of the Silk Road that caused the Iberians to begin the European conquest. There was little in Europe that the Ottomans didn't help shape.

Turkey is European in another sense. Just as its culture infused Europe, Europe has had a profound effect on Turkey. When the Ottoman Empire collapsed after World War I, what remained was the Anatolian Peninsula, Istanbul, and the eastern mountains. Kamal Ataturk took two complementary directions. One was toward founding a nation-state to replace a multinational empire, following the model created by the European Enlightenment. Second, he made the state secular, so that the distinction between public and private became central, and the religious dimension was made part of private life. He remodeled a Muslim state to reflect contemporary European values.

Obviously, Turkey is more than just a European country. It is also a borderland between Europe and the Islamic world. In itself, it melds both dimensions. As a bridge, it continues the Ottoman role of being the transit point between Europe and the Islamic world, economically, politically, and intellectually. It is the translator, not always an effective one, not always a highway without detours and heavy tolls. Still it serves its historical function as well as it can, while obviously seeking to profit from the role. Turkey is no different from any other place in the world. The role of the middleman must bring profit, and the Turks are middlemen, seeking to keep a foot in both worlds, not merely straddling the two worlds, but genuinely belonging to both.

At the Grand Bazaar in Istanbul you can see the melding of the two. It is not simply for tourists, as such places usually are, but citizens of Istanbul come here as well. You can buy goods from Germany, and rugs from Iran. When you enter a shop you are offered a chair and a cup of tea and are looked at with the appraising eye of a man whose DNA came from centuries of men (all men) who sized up customers and readied them for the kill. This is where the Silk Road ended and where the sea lanes to Italy began. It is neither Asian nor European. It is Turkish, but anyone with money is welcome and any language is spoken. It encapsulates what Constantinople, now Istanbul, was and is—the commercial and cultural gateway of Asia to Europe, presided over by Turkey.

The Ottoman Empire's crack troops were called Janissaries. These soldiers, first organized in the fourteenth century, were recruited from Christian families. The key wasn't religion but loyalty to the Pasha. That was guaranteed by both the wages they were paid and the opportunities to rise in power during and after their service. The Ottomans built their power on Christian-born soldiers. It was these soldiers who conquered Europe as far as Buda. The dependence on Christian-born troops to maintain the Ottoman Empire is closely linked to another fact: every Ottoman sultan, save Osman, the founder, was born to a mother who had not been born a Muslim but had converted to it. These were both ways to hold together a diverse empire.

Turkey hasn't been Christian in centuries. That's what strains the Europeans in trying to think of Turkey as European. For all the secularism of Europe, Europe is still the place where Christianity is the religion to reject. To rebel against religion requires that there be a religion to rebel against. In Europe it is for the most part Christianity. Turkey is the place where secularists reject Islam. This has not proven to be a bridge between the two, but a barrier. The underlying religion, declared to be obsolete and dying, still defines both places.

There are two Turkeys. One is Istanbul, the other is the rest of Turkey.

The rest of Turkey is still conservative and Muslim. Istanbul is secular. That, of course, overstates it. Istanbul is a world city, astride one of the critical waterways, the Bosporus Straits, which connect the Mediterranean to the Black Sea. Istanbul is both the bridge between Turkey and the European peninsula, and the bridge between the Mediterranean world and Russia. It is a pivotal city divided by the Bosporus.

Istanbul is a commercial center. The Grand Bazaar represents its older, merchant-based economy. The downtown district represents a newer melding of commerce and industry. Istanbul, and Constantinople before it, was a cosmopolitan city. People of many civilizations, believing many things, but all deeply committed to the art of making money, inhabited it. It therefore is made up of many strands of nationalities and beliefs, bound together by business. From small shopkeepers to senior bankers, it is the city where the deal is the most honored pastime. Such cities have a liberality built into them. It is the liberality of interest where judgments are not made of people who bring cash to the table.

That changed with the fall of the Ottoman Empire. The men who took over, led by Kamal Ataturk, understood that Turkey had to give up its empire and focus on the Anatolian Peninsula. It also understood that it had to become a modern state. Having lost the war to Europeans, Ataturk wanted to make Turkey European. From his point of view, European meant secular, with religion becoming a private matter and public life being devoid of religion and its trappings. In the case of Turkey this meant banning Islamic clothing in government positions and discouraging them in public as well.

Ataturk had a complex view of modernization. He wanted democracy, but he also felt that democracy could be destabilizing in a country undergoing the deep stresses of Turkey. For him there was another tool of modernization, the military. In some sense, the military is the most modern part of a developing country. Its social organization and technology can make it the most advanced institution, and I think that is what Ataturk had in mind. In practical terms, it meant that the military guaranteed—and defined—Turkish stability. He also saw that the military consisted of professionals in the European sense. They were skilled in their craft and followed the ethical imperatives of their profession. As such they were superior to professional politicians, whom Ataturk saw as corrupt and self-interested compared to the honest and duty-bound soldier. And they were superior to the rest of Turkish society, which had not been professionalized. Over the years the military intruded several times into the political process. The army was the guarantor of secularism, stability, and ethics, according to Ataturk's worldview. The military was also the guarantor of the European principle of professionalism and merit, and it was to be the model for Turkish society as a whole.

Ataturk influenced many other countries, including Iran under the shah and Egypt under Gamal Abdul Nasser. The model of secular, militarized states took hold in the region. But starting with the Iranian revolution, and slowly spreading to the Sunni world in the 1990s, the secular model was challenged by Islamic religiosity. In its most extreme forms you can look to Iran or al Qaeda. But throughout the Muslim world, the secular, militaristic state dominating society lost its allure. Partly, the West lost its allure. Partly, the Nasserite derivation of Ataturk's ideas didn't work. I suspect that the idea of a purely private realm that contained religion flew in the face of a people for whom family and clan constituted life itself, indivisible into public and private. Christianity still struggles with the distinction of public and private. It is secularism that has unreserved respect for it. Islam has never truly embraced the distinction, and the world Ataturk created came under pressure.

Turkey was the home of secularism in the Muslim world, but it is complicated even there. Turkey outside Istanbul was still conservative and religious. It was nationalistic, which bound it to Ataturkism, but never completely comfortable with it. In 2000, the Justice and Development Party (AKP) was formed, and in 2002 it won a landslide victory. The AKP was intended to speak for the Muslim majority, easing some of the secularist prohibitions (a woman wearing a head scarf could not work in a government office), while maintaining the desire to join the European Union, protecting secularists, and reining in the army. The secularist CHP party, which feared that beneath its apparent moderation, the AKP was in the process of creating an Islamic state, opposed it. In the superheated politics of Turkey, the claims and counterclaims flew.

We took a walk in a neighborhood in Istanbul called Carsamba. I was told that this was the most religious community in the city. One secularist referred to it as "Saudi Arabia." It is a poor but vibrant community, filled with schools and shops. Children play on the streets, and men cluster in twos and threes, talking and arguing. Women wear burkas and head scarves. There is a large school in the neighborhood where young men go to study the Koran and other religious subjects.

The neighborhood actually reminded me of Williamsburg in the Brooklyn of my youth, before it gentrified. Williamsburg was filled with Hassidic Jews, yeshivas, children on the streets, and men talking outside their shops. The sensibility of community and awareness that I was an outsider revived vivid memories. At this point, I am supposed to write that it shows how much these communities have in common. But the fact is that the commonalities of life in poor, urban, religious neighborhoods don't begin to overcome the profound differences—and importance—of the religions they adhere to.

That said, Carsamba drove home to me the problem the AKP, or any party that planned to govern Turkey, would have to deal with. There are large parts of Istanbul that are European in sensibility and values, and these are significant areas. But there is also Carsamba and the villages and cities of Anatolia, and they have a self-confidence and assertiveness that can't be ignored today.

There is deep concern among some secularists that the AKP intends to impose sharia. This is particularly intense among the professional classes. I had dinner with a physician with deep roots in Turkey who told me that he was going to immigrate to Europe if the AKP kept going the way it was going. Whether he would do it when the time came I couldn't tell, but he was passionate about it after a couple of glasses of wine. This view is extreme even among secularists, many of whom understand the AKP to have no such intentions. Sometimes it appeared to me that the fear was deliberately overdone, in hopes of influencing a foreigner, me, concerning the Turkish government.

But my thoughts go back to Carsamba. The secularists could ignore these people for a long time, but that time has passed. There is no way to rule Turkey without integrating these scholars and shopkeepers into Turkish society. Given the forces sweeping the Muslim world, it is impossible. They represent an increasingly important trend in the Islamic world, and the option is not suppressing them (that's gone) but accommodating them or facing protracted conflict, a kind of conflict that in the rest of the Islamic world is not confined to rhetoric. Carsamba is an extreme case in Istanbul, but it poses the issue most starkly.

Istanbul is a borderland between Europe and the Islamic world, and there is an internal struggle between European and Islamic values. The Europeanists want badly to join the European Union. It is not for economic reasons. Turkey's economy, while slowing now, has done remarkably well for a decade, much better than most of Europe for the past five years. Still, the Europeanists want to join the EU. They see it as a guarantor of secularism and liberal democracy. If they are members, then it will confirm they are European. The Islamists are more casual about it. They know, as the secularists do, that they will not be admitted. Admission will mean free movement, and free movement might mean more Muslim migrants. Europe can't live with that. The European Union is not going to happen, but the question of whether you support membership is the litmus test of the secularist community. The AKP will play their game as they have little to lose.

All this began with the fact that the Ottomans lost World War I. They lost the Arab lands to their south, they lost most of their possessions in the Balkans. They held on to the Anatolian Peninsula, which was the heart of the Ottoman Empire, and the place that ethnic Turks dominated. The true peninsula runs from the Georgian border on the Black

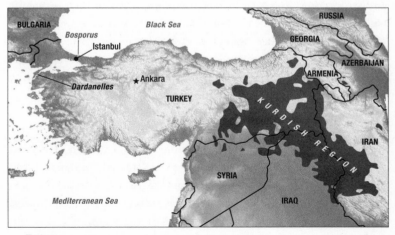

Turkey

Sea to Adana on the Mediterranean, on a steep diagonal. Turkey then stretches east into mountainous terrain bordering on Georgia, Azerbaijan, and Armenia in the north, Iran to the southwest, and Syria and Iraq to the south.

It is mountainous terrain, and the farther east you go the more mountainous it becomes. The surrounding water and the mountainous terrain are what make this into the heartland of the Ottoman Empire and its irreducible core. It is very hard to invade Turkey. It took the Ottomans over a century to take control of the Anatolian Peninsula.

The farther east or west you go, the less important the internal borderland of divergent and hostile groups becomes, and the more important the external borderland of nation-states. In the east, where Asia, the Arab world, and Europe mingle, there is ongoing tension, violence, war, and near war. The Kurdish region, Armenia, Iraq, Azerbaijan, and Syria all border Turkey, and parts of its Kurdish region extend into Iraq. The situation both outside and inside Turkey is characterized by ongoing violence. The farther west you go, to the Bosporus and the European peninsula, the less violence there is, but the political uncertainty is more serious.

The Turks' borders are filled with ethnic groups from across the border, remnants of history. The most significant group, the Kurds, are in the east. Kurds are a nation without a state. They live in Iraq, Iran, Syria, and Turkey, speaking their own language and without their own country. This is one of the fragile borderlands in the region. A single nation submerged in four other nations can constantly destabilize.

There are about 30 million Kurds living in the region. Over half live in Turkey. That means of the roughly 75 million Turks, 20 percent are Kurds. The fact that they are concentrated in the eastern part of the country and have relations with Kurds across the border makes them even more of a problem for Turkey.

Saladin lived in the twelfth century and was a great hero of Islam. He was sultan of Egypt and Syria and fought the Christian crusaders. Dante, in the *Divine Comedy*, ranked Saladin with Homer, Plato, and Julius Caesar as a greathearted non-Christian. He was a hero of Islam and held in awe by Christians. He was also descended from Kurds.

I point this out because it is odd that the Kurds lack their own state.

Following World War I there was serious discussion of the creation of a Kurdish state. It never happened. The basic reason is that none of the major regional powers—Iraq, Turkey, and Syria—wanted one. All of them saw security in borders deeply embedded in the mountains. A Kurdish state would have usurped the space in the central mountains. The Kurdish foreign policy was unpredictable, and there were a lot of Kurds. But a Kurdish state split along internal lines might have been usurped by one of the regional powers. Iran could thrust west into Turkey, Turkey into Iraq, and so forth. Or the Kurds might have grown strong and threatened all three. The Kurdish situation was unclear. Partitioning made sense—for Turkey, Iran, and Iraq.

As we have learned, nations don't go quietly into that good night, and the Kurds have certainly resisted. Living on the edge of Europe, they are an anomaly in many ways, but not in their willingness to resort to violence to assert their national rights. Within Turkey, there are frequently negotiations under way, occasional bombings by the main Kurdish group, the PKK (Kurdish Workers' Party), both in Istanbul and in the Kurdish region, raids by Turkish forces, and so on. The region is poor, Islamic, and hostile to the Turks. The Turks return the favor.

We spent a night in the Kurdish town of Dogubayazit, near the Iranian border. The Turks have decent relations with the Iranians, so when we drove to the border a few miles out of town, trucks were crossing easily, and I had a feeling we could have gone into Iran ourselves. Back in Dogubayazit, the situation was different. The town was much poorer than Erzurum, the last major Turkish town before the Kurdish regions. The change was palpable, on the sidewalks and the hotel.

We went to sleep by nine that night, with nothing else to do and not wanting to walk the streets at night, for no reason other than instinct. A little after lights out, there were two shots, perhaps a few blocks away. They were separated by a couple of seconds. It could have been celebratory fire, but there didn't seem much to celebrate, and that would have been a meager show of joy. It was not a car backfiring. It seemed to be a pistol fired twice. To me it sounded like an execution. I was told later by someone in the larger town of Van that it was not impossible, but likely not political.

The Silk Road lives. This time the product is heroin. It comes into

Turkey from Iran, smuggled by the Kurds, and is then transshipped
to Europe. As in all smuggling, the rules are enforced by the participants. What we thought sounded like an execution probably was, but
most likely about drugs, not politics. In borderlands, as I've said, there
is always something moving from one side of the border to another, in
order to increase value, and this was a very old trail. Who runs the trade
and makes the most money is not something I know or want to know.
But it is not enough to know the politics of this region. You must also
know the economics.

Kurdistan is not Turkey's only flashpoint in the east. The other is
Armenia. We visited a place called Ani on the Turkish side of the border.
It was the medieval capital of Armenia, the first Christian country in the
world, and one that occupied eastern Turkey in the Middle Ages. Ani sits
on a flat, dry, and windy plateau across a river from Armenia. Turks are
excavating the site, much to the anger of the Armenians. When the Ottoman Empire fell and the Turks had to define defensible boundaries, there
was inevitably ethnic cleansing, in which vast numbers of Armenians
were killed. The Armenians have not forgotten it. The Turks will not
admit it, and they make claims of their own about Armenian behavior.
As in Europe, memories are long and a hundred years hardly counts. The
ancient capital is in Turkish hands and Armenia can't do much about it.

As you go northwest from Ani, you arrive at the city of Kars. It is Turkish but the buildings look Russian. In fact the Russians had occupied the
entire region—Armenia, Ani, and Kars—until World War I. During the
war, the Ottomans fought the Russians, who deployed a large force in
Sarikamis in the Allahuekber Daglari, a mountainous region in Turkey
not far from the Russian border. The Turks sent about ninety thousand
troops to attack the Russians in the winter of 1914–15. The battle lasted
about a week, and almost eighty thousand of the Turkish troops died,
according to locals who described it to me one night. They froze to death.
Whether it happened in one night or a few doesn't matter. The slaughter
of the thirty-one years happened here as well. We were still in Europe.

A cousin of a friend in Istanbul met us in the town of Gole (pro-
nounced *Gole-ee*), about an hour's drive from Kars. He took us out at
night through the dirt roads and bare hills of northeastern Turkey to
a small village to meet a man who he said was 110 years old. The man,
who could barely see or hear, was a Laz, a Turkish Georgian, and there

were four generations living in his two-story home built into the side of a hill. His son, who was in his sixties, worked in the town, and his grandson, probably in his early forties, was the muhtar, or leader, of the village. His great-grandson was about four years old, shy but fascinated by these strangers in his home. The Laz were Georgians from the south Caucasus, and there were many more in this village and neighboring villages, living in this remote area under control of Russia, and now under Turkey. This was the wealthiest family in the village because they owned fifty cows. Here borders meant little, and whoever ruled the region at the time was welcome as long as they didn't interfere with local lives.

After our third cup of tea the door opened, and in came the wife of the old man's son, a sturdy woman probably in her sixties. She proudly told us that she had been out tending the cows. They were her responsibility, and they had the most cows of anyone in the village. What she lacked in teeth she made up for in personality and warmth, and the family obviously revolved around her. Despite the remoteness of the area, they had satellite Internet and could get online to find out what was happening beyond their line of hills. Whether the old man was ninety or 110 I have no way of knowing, but this four-generation family knew they were well-off and were proud of it, and proud to show it to strangers from America.

It's worth telling another story from this trip. While visiting Kars and the site of the astounding Battle of Sarikamis, we drove through a valley deserted except for a handful of villages. The villages did not resemble modern Turkey or any surrounding nation. They weren't poor. They were from another time. Their source of energy was dung from the few cattle they owned, and that was their wealth. There were no trees or peat. The dung was piled and shaped like huts, and the piles had symbols embossed on them that I couldn't identify. It was late on a Saturday afternoon, and old women were decorating the piles.

In each village we visited, one house had a clean modern tractor in front of it. That was odder than the dung sculptures, perhaps. Some government program or another had supplied the tractors. But no one supplied electricity or other power and these were the mountains in which eighty thousand men froze to death. We were now on the edge of Europe. The people lived there quietly, tolerating things that Europeans no longer could.

The Silk Road moves not only drugs, but oil as well, and that also involves the Kurds. The war in Iraq fragmented the country. One of the fragments is the Kurdish region in the northeast of Iraq, by Iran and Turkey. It was long known that there was oil there, but no one was prepared to go into Saddam's Iraq to extract it. Once his regime collapsed, the Kurdish region developed a great deal of autonomy, and oil companies began to undertake the risk of extraction.

This put Turkey into an odd position. On the one hand, they were deeply opposed to Kurdish independence. On the other, they were eager to develop sources of energy other than Russia, on whom they are deeply dependent. They saw a Kurdish regional government as a useful instrument for some of their energy needs, but a dangerous precedent for Kurdish nationalism.

The point here is not to examine Turkish energy strategy but to consider the complexities of its Kurdish policies and the manner in which one interest collided with another. There was ideological tension between Iraq and Turkey's Kurds, but they were still Kurdish, and the Kurds in Turkey were attracted by both the autonomy of the Iraqi Kurds and the commercial possibilities. The Turks were and are walking a tightrope.

The Turks walked a similar tightrope in Turkey when a civil war broke out in Syria. They were hostile to the regime led by Bashar al-Assad, a secular government led by members of the Alawite sect. They supported the Sunnis, who were rising against him. But the Sunnis themselves were split, and some factions were extreme jihadists, like the Islamic state. The Turks handled the war gingerly, afraid that it might spill over into Turkey.

All along their eastern and southern borderlands, the Turks proceeded with extreme care. Nothing was simple either in the Caucasus, among the Kurds in Turkey, or the Kurds in Iraq or Syria. They were surrounded by a crescent of instability, sometimes containing seductive opportunities, sometimes only dangers. This crescent was actually one of the boundaries of Europe. To the east was Iran, to the south the Arab countries, none of them European. Here on the edge of Europe, everything was unstable and frequently violent. It was spilling into Europe, and with Turkish immigration, it was moving to some extent into the European peninsula.

During the Cold War, one of the most sensitive potential flashpoints was to the west—the Bosporus and the piece of the European peninsula that Turkey had retained. The Soviets were obsessed with this strait. The

Bosporus, the Sea of Marmara, and the Dardanelles had been a Russian obsession as far back as the eighteenth century. The Mediterranean was the prize, the richest ocean basin in the world, with one last chokepoint keeping the Russian navy out. If the Russians had the straits, they would have access to the Mediterranean and stop being a poor land power. They would transform themselves into a wealthy maritime power and their navy would compete with the British, French, and all the others who crowded there. Unless they had the straits, they would always be guests in the Mediterranean, there only when the Turks or another major naval power let them pass.

The heart of American strategy was the containment of the Soviet Union. One of the indispensable parts of that was making certain that Turkey and Greece did not come under Soviet control. At the same time, Turkey and Greece were sometimes nearly at war over control of islands in the Aegean, the Cyprus crisis, and ancient hatreds.

All that is gone for the moment. The Russians use the Bosporus for shipping oil, and the Turks are buying it. The Greeks are in deep crisis and have no appetite for conflict with Turkey. Along the boundary line of the Anatolian Peninsula, it is quiet and it can remain that way. The same can't be said for the northeastern borders of Turkey and the southern borders of Russia, where the Caucasus Mountains are. For the moment the Mediterranean is no longer a battlefield, save for occasional actions by and against Israel.

However, the Mediterranean is incapable of staying quiet for too long. The ocean and the land that surrounds it are too valuable and too troubled. The tension between the United States and Russia, with a possibly reenergized North Africa facing a fractious and less prosperous southern Europe, opens opportunities for conflict.

But the most important element is that Turkey is rising—not necessarily in a straight line, but it is getting stronger while many of the countries around it are either weakening or in conflict. The idea of a return to the Ottoman Empire is an explosive concept in Turkey, particularly among secularists who see it as shorthand for sharia. However sensitive that notion might be, the power of Turkey is increasing, and over time that power will affect Europe, both in the Caucasus and the Balkans, more than all the Turkish and other Muslim immigrants.

15

Britain

When you stand on the cliffs at Dover, you can pretend to see France and the European peninsula in the distance; I never actually have. You can also pretend to hear the rumble of traffic in the Channel Tunnel underneath your feet. This is the British paradox. On the surface, the English Channel guards the approaches to Britain as it always has, keeping the European peninsula at bay. But the Tunnel now binds Britain to the European peninsula, ignoring the Channel. This paradox crystallizes the fundamental question in British history and strategy: Precisely what was its relation to the peninsula? And the story of the peninsula's future depends at least partly on the answer to that question.

Step back from the Channel and see the entire picture. The Channel connects the Atlantic, the path to empire, and the North Sea, which connects the British Isles with Scandinavia; these are two parts of Europe that are not part of the peninsula, with linked cultures built around Protestantism and the sea. The Normans—or Norse—conquered Britain from France by crossing the Channel in 1066, and redefined England in the process. The British were intimately involved with Scandinavia, the Netherlands, and Belgium, and, for centuries, France. I think of Royal Dutch Shell and dozens of other companies that are Anglo-Dutch. It isn't enough to think of the English Channel in defining Britain's relationship with the peninsula. We must also think of the North Sea and the EFTA, which we discussed earlier—an alternative to the European Community founded by Britain and built around the North Sea.

The North Sea basin draws this part of Europe away from the peninsula, toward the land surrounding it. It is small in terms of population. It does not have sufficient wealth or resources to sustain Germany, but it can draw Denmark, the Netherlands, and a bit of France into a relationship that is an alternative to those they have on the peninsula. Simply in this sense it is a further force fragmenting the European peninsula, not definitively but still another strain on unity.

Britain is by far the most populous and most powerful nation in the region. It has for centuries been the flywheel of the peninsula. Where the peninsula was always focused inward, watching for threats from nearby nations, Britain, surrounded by the sea, developed a global perspective. It was part of the peninsula's affairs, but electively. It involved itself as and when it needed to, unlike France or Germany, who could never choose to ignore what was happening nearby. It controlled its economic and military relationship with them, and in so doing, could frequently define what was happening on the peninsula for its own interest, an interest that always involved encouraging the peninsula's inwardness and tension.

There are many reasons why Europe never united. The North Sea is far from the most significant of these, but the most important reason is nearby. The English Channel, dividing Britain from the European peninsula, is probably the most important reason. It is a narrow body of water, and its narrowness makes it treacherous. The waters from the Atlantic and the North Sea rush in and out of it depending on the tide, making navigation difficult. The weather is cold, wet, windy, yet changeable. It is difficult to cross in either direction.

In June 1944, when the Allies invaded Normandy, the primary consideration in the days before the invasion was the weather and its effect on the Channel. One of the very real military considerations was seasickness. The rough waters of the Channel would likely make infantrymen seasick in their transports and landing craft and unable to fight when they got ashore. The Allies needed optimal conditions for the landing, but they didn't get them. A series of Atlantic storms blew in, and the invasion slipped in between them. The invasion succeeded in spite of mass nausea.

Britain has been successfully invaded, by both the Romans and the Normans. But that was long ago. Since the sixteenth century the Channel has withstood all serious attempts to invade Britain. It defeated the

Spanish in the sixteenth century, Napoleon in the nineteenth century, and Hitler in the twentieth. All had overwhelmingly powerful armies. None had the ability to cross the Channel, land troops, and sustain them. However, it was not just the waves that challenged invaders. For Britain, it was the Royal Navy that preserved the kingdom.

The origin of the Royal Navy had more to do with stealing Spanish treasure than with grand strategy. As wealth flowed to Spain on the Spanish Main from South America, the English had two reasons to be interested. First, the amount being shipped to Spain was staggering, and raiding was lucrative. Second, the growth of the Spanish navy was a direct threat to England. If the Spanish navy could dominate the Atlantic, they could dominate the waters around Britain. If that happened, England was indefensible.

What emerged over time was the most powerful navy in Europe, and after the defeat of Napoleon's navy at the Battle of Trafalgar, the British navy was the only truly global navy in the world. This was the foundation on which Britain built its empire. By the end of the nineteenth century, the British Empire was the largest part of the European imperial system, and it was the British navy that both policed the empire and, most important, kept sea lanes open so that trade within the empire, and between the empire and the rest of the world, could flow.

The security of Britain—the union of England, Scotland, and Ireland, and later just England and Scotland when all but Northern Ireland broke away—depended on maintaining command of the sea. If it lost that, it lost the empire. The best way to defeat an enemy fleet was to prevent the enemy from building one. The best way to prevent them from building one was to make sure that resources were devoted to land warfare rather than building fleets. And the best way to achieve that was to do whatever was necessary to make certain that the peninsula powers distrusted each other. Since the nations of the peninsula really did distrust each other, it took minimal effort for the British to sustain the distrust, shifting their support from one power to the other in an endless balancing act, using peninsula preoccupation to secure Britain.

There was, of course, a problem with this strategy. It didn't always work. Periodically there arose powers that broke out of the system of containment and threatened to dominate the peninsula permanently and threaten Britain. Spain, France, and Germany almost succeeded. In the extreme case, the diplomatic and economic balancing was insufficient, and British command of the sea was, in the long run, threatened. At that point the British had to intervene on the ground.

Britain had a relatively small army that it tried to use as a precision weapon, not fighting extended campaigns but, as at Waterloo, adding the decisive measure to a limited battle that would undermine the rising power. The downside of this strategy was that the enemy could not always be managed with precision. In World War I and World War II, Britain was drawn into a massive war of attrition that ultimately, as we have seen, undermined the strategy and broke British power.

George Orwell once defined the British as "a dull, decent people, cherishing and fortifying their dullness behind a quarter of a million bayonets." A quarter-million bayonets was not much in a continent where millions of bayonets were in use. But what is interesting was that Orwell, who had a superb eye, saw the British as dull and decent. He valued the decency and wasn't bothered by dullness. Still, this was the British view of themselves, but it contains a vast paradox.

For centuries the British manipulated the statesmen of Europe, earning the name "perfidious Albion." Europeans saw their role in Europe as the cold-blooded pursuit of their self-interest without regard to promises and commitments. Hence the term *perfidious*. But even more, behind the manipulative shield the British built an empire. The British dominated hundreds of millions of Indians through alliances, manipulation, guile, and minimum force. They worked their way into a prevailing economic position in China. They dominated the Islamic world. It is hard to see them as dull, and to many they were far from decent. British history was filled with brilliance, cunning, and ruthlessness. Yet Orwell saw them as dull and decent. What was he talking about?

George Bernard Shaw wrote, in *Caesar and Cleopatra*, that Britannus, responding to a description by Theodotus about the rules of marriage in Egypt, says, "Caesar, this is not proper," enraging Theodotus. Caesar tries to calm Theodotus by saying, "Pardon him Theodotus. He is a barbarian and thinks that the customs of his tribe and island are the laws of nature."

The British had conquered much of the world. Every conceivable cul-

ture was contained within their empire. Yet the British remained profoundly provincial. Unlike the Persians, Romans, and Greeks, who had
also created empires, the British did not simply believe in the superiority
of their culture. They went further in believing that its smallest habits
defined civilization. Britannus is shocked at Egyptian royal marriage
customs. It is not simply surprise at differences, but the perception that
decency is being violated. Caesar, a proud Roman, recognizes the pro-
vincialism of Britannus. Every society has its customs and these customs
vary. But the British sometimes seem to believe that in spite of this variation, their customs are the only way it is appropriate to live.

I recall early in my career attending a dinner at a famous British university. I had grown up in a house where eating was a simple matter of
a fork and knife and sometimes a spoon if appropriate. I was stunned
by the complexity of British rituals for eating. What had been a simple
act for me was for the British a complex ritual full of rules that were
completely alien and arbitrary. I had never seen so many utensils, some
whose use was opaque, nor had I ever encountered their etiquette for eating soup, complex and time-consuming. It was assumed, not unkindly,
that anyone sitting at that table, having been educated properly, must
have mastered the proper way of eating. Baffled by what I could touch
with what, and the angle my head should be at while I lifted soup to my
mouth, and the direction the soup should move in the bowl, I made a
mess of it. My hosts were kind and made no mention of the fact that I
was obviously uncultured.

I later married a woman from that part of Australian society that
still takes its bearings from England, and who continued to see the table
manners she had been raised with as the laws of nature. In time we compromised, and I learned to eat as she preferred. She knew that these were
merely customs, yet could not shake the feeling that following them was
the only cultured way to eat. Of course, when she isn't looking, I still
drink my soup from the bowl.

She is far from dull. The dullness of the British that Orwell spoke of
is hard to fathom if you look at their history. But that dullness is what
gave them imperial power. The British accepted that there were many
cultures, and they were interested in all of them. But they believed, in
their souls, that even as trivial a matter as eating soup was not merely
their custom, but the law of nature.

The British clinging to their culture as if it were natural law seemed provincial, the behavior of a barbarian, but it created a fabric of rules that not only bound them together but also helped reshape their colonies in their own image. There was tremendous power in the British dullness. Their unwillingness to countenance variation on customs of everyday life was unimaginative, yet it forced those in the world who wanted to emulate the powerful English to adopt behavior that penetrated the depths of being. Feeling breathtakingly inadequate at a dinner had a power of its own. It was a far more decent weapon of empire than brute force.

The British created the North American colonies in their own image. Even those who were radical dissenters dissented in a very English way. In time, the United States became a challenge to both British culture and British power. America was Britain's first great imperial position. It also became its downfall. Part of it was cultural. The Americans institutionalized British philosophy, and the principles this created then flowed back to British institutions. But more than that, America was founded on immigration, and immigration was constantly changing American culture. Leaving aside the effect that postwar immigration has had on Britain, American culture, its informality and meritocracy, gnawed away at Britain in ways it did not bother the peninsula. Part of the reason was that British insularity and dullness could not survive the growing power of the United States. We can see this in the British loss of control of the seas to the United States, which meant the loss of their empire.

The United States had the same interests as Britain. On a much greater scale than Britain, it was an island that had to be protected from invasion. The greatest threat to the United States was therefore the greatest naval power, Britain. The British had gone to war with the United States in 1812, and there had been periodic crises with the British over Oregon and during the Civil War. It is interesting to note that the United States had developed a series of war plans after World War I. One of them was War Plan Red, a plan for dealing with a British invasion of the United States from Canada. It was, of course, far-fetched, one of those meaningless contingency plans drawn up by military planning staffs. At the same time, the fact that it existed was noteworthy.

The British had no plan to invade the United States. But they were competing for the same body of water: the Atlantic. The United States, a major exporting power then, had to have access to the Atlantic. The British needed it for their empire. Intentions change and capabilities matter more. Though there was no real friction over this, the Americans were uneasy with British control of naval bases in the Western Hemisphere. The British were uneasy with the rise of American naval power since 1900.

Matters came to a head in World War II. The British were under tremendous pressure from Germany after the fall of France. The United States agreed to give the British fifty old destroyers. In return the British agreed to lease land and bases in the Western Hemisphere to the United States for ninety-nine years, including the eastern Bahamas, the southern coast of Jamaica, St. Lucia, western Trinidad, Antigua, parts of British Guiana, and basing rights in Bermuda and Newfoundland.

In return for fifty destroyers the British gave up their naval bases in the Western Hemisphere, eliminating any British threat to the United States as well as their ability to project power anywhere in the North Atlantic. The United States gave the British what they desperately needed, destroyers to fight the U-boat threat. In return for help in containing the Germans, the British allowed a shift in the balance of power with the Americans in the North Atlantic.

After the war, the United States became the first power to control all the world's oceans. It had expelled the Japanese from the Pacific— and the British and French as well. It now dominated the North Atlantic, and through NATO, what was left of the Royal Navy was, in part at least, under American command. This was the end of the British Empire. It was a maritime empire, and the British no longer controlled the sea lanes. The Americans were not interested in securing the British Empire. Therefore, while there were many other reasons for the loss of empire, the fact that the Americans had taken advantage of Britain's plight in 1940 to expel it from North America was pivotal.

With the loss of empire, and U.S. domination of the western European peninsula, Britain became one nation among many. Although a victor in the war, the British lost their most important possessions. This transformed British behavior. Previously it had been focused on maintaining the balance of power. Now it turned to balancing its power between Europe and the United States. It was still balancing, but it was balancing in a more complex way.

Britain has maintained a complex relationship with the European peninsula since the loss of its empire, as discussed in previous chapters of this book. The complexity of the relationship isn't new. Britain has constantly been both intimate with the peninsula and distant from it. In the eighteenth century the European upper classes emulated the French. By the late nineteenth, it was the British, including their dress and manners. This was partly due to the fact that most of Europe's royal houses housed Queen Victoria's offspring. But it was also because Britain was worth emulating. Its global power and industrial revolution made its customs appear magical. By emulating them, someone could share in their power. And by possessing ever more complex customs, customs that you could truly master only if you were born to them, the British upper class—and even the middle class—left the rest of Europe slightly off balance at best. At the same time young British gentlemen made the grand tour, worshipping Athens, Rome, and Paris, more for their history and poetry than for their current inhabitants. Like a marriage that doesn't quite work, the two sides were bound by a passion but divided by lesser matters such as respect, trust, and a sense of a common fate.

After the war the British lost their magic in the European peninsula along with their power. The new focus was on the United States and a profoundly different culture. The British seduced with the complex mystery of their culture. The Americans seduced with the casual openness of theirs. But where the British sought to limit the ability of foreigners and the lower classes to penetrate their culture, the Americans required a friendly but ruthless submission to a culture built around the type of reason embodied in a computer, lunches that were meant to fuel rather than be savored, and success that demanded nothing less than the total dedication of your life. Europeans wanted to live with their extended family. Americans go where their jobs are. My wife and I have four children; each lives in a different city and none in ours. They are American and their careers come first. And we understand because we are like them. Family becomes secondary to mobility in the pursuit of success.

Europeans were as seduced by the Americans as by the British. More so, in that American culture is open to all classes. And more so in that American culture rejects a polite distance. But less so because the demands of being like Americans, open to everyone, were overwhelming and absolute. And the British were caught in between.

During the economic crisis of 2008, the French and Germans spoke of the "Anglo-Saxon" approach to economic policy. Leaving aside their misunderstanding of American ethnicity in the twenty-first century, and leaving aside the ensuing disaster in the EU, it is important to note that the European peninsula places the British in the American camp, adopting American culture and the American economic model that is at the heart of American culture.

The Europeans see the British as different from them. The Americans see the British as different from themselves as well. The British see themselves as both unique and needing to have a foot in both camps. Economically, their biggest trading partner is the European Union as a whole. But the picture looks different if we look at Europe in terms of individual countries. In 2013, the United States purchased more British goods than any other country, buying 13.4 percent of its exports. Germany was second, buying 9.8 percent of its goods. The Netherlands, France, and Ireland followed these two. Together, Germany, the Netherlands, France, and Ireland buy 31 percent of Britain's exports. This means that almost one-third of Britain's exports go to countries with coasts opposite Britain. Another 10 percent of their exports go to Belgium and Scandinavia. Thus, about 40 percent of Britain's exports go to the North Sea basin.

The British, therefore, have two primary economic relationships. The first is in the North Sea basin and other waters surrounding Britain. This is, taken together, the largest relationship. However, in terms of individual countries, the United States is its most important customer. It is not the European Union that Britain depends on as the area that had historically been the core of its national security and influence. Economically, Britain has returned to its geographic core. But in so doing it has sustained its relationship with the United States, its best customer. The rest of the world, including China and the rest of Europe, makes up collectively half of Britain's markets.

The British clearly have no desire to get too deeply entangled with the European Union. They are part of it, but they keep their distance. The reason is not cultural but strategic. Britain no longer has the ability to manage the balance of power in Europe. But at the same time Europe's increasing fragmentation and contradictory needs will tend to draw Britain into circumstances that can damage it. It doesn't want to be dependent on the European Central Bank to sort things out, nor does it want to be caught in the political cross fire between peninsula countries. It is interested in Europe, but particularly interested in the Europe of the North Sea. That is where its most important relationships are. Membership in the European Union allows it easy access to these markets, within the normal pattern of free trade. That is the price of membership. But it is the free-trade zone, not a single currency and certainly not a United States of Europe, that the British are interested in.

To maintain this balance Britain maintains relations with its largest customer, the United States. But it does more than simply maintain an economic relationship. The British maintain a substantial military, substantial for Europe even after planned cuts. But what does all this amount to? The British military is not able to operate alone in most places. The role of the military is to create an American dependency on Britain and thereby give Britain a counterweight to the European Union. This was a process we saw during the last decade's U.S. wars in the Islamic world.

The British force is not trivial. Unlike those of other allies, it is far from symbolic. In particular, the British SAS, its special forces, have been critical in many operations. But the most important benefit for the United States is political. While the French and Germans opposed U.S. operations in Iraq, the British, as well as many smaller European countries, supported it. The British support provided a legitimacy to the alliance that was lacking otherwise.

The willingness of the British to operate in American wars has, of course, been criticized by many there, but the purpose it serves is not trivial. The French frequently speak of a special relationship with the United States, but it is more imagined than real. The British have a genuine special relationship with the United States that is based on British action. The British, therefore, can call on the United States, access American technology, and blend into American successes. In that sense, even though Britain is far from the largest economic power in the European Union, it can punch above its weight, as they say, because the United States is prepared to support it.

The British continue to balance and, as always, their balancing is complex. There are wheels within wheels, but the goal is ultimately the preservation of Britain's ability, to the extent possible, to secure British national interest without being uncontrollably drawn into circumstances it could not manage. Britain, as always, is trying to avoid disaster by manipulating its surroundings. In the end, Britain is manipulating the Americans, the French, the Germans, and the rest, never simply accepting domination. To preserve its power, it uses the strategy of following the American lead into wars. It uses membership in the European Union to guarantee access to markets without submerging itself in the markets.

Britain's danger comes not from its involvement in the European Union but from what it uses to balance Europe: the United States. Britain is a regional power. The United States is a global one. Britain is balancing between Europe and the United States, while the United States is balancing the regions and the global system as a whole. Britain is part of that balancing, and it preserves its room for maneuver by being useful to the United States. This means that Britain is constantly faced with the choice of playing a subsidiary role in American conflicts or losing its influence, and therefore its balance. Britain is in the unique position of needing to engage in conflict in order to indirectly retain its room for maneuver.

The kinds of conflicts that Britain used to engage in are gone. It will influence events on the peninsula but it will not be the decisive force at the end of conflicts. It may engage in peacekeeping in former colonies, but it will not be waging colonial wars. Northern Ireland might experience ethnic strife again, but Britain will not be waging wars to force Ireland to submit. That period of British history is done.

As a result, the English Channel will remain a quiet borderland, not a flashpoint.

As with the Rhine, the probability of conflict is low. But if the Belgians split, and if French politics take an extreme turn, with a far-right or far-left party taking control, the situation might become explosive. But those are great *ifs*. So long as the United States dominates the world's oceans and the British maintain their relationship with the Americans, the strange culture of Britain will endure, fairly peacefully, at least in its own neighborhood.

Britain's flashpoint, therefore, can be anywhere in the world, as was historically the case, but not necessarily of its own choosing. As the

Russian phase of the post–Cold War world intensifies, for example, the United States might find itself deployed on the borderland between Russia and the peninsula. If so, it is likely the British would find themselves next to the Americans. That will be the price it will pay to have a significant role in defining regions and the world after a conflict.

There is, however, one wild card: Scotland, conquered by England in the seventeenth century and drawn into the United Kingdom, whose flag combines the English cross of St. George and the Scottish Cross of St. Andrew. It has been a union in which the English have dominated but in which the Scottish grumbled yet saw little reason to rebel. The Scottish Enlightenment, focused on the practicalities of the market and technology, was the intellectual engine that drove the industrial revolution in Britain and elsewhere. It was also in Scotland that Britain participated in the North Sea oil boom.

There is now a movement for independence in Scotland. Forty-five percent of the vote in a referendum on independence supported leaving the United Kingdom, a startling amount. It reflects the basic revolutionary drive that has defined Europe, as every nationality group claims the right to self-determination and Europe fragments into smaller and smaller parts. The Scottish quest for independence is driven by perceived economic interest, rather than any fierce nationalism. And the British resistance also turns on economic issues, not on the powerful pride and anger that drove centuries of warfare.

What is remarkable is not that Scotland wants to regain its national sovereignty, but rather the lack of passion on both sides. We recall the velvet divorce of the Czechs and the Slovaks, but outsiders invented their unity after World War I. It was never a passionate marriage. But English and Scottish unity was forged in blood, with the Scots the defeated and the British the victor after many battles, intrigues, and betrayals. There ought to be a kind of nuclear energy between the two, the kind in which the massive energy binding an atom together is released in an explosion when the bond is broken. It's not there. Somewhere in the past few centuries, the English and the Scottish lost that energy. The Scottish might want to leave, and if they want, they will. But there is none of the anger and bitterness that there was when Ireland tore itself away from Britain, or during the troubles in Northern Ireland.

It would not be surprising if the Scottish left the Union, or if the

English made things difficult. It would not be surprising if there were no war. The English, as Orwell put it, are decent if dull. And the Scots have been deeply shaped by this. Still, even if there is no flashpoint here, the Scots may prove the rule that nationalism is alive and well in Europe. They may also prove the rule that all nationalism doesn't need to be driven by hatred of the other, as much as by love of one's own.

16

Conclusion

This book has asked three questions. First, how did Europe achieve global domination, politically, militarily, economically, and intellectually? Second, what was the flaw in Europe that caused it to throw away this domination between 1914 and 1945? Third, is the period of peace that followed 1945 what the future of Europe will look like, or will Europe return to its historical ways? The last question couldn't be answered without raising the first two, but answering that question is the real reason I wrote this book.

The short answer is that Europe's history of conflict is far from over. Europe's basic architecture remains the same, a small continent, fragmented into many parts and crowded with many nation-states. Some of these have put their history of resentment and bitterness behind them, but it has not been abolished. In some places it dominates, in some places it hides, but in many places Europe's anger against other Europeans is still there.

The period from 1945 to 1991 was a period of peace, but this was not a European achievement. The peace was imposed by the Americans and Soviets. The period from 1991 to 2008 *was* a European achievement, though it showed only that in a time of extraordinary prosperity and German preoccupation with reunification, Europeans could refrain from war. Even so, there were wars, only not in the heartland of Europe. The test for Europe will come now, after 2008, after the unreasonable expectations about the EU have been revealed for what they were, unease about Germany has spread, and Russia has reasserted itself. The outcome will define Europe, and it is hard to know how it will turn out.

I would not expect another conflagration like the thirty-one years. Europe is no longer the center of the international system or of global culture. The thirty-one years was fueled by the fact that no outside force could contain Europe. Today, the United States is more powerful, and just as it put out the European fire in 1918 and 1945 and contained it during the Cold War, it can do so today. Europe is now a place of small flashpoints, and small fires. A general war in Europe would surprise me. The lack of significant conflict, even between countries where conflict at the moment seems unthinkable, would surprise me even more. Europe is a normal place, and wars are not caused by a failure to learn from history or bad manners. They are caused by divergences of interest so profound that the consequences of not fighting are greater than the consequences of fighting. Over time these conflicts cannot be wished out of existence. Europe cannot escape the human condition by wishing to. This is a tragic truth, but it is, I think, a truth nonetheless.

Europe has lost its former place in the world. It is still a commercial power, but commerce, part of what some Europeans call "soft power," depends on national security—the ability to use the oceans and air freely, the willingness of others to allow you to trade, security for your investments overseas. Europe remains technologically and economically advanced. Relations with some European countries remain beneficial to others, and the ability to withhold these relations can harm other nations. This is not trivial power.

However, the ability to compel other nations to respect European investments and honor agreements all depends on expectations of future investments, future trade, and the rest. The hard power that European global economic power once rested on is gone. Powerful nations like China, Russia, and the United States offer the same benefits as Europe, but the consequences of violating agreements are greater. This may not matter at this moment, but as the global powers diverge and Europe is caught in the middle, the lack of hard power will matter more and more. Being rich and weak is a dangerous combination.

Europe therefore lives in a world with wolves. Some are already out there. Others are emerging. Individual countries like Germany, France, or Britain can play economically in this league, but most of Europe can't, and even those that can have only economic power. They can't compete with the United States, and that really is the most important thing to understand about Europe. Virtually any country that wishes to pose a military challenge can force the Europeans to try to buy their way out of the problem, ignore the problem in the hope it goes away, or capitulate, but not, at the moment, to fight.

The most important conflict has already emerged. It is the battle between the mainland and the peninsula for the borderlands between the two. The main struggle is for Ukraine, since the Baltics are already part of the EU and NATO. The origin of the battle is disputed. The West claims that there was a popular uprising against a corrupt and repressive president. The Russians claim that a legitimately elected president was ousted by a mob underwritten by the United States and Europe.

The truth of either position really doesn't matter. The reality is geopolitical. Ukraine is the buffer to Russia's south. If it becomes part of the European sphere of influence, Volgograd, the Stalingrad the Soviets spent a fortune in lives to defend, is less than two hundred miles from the Ukrainian border. If Ukraine allies with NATO, NATO would have come almost as far as Hitler had in World War II. And if Belarus to the north, sandwiched between the Baltics and Ukraine, were also to change regimes, Smolensk, a city that was at the center of the Russian Empire and the Soviet Union, would now be a border town. The entire European peninsula would be in potentially hostile hands.

The Russians understand that intentions can change quickly. Assume that Europe and the United States have only the most benign intentions. The Russians know from their history how quickly intentions and even capabilities change. Germany was weak, divided, and barely armed in 1932. By 1938 it was the prime military power on the peninsula. Both intentions and capabilities shifted at a dizzying rate. Russia remembers this and other affairs, like the Crimean War. It must assume the worst, as the worst usually happens.

Russia is not particularly powerful now. Its army is a shadow of what it was once. But that army is more powerful than any European military. It therefore doesn't need to invade. The shattered economy of Ukraine, the reluctance of Germany to challenge Russia, and the distance of the United States give Russia a huge advantage. Ukraine matters enormously to Russia. It matters to Europe as well, since Europe needs a buffer zone with Russia too. But it matters far less to the United States. The Europeans are on their own, and this is a case where economic power is not decisive. Not only does Ukraine matter too much to Russia to let economics get in the way, but in addition, Russia has a hammerlock on Europe. Europe must have Russian natural gas. And that comes with a political price.

Russia is trying to rebuild its buffers to the west. The Europeans and Americans would like to deny them those buffers so they can shape Russian behavior. But the lack of European military power makes it an uneven game. The nations along the second tier of the borderland— Poland, Slovakia, Hungary, Romania, and Bulgaria—had accepted the European belief that military power was archaic. But as Russian power moves westward, securing its buffer, the question for these countries is how far the Russians will go.

This question is answered by another: How weak is the eastern frontier of Europe? The Russians don't have to invade to achieve greater power. The Europeans' fragmentation and the weakness of NATO have left them exposed. The unsolved economic crisis in Europe leaves the east open to economic solutions. The Russians have the eighth-largest economy in the world. They have deep economic weaknesses, but it does not take a great deal of investment to benefit a country like Hungary or Slovakia. Simply drawing them into the Russian circle will create a situation where somewhat more powerful countries like Poland and Romania will be isolated and also need to accommodate Russia.

The logical solution for these countries would be to increase their defense capabilities. But this would be a thin alliance. It would cover a long, narrow territory, vulnerable to military action and to economic inducements. This alignment would also require a degree of commitment by the rest of the peninsula. It would need an economic commitment to alleviate its problems, and a military commitment to support its resistance. The key to this, of course, is German support.

Germany is the largest economy in Europe and the fourth largest in the world. It is also the world's third-largest exporter. Consequently Germany looks at the world through an economic lens. It is not merely the catastrophe that came down on Germany in 1945 that drives this. It has achieved a position of economic prosperity and preeminence that makes military adventures irrational. Yet the problem is that military involvement is not entirely up to the Germans. If the Russians exploit the weakness of Eastern Europe, Germany must make a strategic decision. It can attempt an alliance with Russia, but if it remains weak, then that alliance can become a trap. Or it can try to balance Russia, backing an Eastern European coalition. Or it can prepare to roll back the Russians.

The borderland between Germany and Russia is now an active flashpoint. It is not the only one on the Russian periphery. The Caucasus remains a flashpoint, and the Russians have increased the temperature by signing a long-term treaty with Armenia and sending a substantial number of troops there. This puts Georgia, a country supported by the West, in a pincer between Russia and Armenia. And it also threatens Azerbaijan, the major alternative to Russian energy for Europe.

This therefore draws in Turkey. The Turks and Armenians are hostile to each other over very bad memories of slaughter. On the other hand the Turks are dependent on Russian energy, and until they find an alternative—and it will be difficult to replace all Russian oil—Turkey can't challenge Russia. At the same time, the fall of the Soviet Union created a comfortable buffer zone between Turkey and Russia. It is not one that the Turks would like to see disappear with Russian influence returning to its Cold War line. Therefore, the Turks and Russians are dueling politically, particularly in Azerbaijan.

Turkey is in a complex position. It will become a great power, but it is not yet a great power. Turkey is currently passing through a cyclical economic downturn as well as internal political tensions, neither of which will have lasting significance. It will become a great power because of its economic strength and the chaos surrounding it. That chaos gives Turkey economic opportunities for both investment and trade. It also will tend to draw Turkey into conflicts. Turkey has an interest in the future of the Black Sea and therefore has its own interests in Ukraine. It also has interests in Iraq and Syria, and in the Arabian Peninsula, Iran, and the Balkans. With the Black Sea becoming increasingly tense, and either violence or instability to the south and east, the only region on Turkey's periphery that is not at the moment a flashpoint is the Balkans. As we have learned over the centuries, in the Balkans quiet is only temporary. Except for the European peninsula, Turkey is surrounded by flashpoints.

Turkey's relation to the peninsula needs to be considered in terms of the broader relationship between North Africa and the peninsula. There are two dimensions to this. The first is the flow of energy from North Africa to southern Europe, particularly from Libya and Algeria. This flow is extremely important to Europe, both in itself and as an alternative to Russian energy. However, both Libya and Algeria have become unstable, particularly Libya. As a civil war raged in Libya, the French and Italians argued for intervention. The French began air strikes, asking for American support with AWACS aircraft for battle management. It became clear that the French could not sustain the campaign by themselves, and the Americans were drawn into a leading role. This was not a happy experience for the Americans, particularly its aftermath.

The Europeans have relied on the United States to manage situations such as that in Egypt. The United States is not prepared to do so to the extent it was previously, and as we have seen, Egypt's problems can spread. The United States does not have a pressing interest in North Africa beyond addressing radical Islamic movements. Regime change is not something it will attempt. But for Europeans, the flow of energy represents a significant interest, and ensuring that supply is essential.

The second Mediterranean flashpoint is the massive movement of population from North Africa and Turkey into Europe. These immigrants were drawn there deliberately by a Europe looking for cheap labor. Their presence has created substantial internal tension, a tension so profound that it threatens the visa-free zone that the Europeans created around most of the EU. Countries like Denmark want to block Muslims from entering, and there is general consensus that Muslim immigration must be limited. This is a significant issue in North Africa and could generate anti-European feeling, which could translate into trans-Mediterranean terrorism or threats to North African regimes. In that case Europeans will be drawn in whether they want to be or not.

There is another dimension to this in Europe itself—the rise of right-wing parties. One of the inevitable consequences of the financial crisis and massive unemployment has been a loss of trust in existing political parties and the Europeanist ideology. The inevitable result is the rise of a host of right-wing parties, from Hungary to France. These parties have a common hostility to the European Union and a violently anti-immigrant sentiment. They also support the national interests of their own countries, as opposed to the transnational interests of the European elite. These parties have not yet risen to the point where they have the numbers to govern, but some have had to be included in the government in order to create a coalition, and others are growing rapidly.

The old flashpoints of Europe, the Rhine Valley, the English Channel, and the rest, remain generally quiet. Franco-German tension is growing, but it is far from reaching a boiling point. But underneath the surface, the engine of conflict—a romantic nationalism that challenges the legitimacy of transferring authority to multinational institutions and resurrects old national conflicts—is stirring. The right-wing parties are just the tip of the iceberg, although they must not be dismissed in themselves. But beneath the surface, the generalized unease with the consequences of transfers of sovereignty in economic matters is intensifying.

For the moment the flashpoints are on the frontier of the European Union, but that union is itself crumbling. There are four European Unions. There are the German states (Germany and Austria), the rest of northern Europe, the Mediterranean states, and the states in the borderland. The latter face the retaking of their old borderlands by Russia. The Mediterranean Europeans face massive unemployment, in some cases greater than the unemployment experienced by Americans in the Great Depression. The northern European states are doing better but none are doing as well as the Germans.

The dramatic differences in the conditions and concerns of the different parts of the European Union represent the lines along which it is fragmenting. Each region experiences reality in a different way, and the differences are irreconcilable. Indeed, it is difficult to imagine how they might be reconciled. There are four Europes, and these four are fragmenting further, back to the nation-states that compose them, and back into the history they wanted to transcend.

In the end, the problem of Europe is the same problem that haunted its greatest moment, the Enlightenment. It is the Faustian spirit, the desire to possess everything even at the cost of their souls. Today their desire is to possess everything at no cost. They want permanent peace and prosperity. They want to retain their national sovereignty, but they do not want these sovereign states to fully exercise their sovereignty.

They want to be one people, but they do not want to share each other's fate. They want to speak their own language, but they don't believe that this will be a bar to complete mutual understanding. They want to triumph, but they don't want to risk. They want to be completely secure, but they don't wish to defend themselves.

But there is another Europe, as there has always been—the land-locked mainland that is never quite defeated and never quite secure. The story of modern Europe began in 1991, when the Soviet Union died and the European Union was born. In 2014, Russia reemerged, the flashpoint between it and the European Union came alive, and history began again. It is striking how short-lived were Europe's fantasies about what was possible. It is also striking that the return of Europe's most dangerous flashpoint occurred in 2014, one hundred years after the First World War began, one hundred years since Europe began its descent into hell.

It has emerged from that hell. But where Faust was willing to sell his soul for perfect knowledge, modern Europe wants perfection without paying a price. There is always a price, and nothing is more dangerous than not knowing what the price is, except perhaps not wanting to know.

The answer to the most important question, the third question of whether Europe has put the thirty-one years behind it, must be no, but a qualified no. Europe is no longer the center of the world, but a subordinate part of the international system. The stakes are no longer what they once were, and the tendency of outside powers like the United States to suppress conflict if they wish to is even greater than it was in the twentieth century. But the idea that Europe has moved beyond using armed conflict to settle its issues is a fantasy. It was not true in the past generation, and it will remain untrue in the future. We already see the Russian bear rising to reclaim at least some of its place in the world. And we see Germany struggling between its own national interests and those of the EU in a world where the two are no longer one.

Humans do not fight wars because they are fools or haven't learned a lesson. They know the pain that is coming. They fight because they must, because reality has forced them to do so. The Europeans are still human, and they will still encounter terrible choices like those that others face and that they have faced in the past. They will have to choose between war and peace, and as in the past, they will at times choose war. Nothing has ended. For humans nothing significant is ever over.

It has been a year since *Flashpoints* was published, and several years since it was conceived. We have seen numerous frictions in Europe during this time, and the basic idea of this book remains intact.

Europe created the European Union for two reasons. One was to maintain European prosperity. The other was to prevent the recurrence of wars that had torn Europe apart throughout its history, particularly in the thirty-one years from 1914 to 1945. The European Union did this job well until the crisis of 2008, but since then its collective economy has struggled, and the struggle is not evenly distributed. Germany has done well while Southern Europe is in the midst of a depression that it cannot climb out of. As a result, Europe is fragmenting, and the fragmentation is leading to increased nationalism, regional calamities, and increased xenophobia. The flashpoints discussed herein are coming alive.

During the past year, we have seen the Greek crisis, the immigration crisis, increased tension in the Mediterranean, and heightened friction between Russia and its western neighbors and the United States. Let me review briefly here what is actually happening.

The Greek crisis was indeed a crisis, but not about Greece alone. It was about a much broader issue, which is how the rest of Europe can coexist with Germany. Ever since unification in 1871, Germany has posed a problem for Europe. Economically the country has always been a dynamo. But precisely for that reason it has always been insecure. For many years Germany has depended heavily on exports, particularly to Europe, to maintain its economy. This dependency made Germany fearful that other countries would close their markets to German goods, or attack when threatened by Germany's economic power.

The second fear isn't on the table right now, but Germany's fear of losing its European markets certainly is. The EU absorbs about half of German exports, and Germany's total exports are half of its GDP. It must, at all costs, maintain the European free trade zone and the tools that let Germany optimize its export environment: the euro and Brussels regulations. If Greece fails to pay its debts, and is better off for it, then other countries such as Spain, and most of all Italy, might choose the same route. Default means capital controls, and with capital controls come trade restrictions. That is a gun pointed at the German head.

The Greeks can't pay their debts. Default will happen. But the Germans must make sure that the pain of defaulting is so great that it prevents the Greeks from doing so. Or if the Greeks default anyway, the pain must be so considerable that no one else will follow them. Letting the Greeks off the hook would not hurt Germany or Europe at all, as Greece is only 2 percent of Europe's total economy. But it would set a precedent that would endanger the entire European project.

The decisions on Greece have raised other dangers for Europe. The harsh treatment of Greece, along with the relative prosperity of Germany compared with the rest of Europe, has created deep resentments against Germany, emerging in two different spheres. The first is government to government. When the French president meets the German chancellor, they no longer meet primarily as two European leaders from different areas of Europe working toward a common EU goal. It is the president of France presenting France's views to the German chancellor, who speaks only for Germany. A few leaders still try to speak for Europe as a whole, but the EU has become more of an arena for competing interests than a single entity with multiple co-leaders.

Along with the state-level divergences, we see increasing opposition to the EU among the public and the emergence of anti-European parties of the left and particularly the right in countries like Greece, Spain, France, and Britain. Public opinion and these new parties have forced existing governments to take a much harder line on Germany, and on other issues as well.

Among these issues is that of Muslims in Europe. Terrorist attacks emanating from some in the Muslim community have generated anti-

Muslim sentiment and a desire to keep Muslims out. Additionally, the avalanche of Muslim refugees arriving from the Mediterranean to escape the wars of North Africa and the Middle East alarms many Europeans. These fears generate continued calls for border controls, on both the EU's borders with the rest of the world and the interior borders of the EU.

As this book details, the Mediterranean is one of the key flashpoints for Europe and has been for more than a thousand years. Europe was predominantly Christian. North Africa and the Middle East were predominantly Muslim. Armies have crossed and circled the Mediterranean, Muslims conquering Iberia and going as far as Vienna, Europeans dominating the Middle East and North Africa. Since *Flashpoints* was published, a wave of migrants has crossed and circled the Mediterranean seeking refuge in Europe. The Europeans have sought to block their entry. This isn't an army, of course, but the Mediterranean still serves as a crucial barrier to the region.

Following World War I, the Ottoman Empire collapsed, leaving modern Turkey in its wake. The British and French inherited much of the empire and created the modern countries that make up the Levant. Following the U.S. invasion of Iraq, these countries began to disintegrate. The governments became either impotent or simply factions in a raging civil war.

The goal of some of the factions is to create a caliphate, a transnational state governed by a leader functioning under Islamic law. Whereas this was an inconceivable idea a few years ago, it is still unlikely but is no longer inconceivable. The region will reorganize itself, this time with European or significant American involvement, and the course it takes will reignite the flashpoints along the Mediterranean and its shores. The surge of refugees may be simply the forerunner of more serious confrontation in the region. But it is a surge that cuts to the heart of Europe's sense of nationhood. The Europeans are simply unable to manage mass immigration of people of varied cultures. As *Flashpoints* shows, the European nation was built out of different material than the United States.

The other and more immediate flashpoint is the borderland between Russia and the European peninsula. It was on fire when *Flashpoints* was first published but has cooled off in the last year. The first act is over, but not the play. In the first act, Russia confronted the danger of a pro-

Western, well-armed Ukraine. The Americans and Central Europeans feared that a Russian move into Ukraine would threaten Europe. The fact was that the Russian military was in no position to invade Ukraine on a large and deep scale. The Americans, beginning to deploy in Central Europe, could send only military trainers into Ukraine. The Germans were appalled at the thought of a conflict to the east.

Therefore this flashpoint, rhetoric aside, has become relatively quiet. However, that quiet is not permanent. Both sides are building up their forces on the edge of Ukraine and each side anticipates at least another round of confrontation—the degree of which is uncertain—in the region. At the same time, I expect several years of de-escalation before the next round begins.

And finally, the process of national disintegration discussed late in *Flashpoints* is under way. The election in Britain opens the door for an exit from Europe by the U.K. and, even more, reaffirms the divergence of Scotland from England. Such a vote would have been difficult to imagine even five years ago. The Scottish–English division is symptomatic of divisions elsewhere in Europe, with the greatest threat of long-term fragmentation coming from Russia.

This process of disintegration was given a powerful push by the events in Paris in November 2015, when the Islamic State carried out complex operations designed to cause maximum casualties at three targets. The operation succeeded.

The first thing we see is that the Mediterranean flashpoint has become activated in an interesting way. The wars in the Middle East generated a massive outflow of refugees to Europe via Turkey and Greece, the land route along the Mediterranean. This created a significant crisis in the European Union. The land route that was being taken—Greece, Macedonia, Serbia, Hungary—caused these small countries to want to block the flow, but Germany wanted Europe to stay open to migration. This once again pitted Germany against Greece and Hungary. But most importantly it posed another problem that the EU couldn't solve: There was not any joint EU force available to block the refugees nor any agreement on what to do with them.

The attack in Paris turned a serious problem into a crisis. At the time of this writing, some of the terrorists appear to have come from Syria, along with refugees. The refugee problem turned into something linked to terrorism. The first French response after the attack was to close all borders; within hours, other European countries followed suit. The point was to stop and examine the credentials of everyone entering each country. But it was not the EU taking the responsibility. It was each individual country, closing its own border, so that it could control who came in or out.

One of the fundamental principles of the EU is the free movement of peoples. The decision to close borders demonstrated two things: Each nation-state took responsibility for its own security, and free movement took second place to national security. Of course these measures will end when the threat of terrorism goes away, but when will that be?

Before publishing *Flashpoints*, I wrote about intensified nationalism in Europe. That nationalism certainly continues to intensify. It is not only the devolution of existing nation-states, it is also the growing hostility between nations. The intense anti-German feeling we saw in Greece, and the intense contempt for Greece expressed by German leaders, is the tip of the iceberg. Throughout Europe we see increasing tensions within nations and between nations, with the broadest phenomenon being the growing distrust—and even hostility—toward Germany.

Flashpoints revolve around Germany's relationship with Europe. The European Union was supposed to eliminate that tension by making Germany simply one nation among others, all linked together by prosperity. But that prosperity has diminished and the loss has not been shared equally. Germany emerged in the Greek crisis as the real decision maker in Europe, a role that was deeply resented by many.

The point of *Flashpoints* is that the EU created a *temporary* abatement of Europe's core problems, nationalism and power—particularly German power. We are now clearly in the period where that abatement is in the process of failing.

George Friedman
November 2015

Acknowledgments

There are many I need to thank. First, my appreciation goes to Jason Kaufman, my good friend and editor, who has guided me patiently through yet another book, and to Rob Bloom, for his close editing and insightful comments. Second, I thank Jim Hornfischer, another good friend and my literary agent, who has shown me the rules of the business.

I also must thank my colleagues at Stratfor who read and commented on the manuscript, skewering it with their normal vigor. Those colleagues who were particularly devastating include Rodger Baker, Reva Bhalla, Adriano Bosoni, Antonia Colibasanu, Allison Fedirka, Rebecca Keller Friedman, Lauren Goodrich, Karen Hooper, Nate Hughes, Marc Lanthemann, John Minnich, and any others I might have missed. I particularly appreciate my friend and colleague David Judson for his wise counsel and good humor. Also thanks to graphics designer TJ Lensing, who spent hours creating the crucial maps that have clarified many of the important concepts in the book. And thanks to Taylor Christman for helping to keep me organized. I also want to thank Matt Powers for supporting me extensively with his first-rate research.

And finally, and above all, I must thank Meredith, my wife and the coauthor, who chooses not to be mentioned. She *is* mentioned, and therefore has not gotten her way completely. As always, without her this book would not have been written.